Eating Animals

Eating Animals

Jonathan Safran Foer

L **B**

Little, Brown and Company

New York   Boston   London

Little, Brown and Company
Hachette Book Group
237 Park Avenue, New York, NY 10017
www.hachettebookgroup.com

First Edition: November 2009

Little, Brown and Company is a division of Hachette Book Group, Inc. The Little, Brown name and logo are trademarks of Hachette Book Group, Inc.

Chapter opening illustrations by Tom Manning

Library of Congress Cataloging-in-Publication Data
Foer, Jonathan Safran.
    Eating animals / Jonathan Safran Foer. — 1st ed.
        p. cm.
    Includes bibliographical references and index.
    ISBN 978-0-316-06990-8 (hc) / 978-0-316-07267-0 (International ed.)
    1. Vegetarianism — Philosophy.   2. Vegetarianism.   I. Title.
    TX392.F58 2009
    641.3'03 — dc22   2009034434

10 9 8 7 6 5 4 3 2 1

RRD-IN

Printed in the United States of America

for Sam and Eleanor,

trusty compasses

Contents

Americans choose to eat less than
.25% of the known edible food on
the planet.

The Fruits of Family Trees

WHEN I WAS YOUNG, I would often spend the weekend at my grand-mother's house. On the way in, Friday night, she would lift me from the ground in one of her fire-smothering hugs. And on the way out, Sunday afternoon, I was again taken into the air. It wasn't until years later that I realized she was weighing me.

My grandmother survived the War barefoot, scavenging other people's inedibles: rotting potatoes, discarded scraps of meat, skins, and the bits that clung to bones and pits. And so she never cared if I colored outside the lines, as long as I cut coupons along the dashes. And hotel buffets: while the rest of us erected Golden Calves of breakfast, she would make sandwich upon sandwich to swaddle in napkins and stash in her bag for lunch. It was my grandmother who taught me that one tea bag makes as many cups of tea as you're serv-ing, and that every part of the apple is edible.

Money wasn't the point. (Many of those coupons I clipped were for foods she would never buy.)

Health wasn't the point. (She would beg me to drink Coke.)

My grandmother never set a place for herself at family dinners. Even when there was nothing more to be done — no soup bowls to be topped off, no pots to be stirred or ovens checked — she stayed in the kitchen, like a vigilant guard (or prisoner) in a tower. As far as I could tell, the sustenance she got from the food she made didn't require her to eat it.

In the forests of Europe, she ate to stay alive until the next opportunity to eat to stay alive. In America, fifty years later, we ate what pleased us. Our cupboards were filled with food bought on whims, overpriced foodie food, food we didn't need. And when the

expiration date passed, we threw it away without smelling it. Eating was carefree. My grandmother made that life possible for us. But she was, herself, unable to shake the desperation.

Growing up, my brothers and I thought our grandmother was the greatest chef who ever lived. We would literally recite those words when the food came to the table, and again after the first bite, and once more at the end of the meal: "You are the greatest chef who ever lived." And yet we were worldly enough kids to know that the Greatest Chef Who Ever Lived would probably have more than one recipe (chicken with carrots), and that most Great Recipes involved more than two ingredients.

And why didn't we question her when she told us that dark food is inherently healthier than light food, or that most of the nutrients are found in the peel or crust? (The sandwiches of those weekend stays were made with the saved ends of pumpernickel loaves.) She taught us that animals that are bigger than you are very good for you, animals that are smaller than you are good for you, fish (which aren't animals) are fine for you, then tuna (which aren't fish), then vegetables, fruits, cakes, cookies, and sodas. No foods are bad for you. Fats are healthy—all fats, always, in any quantity. Sugars are very healthy. The fatter a child is, the healthier it is—especially if it's a boy. Lunch is not one meal, but three, to be eaten at 11:00, 12:30, and 3:00. You are always starving.

In fact, her chicken and carrots probably *was* the most delicious thing I've ever eaten. But that had little to do with how it was prepared, or even how it tasted. Her food was delicious because we believed it was delicious. We believed in our grandmother's cooking more fervently than we believed in God. Her culinary prowess was one of our family's primal stories, like the cunning of the

grandfather I never met, or the single fight of my parents' marriage. We clung to those stories and depended on them to define us. We were the family that chose its battles wisely, and used wit to get out of binds, and loved the food of our matriarch.

Once upon a time there was a person whose life was so good there was no story to tell about it. More stories could be told about my grandmother than about anyone else I've ever met—her otherwordly childhood, the hairline margin of her survival, the totality of her loss, her immigration and further loss, the triumph and tragedy of her assimilation—and though I will one day try to tell them to my children, we almost never told them to one another. Nor did we call her by any of the obvious and earned titles. We called her the Greatest Chef.

Perhaps her other stories were too difficult to tell. Or perhaps she chose her story for herself, wanting to be identified by her providing rather than her surviving. Or perhaps her surviving is contained within her providing: the story of her relationship to food holds all of the other stories that could be told about her. Food, for her, is not *food*. It is terror, dignity, gratitude, vengeance, joyfulness, humiliation, religion, history, and, of course, love. As if the fruits she always offered us were picked from the destroyed branches of our family tree.

Possible Again

UNEXPECTED IMPULSES STRUCK WHEN I found out I was going to be a father. I began tidying up the house, replacing long-dead lightbulbs, wiping windows, and filing papers. I had my glasses adjusted, bought a dozen pairs of white socks, installed a roof rack on top of the car and a "dog/cargo divider" in the back, had my first physical in half a decade...and decided to write a book about eating animals.

Fatherhood was the immediate impetus for the journey that

would become this book, but I'd been packing my bags for most of my life. When I was two, the heroes of all of my bedtime stories were animals. When I was four, we fostered a cousin's dog for a summer. I kicked it. My father told me we don't kick animals. When I was seven, I mourned the death of my goldfish. I learned that my father had flushed him down the toilet. I told my father — in other, less civil words — we don't flush animals down the toilet. When I was nine, I had a babysitter who didn't want to hurt anything. She put it just like that when I asked her why she wasn't having chicken with my older brother and me: "I don't want to hurt anything."

"*Hurt* anything?" I asked.

"You know that chicken is chicken, right?"

Frank shot me a look: *Mom and Dad entrusted this stupid woman with their precious babies?*

Her intention might or might not have been to convert us to vegetarianism — just because conversations about meat tend to make people feel cornered, not all vegetarians are proselytizers — but being a teenager, she lacked whatever restraint it is that so often prevents a full telling of this particular story. Without drama or rhetoric, she shared what she knew.

My brother and I looked at each other, our mouths full of hurt chickens, and had simultaneous *how-in-the-world-could-I-have-never-thought-of-that-before-and-why-on-earth-didn't-someone-tell-me?* moments. I put down my fork. Frank finished the meal and is probably eating a chicken as I type these words.

What our babysitter said made sense to me, not only because it seemed true, but because it was the extension to food of everything my parents had taught me. We don't hurt family members. We don't hurt friends or strangers. We don't even hurt upholstered furniture. My not having thought to include animals in that list didn't make them the exceptions to it. It just made me a child, ignorant of

the world's workings. Until I wasn't. At which point I had to change my life.

Until I didn't. My vegetarianism, so bombastic and unyielding in the beginning, lasted a few years, sputtered, and quietly died. I never thought of a response to our babysitter's code, but found ways to smudge, diminish, and forget it. Generally speaking, I didn't cause hurt. Generally speaking, I strove to do the right thing. Generally speaking, my conscience was clear enough. Pass the chicken, I'm *starving*.

Mark Twain said that quitting smoking is among the easiest things one can do; he did it all the time. I would add vegetarianism to the list of easy things. In high school I became a vegetarian more times than I can now remember, most often as an effort to claim some identity in a world of people whose identities seemed to come effortlessly. I wanted a slogan to distinguish my mom's Volvo's bumper, a bake sale cause to fill the self-conscious half hour of school break, an occasion to get closer to the breasts of activist women. (And I continued to think it was wrong to hurt animals.) Which isn't to say that I refrained from eating meat. Only that I refrained in public. Privately, the pendulum swung. Many dinners of those years began with my father asking, "Any dietary restrictions I need to know about tonight?"

When I went to college, I started eating meat more earnestly. Not "believing in it"—whatever that would mean—but willfully pushing the questions out of my mind. I didn't feel like having an "identity" right then. And I wasn't around anyone who knew me as a vegetarian, so there was no issue of public hypocrisy, or even having to explain a change. It might well have been the prevalence of vegetarianism on campus that discouraged my own—one is less likely to give money to a street musician whose case is overflowing with bills.

7

But when, at the end of my sophomore year, I became a philosophy major and started doing my first seriously pretentious *thinking*, I became a vegetarian again. The kind of willful forgetting that I was sure meat eating required felt too paradoxical to the intellectual life I was trying to shape. I thought life could, should, and must conform to the mold of reason. You can imagine how annoying this made me.

When I graduated, I ate meat—lots of every kind of meat—for about two years. Why? Because it tasted good. And because more important than reason in shaping habits are the stories we tell ourselves and one another. And I told a forgiving story about myself to myself.

Then I was set up on a blind date with the woman who would become my wife. And only a few weeks later we found ourselves talking about two surprising topics: marriage and vegetarianism.

Her history with meat was remarkably similar to mine: there were things she believed while lying in bed at night, and there were choices made at the breakfast table the next morning. There was a gnawing (if only occasional and short-lived) dread that she was participating in something deeply wrong, and there was the acceptance of both the confounding complexity of the issue and the forgivable fallibility of being human. Like me, she had intuitions that were very strong, but apparently not strong enough.

People get married for many different reasons, but one that animated our decision to take that step was the prospect of explicitly marking a new beginning. Jewish ritual and symbolism strongly encourage this notion of demarcating a sharp division with what came before—the most well-known example being the smashing of the glass at the end of the marriage ceremony. Things were as they were before, but they will be different now. Things will be better. We will be better.

Sounds and feels great, but better how? I could think of endless ways to make myself better (I could learn foreign languages, be more patient, work harder), but I'd already made too many such vows to trust them anymore. I could also think of endless ways to make "us" better, but the meaningful things we can agree on and change in a relationship are few. In actuality, even in those moments when so much feels possible, very little is.

Eating animals, a concern we'd both had and had both forgotten, seemed like a place to start. So much intersects there, and so much could flow from it. In the same week, we became engaged and vegetarian.

Of course our wedding wasn't vegetarian, because we persuaded ourselves that it was only fair to offer animal protein to our guests, some of whom had traveled great distances to share our joy. (Find that logic hard to follow?) And we ate fish on our honeymoon, but we were in Japan, and when in Japan . . . And back in our new home, we did occasionally eat burgers and chicken soup and smoked salmon and tuna steaks. But only every now and then. Only whenever we felt like it.

And that, I thought, was that. And I thought that was just fine. I assumed we'd maintain a diet of conscientious inconsistency. Why should eating be different from any of the other ethical realms of our lives? We were honest people who occasionally told lies, careful friends who sometimes acted clumsily. We were vegetarians who from time to time ate meat.

And I couldn't even feel confident that my intuitions were anything more than sentimental vestiges of my childhood—that if I were to probe deeply, I wouldn't find indifference. I didn't know what animals *were*, or even approximately how they were farmed or killed. The whole thing made me uncomfortable, but that didn't

imply that anyone else should be, or even that I should be. And I felt no rush or need to sort any of this out.

But then we decided to have a child, and that was a different story that would necessitate a different story.

About half an hour after my son was born, I went into the waiting room to tell the gathered family the good news.

"You said he! So it's a boy?"
　"What's his name?"
　　"Who does he look like?"
　　　"Tell us everything!"

I answered their questions as quickly as I could, then went to a corner and turned on my cell phone.

"Grandma," I said. "We have a baby."

Her only phone is in the kitchen. She picked up after the first ring, which meant she had been sitting at the table, waiting for the call. It was just after midnight. Had she been clipping coupons? Preparing chicken and carrots to freeze for someone else to eat at some future meal? I'd never once seen or heard her cry, but tears pushed through her voice as she asked, "How much does it weigh?"

A few days after we came home from the hospital, I sent a letter to a friend, including a photo of my son and some first impressions of fatherhood. He responded, simply, "Everything is possible again." It was the perfect thing to write, because that was exactly how it felt. We could retell our stories and make them better, more representa-

tive or aspirational. Or we could choose to tell different stories. The world itself had another chance.

Eating Animals

PERHAPS THE FIRST DESIRE MY son had, wordlessly and before reason, was the desire to eat. Seconds after being born, he was breastfeeding. I watched him with an awe that had no precedent in my life. Without explanation or experience, he knew what to do. Millions of years of evolution had wound the knowledge into him, as it had encoded beating into his tiny heart, and expansion and contraction into his newly dry lungs.

The awe had no precedent in my life, but it bound me, across generations, to others. I saw the rings of my tree: my parents watching me eat, my grandmother watching my mother eat, my great-grandparents watching my grandmother...He was eating as had the children of cave painters.

As my son began life and I began this book, it seemed that almost everything he did revolved around eating. He was nursing, or sleeping after nursing, or getting cranky before nursing, or getting rid of the milk he had nursed. As I finish this book, he is able to carry on quite sophisticated conversations, and increasingly the food he eats is digested together with stories we tell. Feeding my child is not like feeding myself: it matters more. It matters because food matters (his physical health matters, the pleasure of eating matters), and because the stories that are served with food matter. These stories bind our family together, and bind our family to others. Stories about food are stories about us—our history and our values. Within my family's Jewish tradition, I came to learn that food serves two parallel

purposes: it nourishes and it helps you remember. Eating and storytelling are inseparable—the saltwater is also tears; the honey not only tastes sweet, but makes us think of sweetness; the matzo is the bread of our affliction.

There are thousands of foods on the planet, and explaining why we eat the relatively small selection we do requires some words. We need to explain that the parsley on the plate is for decoration, that pasta is not a "breakfast food," why we eat wings but not eyes, cows but not dogs. Stories establish narratives, and stories establish rules.

At many times in my life, I have forgotten that I have stories to tell about food. I just ate what was available or tasty, what seemed natural, sensible, or healthy—what was there to explain? But the kind of parenthood I always imagined practicing abhors such forgetfulness.

This story didn't begin as a book. I simply wanted to know—for myself and my family—what meat *is*. I wanted to know as concretely as possible. Where does it come from? How is it produced? How are animals treated, and to what extent does that matter? What are the economic, social, and environmental effects of eating animals? My personal quest didn't stay that way for long. Through my efforts as a parent, I came face-to-face with realities that as a citizen I couldn't ignore, and as a writer I couldn't keep to myself. But facing those realities and writing responsibly about them are not the same.

I wanted to address these questions comprehensively. So although upwards of 99 percent of all animals eaten in this country come from "factory farms"—and I will spend much of the rest of the book explaining what this means and why it matters—the other 1 percent of animal agriculture is also an important part of this story. The disproportionate amount of this book that is occupied by discussion of the best family-run animal farms reflects how significant I think they are, but at the same time, how insignificant: they prove the rule.

To be perfectly honest (and to risk losing my credibility on page 13), I assumed, before beginning my research, that I knew what I would find—not the details, but the general picture. Others made the same assumption. Almost always, when I told someone I was writing a book about "eating animals," they assumed, even without knowing anything about my views, that it was a case for vegetarianism. It's a telling assumption, one that implies not only that a thorough inquiry into animal agriculture would lead one away from eating meat, but that most people already know that to be the case. (What assumptions did you make upon seeing the title of this book?)

I, too, assumed that my book about eating animals would become a straightforward case for vegetarianism. It didn't. A straightforward case for vegetarianism is worth writing, but it's not what I've written here.

Animal agriculture is a hugely complicated topic. No two animals, breeds of animals, farms, farmers, or eaters are the same. Looking past the mountains of research—reading, interviewing, seeing firsthand—that was necessary even to begin to think about this stuff seriously, I had to ask myself if it was possible to say something coherent and significant about a practice that is so diverse. Perhaps there is no "meat." Instead, there is *this* animal, raised on *this* farm, slaughtered at *this* plant, sold in *this* way, and eaten by *this* person—but each distinct in a way that prevents them from being pieced together as mosaic.

And eating animals is one of those topics, like abortion, where it is impossible to definitively know some of the most important details (When is a fetus a person, as opposed to a potential person? What is animal experience really like?) and that cuts right to one's deepest discomforts, often provoking defensiveness or aggression. It's a slippery, frustrating, and resonant subject. Each question prompts another, and it's easy to find yourself defending a position far more

extreme than you actually believe or could live by. Or worse, find-ing no position worth defending or living by.

Then there is the difficulty of discerning the difference between how something feels and what something is. Too often, arguments about eating animals aren't arguments at all, but statements of taste. And where there are facts — this is how much pork we eat; these are how many mangrove swamps have been destroyed by aquaculture; this is how a cow is killed — there's the question of what we can actually do with them. Should they be ethically compelling? Com-munally? Legally? Or just more information for each eater to digest as he sees fit?

While this book is the product of an enormous amount of research, and is as objective as any work of journalism can be — I used the most conservative statistics available (almost always from government, and peer-reviewed academic and industry sources) and hired two outside fact-checkers to corroborate them — I think of it as a story. There's plenty of data to be found, but it is often thin and malleable. Facts are important, but they don't, on their own, provide meaning — especially when they are so bound to linguistic choices. What does a precisely measured pain response in chickens mean? Does it mean pain? What does pain mean? No matter how much we learn about the physiology of the pain — how long it per-sists, the symptoms it produces, and so forth — none of it will tell us anything definitive. But place facts in a story, a story of compassion or domination, or maybe both — place them in a story about the world we live in and who we are and who we want to be — and you can begin to speak meaningfully about eating animals.

We are made of stories. I'm thinking of those Saturday afternoons at my grandmother's kitchen table, just the two of us — black bread in the glowing toaster, a humming refrigerator that couldn't be seen through its veil of family photographs. Over pumpernickel ends and

Coke, she would tell me about her escape from Europe, the foods she had to eat and those she wouldn't. It was the story of her life—"Listen to me," she would plead—and I knew a vital lesson was being transmitted, even if I didn't know, as a child, what that lesson was.

I know, now, what it was. And though the particulars couldn't be more different, I am trying, and will try, to transmit her lesson to my son. This book is my most earnest attempt to do so. I feel great trepidation as I begin, because there is so much reverberation. Putting aside, for a moment, the more than ten billion land animals slaughtered for food every year in America, and putting aside the environment, and workers, and such directly related issues as world hunger, flu epidemics, and biodiversity, there is also the question of how we think of ourselves and one another. We are not only the tellers of our stories, we are the stories themselves. If my wife and I raise our son as a vegetarian, he will not eat his great-grandmother's singular dish, will never receive that unique and most direct expression of her love, will perhaps never think of her as the Greatest Chef Who Ever Lived. Her primal story, our family's primal story, will have to change.

My grandmother's first words upon seeing my son for the first time were "My revenge." Of the infinite number of things she could have said, that was what she chose, or was chosen for her.

Listen to Me:

"We weren't rich, but we always had enough. Thursday we baked bread, and challah and rolls, and they lasted the whole week. Friday we had pancakes. Shabbat we always had a chicken, and soup with noodles. You would go to the butcher and ask for a little more fat. The fattiest piece was the best piece. It wasn't like now. We didn't have refrigerators, but we had milk and cheese. We didn't

have every kind of vegetable, but we had enough. The things that you have here and take for granted...But we were happy. We didn't know any better. And we took what we had for granted, too.

"Then it all changed. During the War it was hell on earth, and I had nothing. I left my family, you know. I was always running, day and night, because the Germans were always right behind me. If you stopped, you died. There was never enough food. I became sicker and sicker from not eating, and I'm not just talking about being skin and bones. I had sores all over my body. It became difficult to move. I wasn't too good to eat from a garbage can. I ate the parts others wouldn't eat. If you helped yourself, you could survive. I took whatever I could find. I ate things I wouldn't tell you about.

"Even at the worst times, there were good people, too. Someone taught me to tie the ends of my pants so I could fill the legs with any potatoes I was able to steal. I walked miles and miles like that, because you never knew when you would be lucky again. Someone gave me a little rice once, and I traveled two days to a market and traded it for some soap, and then traveled to another market and traded the soap for some beans. You had to have luck and intuition.

"The worst it got was near the end. A lot of people died right at the end, and I didn't know if I could make it another day. A farmer, a Russian, God bless him, he saw my condition, and he went into his house and came out with a piece of meat for me."

"He saved your life."

"I didn't eat it."

"You didn't eat it?"

"It was pork. I wouldn't eat pork."

"Why?"

"What do you mean why?"

"What, because it wasn't kosher?"

"Of course."

"But not even to save your life?"

"If nothing matters, there's nothing to save."

All
or Nothing
or Something
Else

Modern industrial fishing lines can
be as long as 75 miles—the same
distance as from sea level to space.

1.

George

I SPENT THE FIRST TWENTY-SIX years of my life disliking animals. I thought of them as bothersome, dirty, unapproachably foreign, frighteningly unpredictable, and plain old unnecessary. I had a particular lack of enthusiasm for dogs — inspired, in large part, by a related fear that I inherited from my mother, which she inherited from my grandmother. As a child I would agree to go over to friends' houses only if they confined their dogs in some other room. If a dog approached in the park, I'd become hysterical until my father hoisted me onto his shoulders. I didn't like watching television shows that featured dogs. I didn't understand — I *disliked* — people who got excited about dogs. It's possible that I even developed a subtle prejudice against the blind.

And then one day I became a person who loved dogs. I became a dog person.

George came very much out of the blue. My wife and I hadn't broached the subject of getting a dog, much less set about looking for one. (Why would we? I disliked dogs.) In this case, the first day of the rest of my life was a Saturday. Strolling down Seventh Avenue in our Brooklyn neighborhood, we came upon a tiny black puppy, asleep on the curb, curled into its ADOPT ME vest like a question mark. I don't believe in love at first sight or fate, but I loved that damned dog and it was meant to be. Even if I wouldn't touch it.

Suggesting we adopt the puppy might have been the most unpredictable thing I'd ever done, but here was a beautiful little animal, the sort that even a hard-hearted dog skeptic would find irresistible.

21

Of course, people find beauty in things without wet noses, too. But there is something unique about the ways in which we fall in love with animals. Unwieldy dogs and minuscule dogs and long-haired and sleek dogs, snoring Saint Bernards, asthmatic pugs, unfolding shar-peis, and depressed-looking basset hounds — each with devoted fans. Bird-watchers spend frigid mornings scanning skies and scrub for the feathered objects of their fascination. Cat lovers display an intensity lacking — thank goodness — in most human relationships. Children's books are constellated with rabbits and mice and bears and caterpillars, not to mention spiders, crickets, and alligators. Nobody ever had a plush toy shaped like a rock, and when the most enthusiastic stamp collector refers to loving stamps, it is an altogether different kind of affection.

We took the puppy home. I hugged it—her—from across the room. Then, because it—she—gave me reason to think I wouldn't lose digits in the process, I graduated to feeding her from my palm. Then I let her lick my hand. And then I let her lick my face. And then I licked her face. And now I love all dogs and will live happily ever after.

Sixty-three percent of American households have at least one pet. This prevalence is most impressive because of its newness. Keeping companion animals became common only with the rise of the middle class and urbanization, perhaps because of the deprivation of other contact with animals, or simply because pets cost money and are therefore a signifier of extravagance (Americans spend $34 billion on their companion animals every year). Oxford historian Sir Keith Thomas, whose encyclopedic work *Man and the Natural World* is now considered a classic, argues that

> the spread of pet-keeping among the urban middle classes in the early modern period is...a development of genuine social, psychological, and indeed commercial importance....It also had

intellectual implications. It encouraged the middle classes to form optimistic conclusions about animal intelligence; it gave rise to innumerable anecdotes about animal sagacity; it stimulated the notion that animals could have character and individual personality; and it created the psychological foundation for the view that some animals at least were entitled to moral consideration.

It wouldn't be right to say that my relationship with George has revealed to me the "sagacity" of animals. Beyond her most basic desires, I don't have the faintest clue what's going on in her head. (Although I have become convinced that much, beyond basic desires, is going on.) I'm surprised by her lack of intelligence as often as I'm surprised by her intelligence. The differences between us are always more present than the similarities.

And George isn't a kumbaya being who wants only to give and receive affection. As it turns out, she is a major pain in the ass an awful lot of the time. She compulsively pleasures herself in front of guests, eats my shoes and my son's toys, is monomaniacally obsessed with squirrel genocide, has the savant-like ability to find her way between the camera lens and the subject of every photo taken in her vicinity, lunges at skateboarders and Hasids, humiliates menstruating women (and is the worst nightmare of menstruating Hasids), backs her flatulent ass into the least interested person in the room, digs up the freshly planted, scratches the newly bought, licks the about-to-be-served, and occasionally exacts revenge (for *what?*) by shitting in the house.

Our various struggles—to communicate, to recognize and accommodate each other's desires, simply to coexist—force me to encounter and interact with something, or rather someone, entirely other. George can respond to a handful of words (and choose to

ignore a slightly larger handful), but our relationship takes place almost entirely outside of language. She seems to have thoughts and emotions. Sometimes I think I understand them, but often I don't. Like a photograph, she cannot say what she lets me see. She is an embodied secret. And I must be a photograph to her.

Just last night, I looked up from my reading to find George staring at me from across the room. "When did you come in here?" I asked. She lowered her eyes and lumbered away from me, down the hall—not a silhouette so much as a kind of negative space, a form cut out of the domesticity. Despite our patterns, which are more regular than anything I share with another person, she still feels unpredictable to me. And despite our closeness, I am occasionally thrilled, and even a bit scared, by the foreignness of her. Having a child greatly exacerbated this, as there was absolutely no guarantee—beyond the one I felt absolutely—that she wouldn't maul the baby.

The list of our differences could fill a book, but like me, George fears pain, seeks pleasure, and craves not just food and play, but companionship. I don't need to know the details of her moods and preferences to know that she has them. Our psychologies are not the same or similar, but each of us has a perspective, a way of processing and experiencing the world that is intrinsic and unique.

I wouldn't eat George, because she's mine. But why wouldn't I eat a dog I'd never met? Or more to the point, what justification might I have for sparing dogs but eating other animals?

A Case for Eating Dogs

DESPITE THE FACT THAT IT's perfectly legal in forty-four states, eating "man's best friend" is as taboo as a man eating his best friend. Even the most enthusiastic carnivores won't eat dogs. TV guy and

sometimes cooker Gordon Ramsay can get pretty macho with baby animals when doing publicity for something he's selling, but you'll never see a puppy peeking out of one of his pots. And though he once said he'd electrocute his children if they became vegetarian, I wonder what his response would be if they poached the family pooch.

Dogs are wonderful, and in many ways unique. But they are remarkably unremarkable in their intellectual and experiential capacities. Pigs are every bit as intelligent and feeling, by any sensible definition of the words. They can't hop into the back of a Volvo, but they can fetch, run and play, be mischievous, and reciprocate affection. So why don't they get to curl up by the fire? Why can't they at least be spared being tossed on the fire?

Our taboo against dog eating says something about dogs and a great deal about us.

The French, who love their dogs, sometimes eat their horses.

The Spanish, who love their horses, sometimes eat their cows.

The Indians, who love their cows, sometimes eat their dogs.

While written in a much different context, George Orwell's words (from *Animal Farm*) apply here: "All animals are equal, but some animals are more equal than others." The protective emphasis is not a law of nature; it comes from the stories we tell about nature.

So who's right? What might be the reasons to exclude canine from the menu? The selective carnivore suggests:

Don't eat companion animals. But dogs aren't kept as companions in all of the places they are eaten. And what about our petless neighbors? Would we have any right to object if they had dog for dinner?

OK, then:

Don't eat animals with significant mental capacities. If by "significant mental capacities" we mean what a dog has, then good for the

dog. But such a definition would also include the pig, cow, chicken, and many species of sea animals. And it would exclude severely impaired humans.

Then:

It's for good reason that the eternal taboos—don't fiddle with your shit, kiss your sister, or eat your companions—are taboo. Evolutionarily speaking, those things are bad for us. But dog eating hasn't been and isn't a taboo in many places, and it isn't in any way bad for us. Properly cooked, dog meat poses no greater health risks than any other meat, nor does such a nutritious meal foster much objection from the physical component of our selfish genes.

And dog eating has a proud pedigree. Fourth-century tombs contain depictions of dogs being slaughtered along with other food animals. It was a fundamental enough habit to have informed language itself: the Sino-Korean character for "fair and proper" (*yeon*) literally translates into "as cooked dog meat is delicious." Hippocrates praised dog meat as a source of strength. The Romans ate "suckling puppy," Dakota Indians enjoyed dog liver, and not so long ago Hawaiians ate dog brains and blood. The Mexican hairless dog was the *principal food species* of the Aztecs. Captain Cook ate dog. Roald Amundsen famously ate his sled dogs. (Granted, he was *really* hungry.) And dogs are still eaten to overcome bad luck in the Philippines; as medicine in China and Korea; to enhance libido in Nigeria; and in numerous places, on every continent, because they taste good. For centuries, the Chinese have raised special breeds of dogs, like the black-tongued chow, for chow, and many European countries still have laws on the books regarding postmortem examination of dogs intended for human consumption.

Of course, something having been done just about everywhere just about always is no kind of justification for doing it now. But unlike all farmed meat, which requires the creation and maintenance

of animals, dogs are practically begging to be eaten. Three to four million dogs and cats are euthanized annually. This amounts to millions of pounds of meat now being thrown away every year. The simple disposal of these euthanized dogs is an enormous ecological and economic problem. It would be demented to yank pets from homes. But eating those strays, those runaways, those not-quite-cute-enough-to-take and not-quite-well-behaved-enough-to-keep dogs would be killing a flock of birds with one stone and eating it, too.

In a sense it's what we're doing already. Rendering—the conversion of animal protein unfit for human consumption into food for livestock and pets—allows processing plants to transform useless dead dogs into productive members of the food chain. In America, millions of dogs and cats euthanized in animal shelters every year become the food for our food. (Almost twice as many dogs and cats are euthanized as are adopted.) So let's just eliminate this inefficient and bizarre middle step.

This need not challenge our civility. We won't make them suffer any more than necessary. While it's widely believed that adrenaline makes dog meat taste better—hence the traditional methods of slaughter: hanging, boiling alive, beating to death—we can all agree that if we're going to eat them, we should kill them quickly and painlessly, right? For example, the traditional Hawaiian means of holding the dog's nose shut—in order to conserve blood—must be regarded (socially if not legally) as a no-no. Perhaps we could include dogs under the Humane Methods of Slaughter Act. That doesn't say anything about how they're treated during their lives, and isn't subject to any meaningful oversight or enforcement, but surely we can rely on the industry to "self-regulate," as we do with other eaten animals.

Few people sufficiently appreciate the colossal task of feeding a

world of billions of omnivores who demand meat with their potatoes. The inefficient use of dogs—conveniently already in areas of high human population (take note, local-food advocates)—should make any good ecologist blush. One could argue that various "humane" groups are the worst hypocrites, spending enormous amounts of money and energy in a futile attempt to *reduce* the number of unwanted dogs while at the very same time propagating the irresponsible no-dog-for-dinner taboo. If we let dogs be dogs, and breed without interference, we would create a sustainable, local meat supply with low energy inputs that would put even the most efficient grass-based farming to shame. For the ecologically minded it's time to admit that dog is realistic food for realistic environmentalists.

Can't we get over our sentimentality? Dogs are plentiful, good for you, easy to cook, and tasty, and eating them is vastly more reasonable than going through all the trouble of processing them into protein bits to become the food for the other species that become our food.

For those already convinced, here's a classic Filipino recipe. I haven't tried it myself, but sometimes you can read a recipe and just know.

STEWED DOG, WEDDING STYLE

First, kill a medium-sized dog, then burn off the fur over a hot fire. Carefully remove the skin while still warm and set aside for later (may be used in other recipes). Cut meat into 1" cubes. Marinate meat in mixture of vinegar, peppercorn, salt, and garlic for 2 hours. Fry meat in oil using a large wok over an open fire, then add onions and chopped pineapple and sauté until tender. Pour in tomato sauce and boiling water, add green pepper, bay leaf, and Tabasco. Cover and simmer over warm coals

28

until meat is tender. Blend in puree of dog's liver and cook for additional 5–7 minutes.

A simple trick from the backyard astronomer: if you are having trouble seeing something, look slightly away from it. The most light-sensitive parts of our eyes (those we need to see dim objects) are on the edges of the region we normally use for focusing.

Eating animals has an invisible quality. Thinking about dogs, and their relationship to the animals we eat, is one way of looking askance and making something invisible visible.

2.

Friends and Enemies

DOGS AND FISH DON'T GO together. Dogs go with cats, kids, and firemen. We share our food and beds with them, bring them on planes and to doctors, take joy in their joy, and mourn their deaths. Fish go in aquariums, with tartar sauce, between chopsticks, and at the far end of human regard. They are divided from us by surfaces and silence.

The differences between dogs and fish couldn't seem more profound. *Fish* signifies an unimaginable plurality of kinds, an ocean of more than 31,000 different species unleashed by language each time we use the word. *Dogs*, by contrast, are decisively singular: one species and often known by personal names, e.g., George. I am among the 95 percent of male dog owners who talk to their

dogs—if not the 87 percent who believe their dogs talk back. But it's hard to imagine what a fish's internal experience of perception is like, much less try to engage with it. Fish are precisely attuned to changes in water pressure, can cue in to a diverse array of chemicals released by the bodies of other sea animals, and respond to sounds from as far away as twelve miles. Dogs are *here*, padding mud-pawed through our living rooms, snoring under our desks. Fish are always in another element, silent and unsmiling, legless and dead-eyed. They were created, in the Bible, on a different day, and are thought of as an unflatteringly early stop in the evolutionary march toward the human.

Historically, tuna—I'll use the tuna as the ambassador of the fish world, as it's the most eaten fish in the United States—were caught with individual hooks and lines, ultimately controlled by individual fishermen. A hooked fish might bleed to death or drown (fish drown when unable to move), and then be hauled into the boat. Larger fish (including not only tuna, but swordfish and marlin) would often only be injured by the hook, their wounded bodies still more than capable of resisting the pull of the line for hours or days. The massive power of larger fish meant that two and sometimes three men were required to pull in a single animal. Special pickax tools called gaffs were (and still are) used to pull in large fish once they were within reach. Slamming a gaff into the side, fin, or even the eye of a fish creates a bloody but effective handle to help haul it on deck. Some claim that it's most effective to place the hook of the gaff under the backbone. Others—like the authors of a United Nations manual for fishing—argue, "If possible gaff it by the head."

In the old days, fishermen painstakingly located schools of tuna and then muscled in one after another with pole, line, and gaff. The tuna on our plates today, though, is almost never caught with simple "pole and line" equipment, but with one of two modern methods:

the purse seine or the longline. Since I wanted to learn about the most common techniques for bringing the most commonly eaten sea animals to market, my research ultimately turned to these dominant methods of tuna fishing—and I'll describe them later. But I had plenty to consider first.

The Internet is overflowing with video footage of fishing. Shitty B rock as soundtracks to men behaving as if they just saved someone's life after reeling in a wearied marlin or bluefin. And then there are the subgenres of bikini-clad women gaffing, very young children gaffing, first-time gaffers. Looking past the bizarre ritualism, my mind kept returning to the fish in these videos, to the moment when the gaff is between the fisher's hand and the creature's eye....

No reader of this book would tolerate someone swinging a pickax at a dog's face. Nothing could be more obvious or less in need of explanation. Is such concern morally out of place when applied to fish, or are we silly to have such unquestioning concern about dogs? Is the suffering of a drawn-out death something that is cruel to inflict on any animal that can experience it, or just some animals?

Can the familiarity of the animals we have come to know as companions be a guide to us as we think about the animals we eat? Just how distant are fish (or cows, pigs, or chickens) from us in the scheme of life? Is it a chasm or a tree that defines the distance? Are nearness and distance even relevant? If we were to one day encounter a form of life more powerful and intelligent than our own, and it regarded us as we regard fish, what would be our argument against being eaten?

The lives of billions of animals a year and the health of the largest ecosystems on our planet hang on the thinly reasoned answers we give to these questions. Such global concerns can themselves feel distant, though. We care most about what's close to us, and

have a remarkably easy time forgetting everything else. We also have a strong impulse to do what others around us are doing, especially when it comes to food. Food ethics are so complex because food is bound to both taste buds and *taste*, to individual biographies and social histories. The choice-obsessed modern West is probably more accommodating to individuals who choose to eat differently than any culture has ever been, but ironically, the utterly unselective omnivore—"I'm easy; I'll eat anything"—can appear more socially sensitive than the individual who tries to eat in a way that is good for society. Food choices are determined by many factors, but reason (even consciousness) is not generally high on the list.

There is something about eating animals that tends to polarize: never eat them or never sincerely question eating them; become an activist or disdain activists. These opposing positions—and the closely related unwillingness to take a position—converge in suggesting that eating animals matters. If and how we eat animals cuts to something deep. Meat is bound up with the story of who we are and who we want to be, from the book of Genesis to the latest farm bill. It raises significant philosophical questions and is a $140 billion–plus a year industry that occupies nearly a third of the land on the planet, shapes ocean ecosystems, and may well determine the future of earth's climate. And yet we seem able to think only about the edges of the arguments—the logical extremes rather than the practical realities. My grandmother said she wouldn't eat pork to save her life, and though the context of her story is as extreme as it gets, many people seem to fall back on this all-or-nothing framework when discussing their everyday food choices. It's a way of thinking that we would never apply to other ethical realms. (Imagine always or never lying.) I can't count the times that upon telling someone I am vegetarian, he or she responded by pointing out an inconsistency in my lifestyle or trying to find a flaw

in an argument I never made. (I have often felt that my vegetarian-ism matters more to such people than it does to me.)

We need a better way to talk about eating animals. We need a way that brings meat to the center of public discussion in the same way it is often at the center of our plates. This doesn't require that we pretend we are going to have collective agreement. How-ever strong our intuitions are about what's right for us personally and even about what's right for others, we all know in advance that our positions will clash with those of our neighbors. What do we do with that most inevitable reality? Drop the conversation, or find a way to reframe it?

War

FOR EVERY TEN TUNA, SHARKS, and other large predatory fish that were in our oceans fifty to a hundred years ago, only one is left. Many scientists predict the total collapse of all fished species in less than fifty years—and intense efforts are under way to catch, kill, and eat even more sea animals. Our situation is so extreme that research scientists at the Fisheries Centre of the University of British Columbia argue that "our interactions with fisheries resources [also known as *fish*] have come to resemble...wars of extermination."

As I came to see, *war* is precisely the right word to describe our relationship to fish—it captures the technologies and techniques brought to bear against them, and the spirit of domination. As my experience with the world of animal agriculture deepened, I saw that the radical transformations fishing has undergone in the past fifty years are representative of something much larger. We have waged war, or rather let a war be waged, against all of the animals we eat. This war is new and has a name: factory farming.

Like pornography, factory farming is hard to define but easy to identify. In a narrow sense it is a system of industrialized and intensive agriculture in which animals—often housed by the tens or even hundreds of thousands—are genetically engineered, restricted in mobility, and fed unnatural diets (which almost always include various drugs, like antimicrobials). Globally, roughly 450 billion land animals are now factory farmed every year. (There is no tally of fish.) Ninety-nine percent of all land animals eaten or used to produce milk and eggs in the United States are factory farmed. So although there are important exceptions, to speak about eating animals today is to speak about factory farming.

More than any set of practices, factory farming is a mind-set: reduce production costs to the absolute minimum and systematically ignore or "externalize" such costs as environmental degradation, human disease, and animal suffering. For thousands of years, farmers took their cues from natural processes. Factory farming considers nature an obstacle to be overcome.

Industrial fishing is not exactly factory *farming*, but it belongs in the same category and needs to be part of the same discussion—it is part of the same agricultural coup. This is most obvious for aquaculture (farms on which fish are confined to pens and "harvested") but is every bit as true for wild fishing, which shares the same spirit and intensive use of modern technology.

Captains of fishing vessels today are more Kirk than Ahab. They watch fish from electronics-filled rooms and plot the best moment to rope in entire schools at a time. If fish are missed, the captains know it and take a second pass. And these fishers aren't just able to look at the schools of fish that are within a certain distance of their boats. GPS monitors are deployed along with "fish-attracting devices" (FADs) across the ocean. The monitors transmit informa-

tion to the control rooms of fishing boats about how many fish are present and the exact location of the floating FADs.

Once the picture of industrial fishing is filled in — the 1.4 *billion* hooks deployed annually on longlines (on each of which is a chunk of fish, squid, or dolphin flesh used as bait); the 1,200 nets, each one thirty miles in length, used by only one fleet to catch only one species; the ability of a single vessel to haul in fifty *tons* of sea animals in a few minutes — it becomes easier to think of contemporary fishers as factory farmers rather than fishermen.

Technologies of war have literally and systematically been applied to fishing. Radar, echo sounders (once used to locate enemy submarines), navy-developed electronic navigation systems, and, in the last decade of the twentieth century, satellite-based GPS give fishers unprecedented abilities to identify and return to fish hot spots. Satellite-generated images of ocean temperatures are used to identify fish schools.

Factory farming's success depends on consumers' nostalgic images of food production — the fisherman reeling in fish, the pig farmer knowing each of his pigs as individuals, the turkey rancher watching beaks break through eggs — because these images correspond to something we respect and trust. But these persistent images are also factory farmers' worst nightmares: they have the power to remind the world that what is now 99 percent of farming was not long ago less than 1 percent. The takeover of the factory farm could itself be taken over.

What might inspire such change? Few know the details about the contemporary meat and seafood industries, but most know the gist — at least that something isn't right. The details are important, but they probably won't, on their own, persuade most people to change. Something else is needed.

3.

Shame

AMONG MANY OTHER THINGS WE could say about his wide-ranging explorations of literature, Walter Benjamin was the most penetrating interpreter of Franz Kafka's animal tales.

Shame is crucial in Benjamin's reading of Kafka and is imagined as a unique moral sensibility. Shame is both intimate—felt in the depths of our inner lives—and, at the same time, social—something we feel strictly before others. For Kafka, shame is a response and a responsibility before invisible others—before "unknown family," to use a phrase from *The Trial*. It is the core experience of the ethical.

Benjamin emphasizes that Kafka's ancestors—his *unknown family*—include animals. Animals are part of the community in front of which Kafka might blush, a way of saying that they are within Kafka's sphere of moral concern. Benjamin also tells us that Kafka's animals are "receptacles of forgetting," a remark that is, at first, puzzling.

I mention these details here to frame a small story about Kafka's glance falling upon some fish in a Berlin aquarium. As told by Kafka's close friend Max Brod:

Suddenly he began to speak to the fish in their illuminated tanks. "Now at last I can look at you in peace, I don't eat you anymore." It was the time that he turned strict vegetarian. If you have never heard Kafka saying things of this sort with his own lips, it is difficult to imagine how simply and easily, without any affectation, without the least sentimentality—which was something almost completely foreign to him—he brought them out.

What had moved Kafka to become vegetarian? And why is it a comment about fish that Brod records to introduce Kafka's diet? Surely Kafka also made comments about land animals in the course of becoming vegetarian.

A possible answer lies in the connection that Benjamin makes, on the one hand, between animals and shame, and on the other, between animals and forgetting. Shame is the work of memory against forgetting. Shame is what we feel when we almost entirely—yet not entirely—forget social expectations and our obligations to others in favor of our immediate gratification. Fish, for Kafka, must have been the very flesh of forgetting: their lives are forgotten in a radical manner that is much less common in our thinking about farmed land animals.

Beyond this literal forgetting of animals by eating them, animal bodies were, for Kafka, burdened with the forgetting of all those parts of ourselves we want to forget. If we wish to disavow a part of our nature, we call it our "animal nature." We then repress or conceal that nature, and yet, as Kafka knew better than most, we sometimes wake up and find ourselves, still, only animals. And this seems right. We do not, so to speak, blush with shame before fish. We can recognize parts of ourselves in fish—spines, nociceptors (pain receptors), endorphins (that relieve pain), all of the familiar pain responses—but then deny that these animal similarities matter, and thus equally deny important parts of our humanity. What we forget about animals we begin to forget about ourselves.

Today, at stake in the question of eating animals is not only our basic ability to respond to sentient life, but our ability to respond to parts of our own (animal) being. There is a war not only between us and them, but between us and us. It is a war as old as story and more unbalanced than at any point in history. As philosopher and social critic Jacques Derrida reflects, it is

37

an unequal struggle, a war (whose inequality could one day be reversed) being waged between, on the one hand, those who violate not only animal life but even and also this sentiment of compassion, and, on the other hand, those who appeal for an irrefutable testimony to this pity.

War is waged over the matter of pity. This war is probably ageless but...it is passing through a critical phase. We are passing through that phase, and it passes through us. To think the war we find ourselves waging is not only a duty, a responsibility, an obligation, it is also a necessity, a constraint that, like it or not, directly or indirectly, no one can escape....The animal looks at us, and we are naked before it.

Silently the animal catches our glance. The animal looks at us, and whether we look away (from the animal, our plate, our concern, ourselves) or not, we are exposed. Whether we change our lives or do nothing, we have responded. To do nothing is to do something.

Perhaps the innocence of young children and their freedom from certain responsibilities allow them to absorb an animal's silence and gaze with more ease than adults. Perhaps our children, at least, have not taken a side in our war, only the spoils.

My family lived in Berlin in the spring of 2007, and we spent several afternoons at the aquarium. We stared into the tanks — or tanks just like the tanks — that Kafka had stared into. I was particularly taken by the sight of sea horses — those strange, chessman-like creatures that are a favorite of the popular animal imaginaire. Sea horses come not only in the chessman variety, but also in soda straw and plantlike shapes, and range in size from one to eleven inches. I am clearly not the only one fascinated by the perpetually startling appearance of these fish. (We desire to look at them so much that millions die in the aquarium and souvenir trade.) And it is just this

odd aesthetic bias that makes me spend time on them here, while I pass over so many other animals—animals closer to our realm of concern. Sea horses are the extreme of the extreme.

Sea horses, more than most animals, inspire wonder—they draw our attention to the astonishing similarities and discontinuities between each kind of creature and every other. They can change color to blend in with their surroundings, and beat their dorsal fins nearly as fast as a hummingbird beats its wings. Because they have no teeth or stomach, food moves through them almost instantly, requiring them to eat constantly. (Hence such adaptations as eyes that move independently, which allow them to search for prey without turning their heads.) Not terribly good swimmers, they can die of exhaustion when caught in even small currents, so they prefer to anchor themselves to sea grasses or coral, or to each other—they like to swim in pairs, linked by their prehensile tails. Sea horses have complicated routines for courtship, and tend to mate under full moons, making musical sounds while doing so. They live in long-term monogamous partnerships. What is perhaps most unusual, though, is that it is the male sea horse that carries the young for up to six weeks. Males become properly "pregnant," not only carrying, but fertilizing and nourishing the developing eggs with fluid secretions. The image of males giving birth is perpetually mind-blowing: a turbid liquid bursts forth from the brood pouch, and like magic, minuscule but fully formed sea horses appear out of the cloud.

My son was not impressed. He should have loved the aquarium, but was terrified and spent our time there pleading to go home. Perhaps he encountered something in what were, for me, the mute faces of sea animals. More likely he was afraid of the wet dimness, or the throat clearing of the whirring pumps, or the crowds. I figured if we went enough times, and stayed long enough, he would

realize—eureka!—that in fact he enjoyed being there. It never happened.

As a writer aware of that Kafka story, I came to feel a certain kind of shame at the aquarium. The reflection in the tanks wasn't Kafka's face. It belonged to a writer who, when held up to his hero, was grossly, shamefully inadequate. And as a Jew in Berlin, I felt other shades of shame. And there was the shame that came with being a tourist, and with being an American as photos of Abu Ghraib proliferated. And there was shame in being human: the shame of knowing that twenty of the roughly thirty-five classified species of sea horse worldwide are threatened with extinction because they are killed "unintentionally" in seafood production. The shame of indiscriminate killing for no nutritional necessity or political cause or irrational hatred or intractable human conflict. I felt shame in the deaths my culture justified by so thin a concern as the taste of canned tuna (sea horses are one of the more than one hundred sea animal species killed as "bycatch" in the modern tuna industry) or the fact that shrimp make convenient *hors d'oeuvres* (shrimp trawling devastates sea horse populations more than any other activity). I felt shame for living in a nation of unprecedented prosperity—a nation that spends a smaller percentage of income on food than any other civilization has in human history—but in the name of affordability treats the animals it eats with cruelty so extreme it would be illegal if inflicted on a dog.

And nothing inspires as much shame as being a parent. Children confront us with our paradoxes and hypocrisies, and we are exposed. You need to find an answer for every why—*Why do we do this? Why don't we do that?*—and often there isn't a good one. So you say, simply, *because.* Or you tell a story that you know isn't true. And whether or not your face reddens, you blush. The shame of parenthood—which is a *good* shame—is that we want our children to be

more whole than we are, to have satisfactory answers. My son not only inspired me to reconsider what kind of eating animal I would be, but shamed me into reconsideration.

And then there's George, asleep at my feet while I type these words, her body contorted to fit the rectangle of sun on the floor. Her paws are paddling in the air, so she is probably dreaming about running: Chasing a squirrel? Playing with another dog in the park? Maybe she's dreaming about swimming. I'd love to get inside that oblong skull of hers and see what mental baggage she's trying to sort through or unload. Occasionally, when dreaming, she'll let out a little yelp—sometimes loud enough to wake herself up, sometimes loud enough to rouse my son. (She always falls back asleep; he never does.) Sometimes she'll wake from a dream panting, jump to her feet, get right up near me—her hot breath pushing against my face—and look directly into my eyes. Between us is...*what?*

Words

Meaning

Animal agriculture makes a 40% greater contribution to global warming than all transportation in the world combined; it is the number one cause of climate change.

ANIMAL

Before visiting any farms, I spent more than a year wading through literature about eating animals: histories of agriculture, industry and United States Department of Agriculture (USDA) materials, activist pamphlets, relevant philosophical works, and the numerous existing books about food that touch on the subject of meat. I frequently found myself confused. Sometimes my disorientation was the result of the slipperiness of terms like *suffering, joy,* and *cruelty.* Sometimes it seemed to be a deliberate effect. Language is never fully trustworthy, but when it comes to eating animals, words are as often used to misdirect and camouflage as they are to communicate. Some words, like *veal,* help us forget what we are actually talking about. Some, like *free-range,* can mislead those whose consciences seek clarification. Some, like *happy,* mean the opposite of what they would seem. And some, like *natural,* mean next to nothing.

Nothing could seem more "natural" than the boundary between humans and animals (*see:* SPECIES BARRIER). It happens, though, that not all cultures even have the category *animal* or any equivalent word in their vocabulary—the Bible, for example, lacks any word that parallels the English *animal.* Even by the dictionary definition, humans both are and are not animals. In the first sense, humans are members of the animal kingdom. But more often, we casually use the word *animal* to signify all creatures—from orangutan to dog to shrimp—except humans. Within a culture, even within a family, people have their own understandings of what an animal is. Within each of us there are probably several different understandings.

What is an animal? Anthropologist Tim Ingold posed the question to a diverse group of scholars from the disciplines of social and

45

cultural anthropology, archaeology, biology, psychology, philosophy, and semiotics. It proved impossible for them to reach a consensus on the meaning of the word. Tellingly, though, there were two important points of agreement: "First, that there is a strong emotional undercurrent to our ideas about animality; and, second, that to subject these ideas to critical scrutiny is to expose highly sensitive and largely unexplored aspects of the understanding of our own humanity." To ask "What is an animal?"—or, I would add, to read a child a story about a dog or to support animal rights—is inevitably to touch upon how we understand what it means to be us and not them. It is to ask, "What is a human?"

ANTHROPOCENTRISM

The conviction that humans are the pinnacle of evolution, the appropriate yardstick by which to measure the lives of other animals, and the rightful owners of everything that lives.

ANTHROPODENIAL

The refusal to concede significant experiential likeness between humans and the other animals, as when my son asks if George will be lonely when we leave the house without her, and I say, "George doesn't get lonely."

ANTHROPOMORPHISM

The urge to project human experience onto the other animals, as when my son asks if George will be lonely.

The Italian philosopher Emanuela Cenami Spada wrote:

> Anthropomorphism is a risk we must run, because we must refer
> to our own human experience in order to formulate questions

about animal experience....The only available "cure" [for anthropomorphism] is the continuous critique of our working definitions in order to provide more adequate answers to our questions, and to that embarrassing problem that animals present to us.

What is that embarrassing problem? That we don't simply project human experience onto animals; we are (and are not) animals.

BATTERY CAGE

Is it anthropomorphism to try to imagine yourself into a farmed animal's cage? Is it anthropodenial not to?

The typical cage for egg-laying hens allows each sixty-seven square inches of floor space—somewhere between the size of this page and a sheet of printer paper. Such cages are stacked between three and nine tiers high—Japan has the world's highest battery cage unit, with cages stacked eighteen tiers high—in windowless sheds.

Step your mind into a crowded elevator, an elevator so crowded you cannot turn around without bumping into (and aggravating) your neighbor. The elevator is so crowded you are often held aloft. This is a kind of blessing, as the slanted floor is made of wire, which cuts into your feet.

After some time, those in the elevator will lose their ability to work in the interest of the group. Some will become violent; others will go mad. A few, deprived of food and hope, will become cannibalistic.

There is no respite, no relief. No elevator repairman is coming. The doors will open once, at the end of your life, for your journey to the only place worse (see: PROCESSING).

BROILER CHICKENS

Not all chickens have to endure battery cages. In this way only, it could be said that *broilers*—chickens that become meat (as opposed to *layers*, chickens that lay eggs)—are lucky: they tend to get close to a single square foot of space.

If you aren't a farmer, what I've just written probably confuses you. You probably thought that chickens were chickens. But for the past half century, there have actually been two kinds of chickens—broilers and layers—each with distinct genetics. We call them both chickens, but they have starkly different bodies and metabolisms, engineered for different "functions." Layers make eggs. (Their egg output has more than doubled since the 1930s.) Broilers make flesh. (In the same period, they have been engineered to grow more than twice as large in less than half the time. Chickens once had a life expectancy of fifteen to twenty years, but the modern broiler is typically killed at around six weeks. Their daily growth rate has increased roughly 400 percent.)

This raises all kinds of bizarre questions—questions that before I learned about our two types of chickens, I'd never had reason to ask—like, *What happens to all of the male offspring of layers?* If man hasn't designed them for meat, and nature clearly hasn't designed them to lay eggs, what function do they serve?

They serve no function. Which is why all male layers—half of all the layer chickens born in the United States, more than 250 million chicks a year—are destroyed.

Destroyed? That seems like a word worth knowing more about.

Most male layers are destroyed by being sucked through a series of pipes onto an electrified plate. Other layer chicks are destroyed in other ways, and it's impossible to call those animals more or less fortunate. Some are tossed into large plastic containers. The weak are trampled to the bottom, where they suffocate slowly. The strong

suffocate slowly at the top. Others are sent fully conscious through macerators (picture a wood chipper filled with chicks).

Cruel? Depends on your definition of cruelty (*see:* CRUELTY).

BULLSHIT

1) The shit of a bull (*see also:* ENVIRONMENTALISM)

2) Misleading or false language and statements, such as:

BYCATCH

Perhaps the quintessential example of bullshit, *bycatch* refers to sea creatures caught by accident—except not really "by accident," since bycatch has been consciously built into contemporary fishing methods. Modern fishing tends to involve much technology and few fishers. This combination leads to massive catches with massive amounts of bycatch. Take shrimp, for example. The average shrimp-trawling operation throws 80 to 90 percent of the sea animals it captures overboard, dead or dying, as bycatch. (Endangered species amount to much of this bycatch.) Shrimp account for only 2 percent of global seafood by weight, but shrimp trawling accounts for 33 percent of global bycatch. We tend not to think about this because we tend not to know about it. What if there were labeling on our food letting us know how many animals were killed to bring our desired animal to our plate? So, with trawled shrimp from Indonesia, for example, the label might read: 26 POUNDS OF OTHER SEA ANIMALS WERE KILLED AND TOSSED BACK INTO THE OCEAN FOR EVERY 1 POUND OF THIS SHRIMP.

Or take tuna. Among the other 145 species regularly killed—gratuitously—while killing tuna are: manta ray, devil ray, spotted skate, bignose shark, copper shark, Galapagos shark, sandbar shark, night shark, sand tiger shark, (great) white shark, hammerhead shark, spurdog fish, Cuban dogfish, bigeye thresher, mako, blue shark, wahoo, sailfish, bonito, king mackerel, Spanish mackerel,

longbill spearfish, white marlin, swordfish, lancet fish, grey trigger-fish, needlefish, pomfret, blue runner, black ruff, dolphin fish, bigeye cigarfish, porcupine fish, rainbow runner, anchovy, grouper, flying fish, cod, common sea horse, Bermuda chub, opah, escolar, leerfish, tripletail, goosefish, monkfish, sunfish, Murray eel, pilotfish, black gemfish, stone bass, bluefish, cassava fish, red drum, greater amber-jack, yellowtail, common sea bream, barracuda, puffer fish, logger-head turtle, green turtle, leatherback turtle, hawksbill turtle, Kemp's ridley turtle, Atlantic yellow-nosed albatross, Audouin's gull, balearic shearwater, black-browed albatross, great black-backed gull, great shearwater, great-winged petrel, grey petrel, herring gull, laughing gull, northern royal albatross, shy albatross, sooty shearwater, south-ern fulmar, Yelkouan shearwater, yellow-legged gull, minke whale, sei whale, fin whale, common dolphin, northern right whale, pilot whale, humpback whale, beaked whale, killer whale, harbor porpoise, sperm whale, striped dolphin, Atlantic spotted dolphin, spinner dol-phin, bottlenose dolphin, and goose-beaked whale.

Imagine being served a plate of sushi. But this plate also holds all of the animals that were killed for your serving of sushi. The plate might have to be five feet across.

CAFO

Concentrated Animal Feeding Operation, a.k.a. factory farm. Tell-ingly, this formal designation was created not by the meat industry but by the Environmental Protection Agency (*see also:* ENVIRON-MENTALISM). All CAFOs harm animals in ways that would be illegal according to even relatively weak animal welfare legislation. Thus:

CFE

Common Farming Exemptions make legal any method of rais-ing farmed animals so long as it is commonly practiced within

the industry. In other words, farmers—*corporations* is the right word—have the power to define cruelty. If the industry adopts a practice—hacking off unwanted appendages with no painkillers, for example, but you can let your imagination run with this—it automatically becomes legal.

CFEs are enacted state by state and range from the disturbing to the absurd. Take Nevada. Under its CFE, the state's welfare laws cannot be enforced to "prohibit or interfere with established methods of animal husbandry, including the raising, handling, feeding, housing, and transporting, of livestock or farm animals." What happens in Vegas stays in Vegas.

Lawyers David Wolfson and Mariann Sullivan, experts on the issue, explain:

> Certain states exempt specific practices, rather than all customary farming practices.... Ohio exempts farmed animals from requirements for "wholesome exercise and a change of air," and Vermont exempts farmed animals from the section in its criminal anticruelty statute that deems it illegal to "tie, tether and restrain" an animal in a manner that is "inhumane or detrimental to its welfare." One cannot help but assume that in Ohio farmed animals are denied exercise and air, and that in Vermont they are tied, tethered or restrained in a manner that is inhumane.

COMFORT FOOD

One night, when my son was four weeks old, he developed a slight fever. By the next morning he was having trouble breathing. On our pediatrician's recommendation, we took him to the emergency room, where he was diagnosed with RSV (respiratory syncytial virus), which often expresses itself in adults as the common cold,

but in babies can be extremely dangerous, even life threatening. We ended up spending a week in the pediatric intensive-care unit, my wife and I taking turns sleeping in the armchair in our son's room, and on the waiting-room recliner.

On the second, third, fourth, and fifth days, our friends Sam and Eleanor brought us food. Lots of food, far more than we could eat: lentil salad, chocolate truffles, roasted vegetables, nuts and berries, mushroom risotto, potato pancakes, green beans, nachos, wild rice, oatmeal, dried mango, pasta primavera, chili—all of it comfort food. We could have eaten in the cafeteria or ordered in. And they could have expressed their love with visits and kind words. But they brought all of that food, and it was a small, good thing that we needed. That, more than any other reason—and there are many other reasons—is why this book is dedicated to them.

COMFORT FOOD, CONT.

On the sixth day, my wife and I were able, for the first time since arriving, to leave the hospital together. Our son was clearly over the hump, and doctors thought we'd be able to take him home the following morning. We could hear the bullet we'd dodged whistle past. So as soon as he'd fallen asleep (with my in-laws by his bedside), we took the elevator down and reemerged into the world.

It was snowing. The snowflakes were surreally large, distinct and durable: like the ones children cut out of white paper. We glided like sleepwalkers down Second Avenue, no destination in mind, and ended up in a Polish diner. Massive glass windows faced the street, and the snowflakes clung for several seconds before descending. I can't remember what I ordered. I can't remember if the food was any good. It was the best meal of my life.

CRUELTY

Not only the willful causing of unnecessary suffering, but the indifference to it. It's much easier to be cruel than one might think.

It's often said that nature, "red in tooth and claw," is cruel. I heard this again and again from ranchers, who tried to persuade me that they were protecting their animals from what lay outside the enclosures. Nature is no picnic, true. (*Picnics* are rarely picnics.) And it's also true that animals on the very best farms often have better lives than they would in the wild. But nature isn't cruel. And neither are the animals in nature that kill and occasionally even torture one another. Cruelty depends on an understanding of cruelty, and the ability to choose against it. Or to choose to ignore it.

DESPERATION

There are sixty pounds of flour in my grandmother's basement. On a recent weekend visit, I was sent down to retrieve a bottle of Coke and discovered the sacks lining the wall, like sandbags on the banks of a rising river. Why would a ninety-year-old woman need so much flour? And why the several dozen two-liter bottles of Coke, or the pyramid of Uncle Ben's, or the wall of pumpernickel loaves in the freezer?

"I noticed you have an awful lot of flour in the basement," I said, returning to the kitchen.

"Sixty pounds."

I couldn't read her tone. Was that pride I heard? A hint of challenge? Shame?

"Can I ask why?"

She opened a cabinet and took down a thick stack of coupons, each of which offered a free sack of flour for every bag purchased.

"How did you get so many of these?" I asked.

"It wasn't a problem."

"What are you going to do with all of that flour?"

"I'll make some cookies."

I tried to imagine how my grandmother, who has never driven a car in her life, managed to schlep all of those sacks from the supermarket to her house. Someone drove her, as always, but did she load down any one car with all sixty, or did she make multiple trips? Knowing my grandmother, she probably calculated how many sacks she could get in one car without overly inconveniencing the driver. She then contacted the necessary number of friends and made that many trips to the supermarket, likely in one day. Was this what she meant by ingenuity, all those times she told me that it was her luck and ingenuity that got her through the Holocaust?

I've been an accomplice on many of my grandmother's food-acquisition missions. I remember a sale of some pelleted bran cereal, for which the coupon limited three boxes per customer. After buying three boxes herself, my grandmother sent my brother and me to buy three boxes each while she waited at the door. What must I have looked like to the cashier? A five-year-old boy using a coupon to buy multiple boxes of a foodstuff that not even a genuinely starving person would willfully eat? We went back an hour later and did it again.

The flour demanded answers. For what population was she planning on baking all of these cookies? Where was she hiding the 1,400 cartons of eggs? And most obviously: How did she get all of those sacks into the basement? I've met enough of her decrepit chauffeurs to know they weren't doing the hauling.

"One bag at a time," she said, dusting the table with her palm.

One bag at a time. My grandmother has trouble making it from the car to the front door one step at a time. Her breathing is slow and labored, and on a recent visit to the doctor, it was discovered that she shares a heart rate with the great blue whale.

Her perpetual wish is to live to the next bar mitzvah, but I expect her to live another decade, at least. She's not the kind of person who dies. She could live to be 120, and there's no way she'll use up half of the flour. And she must know that.

DISCOMFORT FOOD

Sharing food generates good feeling and creates social bonds. Michael Pollan, who has written as thoughtfully about food as anyone, calls this "table fellowship" and argues that its importance, which I agree is significant, is a vote against vegetarianism. At one level, he's right.

Let's assume you're like Pollan and are opposed to factory-farmed meat. If you're at the guest end, it stinks not to eat food that was prepared for you, especially (although he doesn't get into this) when the grounds for refusal are ethical. But how much does it stink? It's a classic dilemma: How much do I value creating a socially comfortable situation, and how much do I value acting socially responsible? The relative importance of ethical eating and table fellowship will be different in different situations (declining my grandmother's chicken with carrots is different from passing on microwaved buffalo wings).

More important, though, and what Pollan curiously doesn't emphasize, is that attempting to be a selective omnivore is a much heavier blow to table fellowship than vegetarianism. Imagine an acquaintance invites you to dinner. You could say, "I'd love to come. And just so you know, I'm a vegetarian." You could also say, "I'd love to come. But I only eat meat that is produced by family farmers." Then what do you do? You'll probably have to send the host a web link or list of local shops to even make the request intelligible, let alone manageable. This effort might be well-placed, but it is certainly more invasive than asking for vegetarian food (which these days requires no explanation). The entire food industry (restaurants, airline and college

food services, catering at weddings) is set up to accommodate vegetarians. There is no such infrastructure for the selective omnivore.

And what about being at the host end of a gathering? Selective omnivores also eat vegetarian fare, but the reverse is obviously not true. What choice promotes greater table fellowship?

And it isn't just what we put into our mouths that creates table fellowship, but what comes out. There is also the possibility that a conversation about what we believe would generate more fellowship—even when we believe different things—than any food being served.

DOWNER

1) Something or someone depressing.

2) An animal that collapses from poor health and is unable to stand back up. This does not imply grave illness any more than a fallen person does. Some downed animals are seriously ill or injured, but often enough they require little more than water and rest to be spared a slow, painful death. There aren't reliable statistics available about downers (who would report them?), but estimates put the number of downed cows at around 200,000 a year—about two cows for every word in this book. When it comes to animal welfare, the absolute bare minimum, the least we could conceivably give, would seem to be euthanizing downed animals. But that costs money, and downers have no use and so earn no regard or mercy. In most of America's fifty states it is perfectly legal (and perfectly common) to simply let downers die of exposure over days or toss them, live, into dumpsters.

My first research visit for this book was to Farm Sanctuary in Watkins Glen, New York. Farm Sanctuary is not a farm. Nothing is grown or raised there. Founded in 1986, by Gene Baur and his then-wife, Lorri Houston, it was created as a place for rescued farmed animals to live out their unnatural lives. (*Natural lives* would be an awkward expression to use in reference to animals designed to be

slaughtered in their adolescence. Farmed pigs, for example, are usually slaughtered at about 250 pounds. Let these genetic mutants live on, as they do at Farm Sanctuary, and they can exceed 800 pounds.)

Farm Sanctuary has become one of the most important animal protection, education, and lobbying organizations in America. Once funded by the sales of veggie hot dogs off the back of a VW van at Grateful Dead concerts—there's no real need to make a joke here—Farm Sanctuary has expanded to occupy 175 acres in upstate New York and another 300-acre sanctuary in northern California. It has more than 200,000 members, an annual budget of about $6 million, and the ability to help shape local and national legislation. But none of that is why I chose to begin there. I simply wanted to interact with farmed animals. In my thirty years of life, the only pigs, cows, and chickens I had touched were dead and cut up.

As we walked the pasture, Baur explained that Farm Sanctuary was less his dream or big idea than it was the product of a fortuitous event.

"I was driving around the Lancaster stockyard, and saw, around back, a pile of downers. I approached, and one of the sheep moved her head. I realized she was still alive, left there to suffer. So I put her in the back of my van. I'd never done anything like that before, but I couldn't leave her like that. I took her to the vet, expecting she'd be euthanized. But after a bit of prodding, she just stood right up. We took her to our house in Wilmington, and then, when we got the farm, we took her here. She lived ten years. *Ten*. Good years."

I mention this story not to promote additional farm sanctuaries. They do plenty of good, but that good is educational (offering exposure to people like me) and not practical in the sense of actually rescuing and caring for a significant number of animals. Baur would be the first to acknowledge this. I mention the story to illustrate just how close to health downed animals can be. Any individual that close needs either to be saved or mercifully killed.

ENVIRONMENTALISM

Concern for the preservation and restoration of natural resources and the ecological systems that sustain human life. There are grander definitions I could get more excited about, but this is in fact what is usually meant by the term, at least for the moment. Some environmentalists include animals as resources. What is meant by *animals* here is usually endangered or hunted species, rather than those most populous on earth, which are most in need of preservation and restoration.

A University of Chicago study recently found that our food choices contribute at least as much as our transportation choices to global warming. More recent and authoritative studies by the United Nations and the Pew Commission show conclusively that globally, farmed animals contribute *more* to climate change than transport. According to the UN, the livestock sector is responsible for 18 percent of greenhouse gas emissions, around 40 percent more than the entire transport sector—cars, trucks, planes, trains, and ships—combined. Animal agriculture is responsible for 37 percent of anthropogenic methane, which offers twenty-three times the global warming potential (GWP) of CO_2, as well as 65 percent of anthropogenic nitrous oxide, which provides a staggering 296 times the GWP of CO_2. The most current data even quantifies the role of diet: omnivores contribute seven times the volume of greenhouse gases that vegans do.

The UN summarized the environmental effects of the meat industry this way: raising animals for food (whether on factory or traditional farms) "is one of the top two or three most significant contributors to the most serious environmental problems, at every scale from local to global.... [Animal agriculture] should be a major policy focus when dealing with problems of land degradation, climate change and air pollution, water shortage and water pollution and loss

of biodiversity. Livestock's contribution to environmental problems is on a massive scale." In other words, if one cares about the environment, and if one accepts the scientific results of such sources as the UN (or the Intergovernmental Panel on Climate Change, or the Center for Science in the Public Interest, or the Pew Commission, or the Union of Concerned Scientists, or the Worldwatch Institute...), one *must* care about eating animals.

Most simply put, someone who regularly eats factory-farmed animal products cannot call himself an environmentalist without divorcing that word from its meaning.

FACTORY FARM

This term is sure to fall out of use in the next generation or so, either because there will be no more factory farms, or because there will be no more family farms to compare them to.

FAMILY FARM

A family farm is typically defined as a farm where a family owns the animals, manages the operations, and contributes labor on a day-to-day basis. Two generations ago, virtually all farms were family farms.

FEED CONVERSION

By necessity, both factory and family farmers are concerned with the ratio of edible animal flesh, eggs, or milk produced per unit of food a farmed animal is fed. It's the disparity of their concern — and the very different lengths to which they will go to increase profitability — that distinguishes the two kinds of farmers. For example:

FOOD AND LIGHT

Factory farms commonly manipulate food and light to increase productivity, often at the expense of the animals' welfare. Egg

farmers do this to reboot birds' internal clocks so they start laying valuable eggs faster and, crucially, at the same time. Here's how one poultry farmer described the situation to me:

> As soon as females mature—in the turkey industry at twenty-three to twenty-six weeks and with chickens sixteen to twenty—they're put into barns and they lower the light; sometimes it's total darkness twenty-four/seven. And then they put them on a very low-protein diet, almost a starvation diet. That will last about two or three weeks. Then they turn the lights on sixteen hours a day, or twenty with chickens, so she thinks it's spring, and they put her on high-protein feed. She immediately starts laying. They have it down to such a science that they can stop it, start it, and everything. See, in the wild, when spring comes, the bugs come and the grass comes and the days get longer—that's a key to tell the birds, "Well, I better start laying. Spring is coming." So man has tapped into that already built-in thing. And by controlling the light, the feed, and when they eat, the industry can force the birds to lay eggs year-round. So that's what they do. Turkey hens now lay 120 eggs a year and chickens lay over 300. That's two or even three times as many as in nature. After that first year, they are killed because they won't lay as many eggs in the second year—the industry figured out that it's cheaper to slaughter them and start over than it is feed and house birds that lay fewer eggs. These practices are a big part of why poultry meat is so cheap today, but the birds suffer for it.

While most people know the vague outlines of the cruelty of factory farms—the cages are small, the slaughter is violent—certain widely practiced techniques have eluded the public consciousness. I had never heard about food and light deprivation. And after learning

about it, I didn't want to eat a conventional egg ever again. Thank goodness for free-range. Right?

FREE-RANGE

Applied to meat, eggs, dairy, and every now and then even fish (tuna on the range?), the free-range label is bullshit. It should provide no more peace of mind than "all-natural," "fresh," or "magical."

To be considered free-range, chickens raised for meat must have "access to the outdoors," which, if you take those words literally, means nothing. (Imagine a shed containing thirty thousand chickens, with a small door at one end that opens to a five-by-five dirt patch—and the door is closed all but occasionally.)

The USDA doesn't even have a definition of free-range for laying hens and instead relies on producer testimonials to support the accuracy of these claims. Very often, the eggs of factory-farmed chickens—chickens packed against one another in vast barren barns—are labeled free-range. ("Cage-free" is regulated but means no more or less than what it says—they are literally not in cages.) One can reliably assume that most "free-range" (or "cage-free") laying hens are debeaked, drugged, and cruelly slaughtered once "spent." I could keep a flock of hens under my sink and call them free-range.

FRESH

More bullshit. According to the USDA, "fresh" poultry has never had an internal temperature below 26 degrees or above 40 degrees Fahrenheit. Fresh chicken can be frozen (thus the oxymoron "fresh frozen"), and there is no time component to food freshness. Pathogen-infested, feces-splattered chicken can technically be fresh, cage-free, and free-range, and sold in the supermarket legally (the shit does need to be rinsed off first).

HABIT, THE POWER OF

My father, who did just about all of the cooking in our house, raised us on exotics. We ate tofu before tofu was tofu. It's not that he liked the taste, or even that the supposed health benefits were touted as they are now. He simply liked eating something that no one else ate. And it wasn't enough to use an unfamiliar food according to its typical preparation. No, he made portobello "fingers," falafel "ragu," seitan "scramblers."

Much of my father's scare-quote cooking involved food substitution, sometimes in the interest of placating my mother by replacing a gratuitously unkosher food with a more subtly unkosher one (bacon→turkey bacon), an unhealthy food with a more subtly unhealthy one (turkey bacon→fakin' bacon), and sometimes simply to prove it could be done (flour→buckwheat). A few of his substitutions seemed to be nothing less than flipped middle fingers at nature itself.

On a recent trip home, I found the following foods in my parents' refrigerator: faux chicken patties, nuggets, and strips; fake sausage links and patties; butter and egg substitutes, veggie burgers, and vegetarian kielbasa. You might assume that someone with a dozen varieties of imitation animal products was a vegan, but that would not only be incorrect—my father eats meat all the time—it would miss the point entirely. My father has always cooked against the grain. His cuisine is as existential as it is gastronomic.

We never questioned it, and might even have liked it—even if we never wanted to have friends come over for dinner. We might even have thought of him as a Great Chef. But as with my grandmother's cooking, the food wasn't food. It was story: ours was the dad who liked to take safe chances, who encouraged us to try the new thing because it was new, who liked it when people laughed at his mad-scientist cooking, because the laughter was more valuable than the taste of food could ever be.

One thing that never followed dinner was dessert. I lived with my parents for eighteen years and cannot remember a single family meal that included something sweet. My father wasn't trying to protect our teeth. (I don't remember being asked to brush much in those years.) He just didn't think of dessert as necessary. Savory foods were clearly superior, so why waste stomach real estate? The amazing thing is that we believed him. My tastes—not only my ideas about foods, but my preconscious cravings—were formed around his lessons. To this day, I get less excited about dessert than anyone I know, and would always choose a slice of black bread over one of yellow cake.

Around what lessons will my son's cravings be formed? Although my taste for meat has almost entirely gone away—I often find the sight of red meat repulsive—the smell of a summer barbecue still makes my mouth water. What will it do to my son? Will he be among the first of a generation that doesn't crave meat because it never tasted it? Or will he crave it even more?

HUMAN

Humans are the only animals that have children on purpose, keep in touch (or don't), care about birthdays, waste and lose time, brush their teeth, feel nostalgia, scrub stains, have religions and political parties and laws, wear keepsakes, apologize years after an offense, whisper, fear themselves, interpret dreams, hide their genitalia, shave, bury time capsules, and can choose not to eat something for reasons of conscience. The justifications for eating animals and for not eating them are often identical: we are not them.

INSTINCT

Most of us are familiar with the remarkable navigational abilities of migrating birds, which are able to find their way to specific nesting

grounds across continents. When I learned about this, I was told that it was "instinct." ("Instinct" continues to be the explanation of choice whenever animal behavior implies too much intelligence [*see:* INTELLIGENCE].) Instinct, though, wouldn't go very far in explaining how pigeons use human transportation routes to navigate. Pigeons follow highways and take particular exits, likely following many of the same landmarks as the humans driving below.

Intelligence used to be narrowly defined as intellectual ability (book smarts); we now consider multiple intelligences, such as visual-spatial, interpersonal, emotional, and musical. A cheetah is not intelligent because it can run fast. But its uncanny ability to map space—to find the hypotenuse, to anticipate and counter the movements of prey—is a kind of mental work that matters. To write this off as instinct makes as much sense as equating the kick that results from a physician's mallet tapping your knee to your being able to successfully take a penalty kick in a soccer game.

INTELLIGENCE

Generations of farmers have known that clever pigs will learn to undo the latches of their pens. Gilbert White, the British naturalist, wrote in 1789 of one such pig, a female, who, after undoing her own latch, "used to open all the intervening gates, and march, by herself, up to a distant farm where [a male] was kept; and when her purpose was served"—a great way of putting it—"would return home by the same means."

Scientists have documented a pig language of sorts, and pigs will come when called (to humans or one another), will play with toys (and have favorites), and have been observed coming to the aid of other pigs in distress. Dr. Stanley Curtis, an animal scientist friendly to the industry, empirically evaluated the cognitive abilities of pigs by training them to play a video game with a joystick modified

for snouts. They not only learned the games, but did so as fast as chimpanzees, demonstrating a surprising capacity for abstract representation. And the legend of pigs undoing latches continues. Dr. Ken Kephart, a colleague of Curtis's, not only confirms the ability of pigs to do this, but adds that pigs often work in pairs, are usually repeat offenders, and in some cases undo the latches of fellow pigs. If pig intelligence has been part of America's barnyard folklore, that same lore has imagined fish and chickens as especially stupid. Are they?

INTELLIGENCE?

In 1992, only 70 peer-reviewed papers had reported on fish learning—a decade later there were 500 such papers (today it tops 640). Our knowledge of no other animal has been so quickly and dramatically revised. If you were the world expert on fish mental capacities in the 1990s, you're at best a novice today.

Fish build complex nests, form monogamous relationships, hunt cooperatively with other species, and use tools. They recognize one another as individuals (and keep track of who is to be trusted and who is not). They make decisions individually, and monitor social prestige and vie for better positions (to quote from the peer review journal *Fish and Fisheries:* they use "Machiavellian strategies of manipulation, punishment and reconciliation"). They have significant long-term memories, are skilled in passing knowledge to one another through social networks, and can also pass on information generationally. They even have what the scientific literature calls "long-standing 'cultural traditions' for particular pathways to feeding, schooling, resting or mating sites."

And chickens? There has been a revolution in scientific understanding here as well. Dr. Lesley Rogers, a prominent animal physiologist, discovered the lateralization of avian brains—the separation of the brain into left and right hemispheres with different

specialties—at a time when this was believed to be a unique property of the human brain. (Scientists now agree that lateralization is present throughout the animal kingdom.) Building on forty years of research experience, Rogers argues that our present knowledge of bird brains has made it "clear that birds have cognitive capacities equivalent to those of mammals, even primates." She argues they have sophisticated memories that are "written down according to some sort of chronological sequence that becomes a unique autobiography." Like fish, chickens can pass information generationally. They also deceive one another and can delay satisfaction for larger rewards.

Such research has altered our understanding of birds' brains so much that in 2005, scientific experts from around the world convened to begin the process of renaming the parts of avian brains. They aimed to replace old terms that implied "primitive" functions with the new realization that bird brains process information in a manner analogous to (but different from) the human cerebral cortex.

The image of hard-nosed physiologists standing over diagrams of brains and arguing for a renaming has a larger resonance. Think of the beginning of the story of the beginning of everything: Adam (without Eve and without divine guidance) names the animals. Continuing his work, we call stupid people bird-brained, cowardly people chickens, fools turkeys. Are these the best names we have to offer? If we can revise the notion of women coming from a rib, can't we revise our categorizations of the animals that, draped with barbecue sauce, end up as the ribs on our dinner plates—or for that matter, the KFC in our hands?

KFC

Formerly signifying Kentucky Fried Chicken, now signifying nothing, KFC is arguably the company that has increased the sum total

of suffering in the world more than any other in history. KFC buys nearly a billion chickens a year—if you packed those chickens body to body, they would blanket Manhattan from river to river and spill from the windows of the higher floors of office buildings—so its practices have profound ripple effects throughout all sectors of the poultry industry.

KFC insists it is "committed to the well-being and humane treatment of chickens." How trustworthy are these words? At a slaughterhouse in West Virginia that supplies KFC, workers were documented tearing the heads off live birds, spitting tobacco into their eyes, spray-painting their faces, and violently stomping on them. These acts were witnessed dozens of times. This slaughter-house was not a "bad apple," but a "Supplier of the Year." Imagine what happens at the bad apples when no one is looking.

On KFC's website, the company claims, "We are monitoring our suppliers on an ongoing basis to determine whether our suppliers are using humane procedures for caring for and handling animals they supply to us. As a consequence, it is our goal to only deal with suppliers who promise to maintain our high standards and share our commitment to animal welfare." That is half true. KFC does deal with suppliers that *promise* to ensure welfare. What KFC doesn't tell you is that anything the suppliers practice is necessarily considered welfare (*see:* CFE).

A similar half-truth is the claim that KFC conducts welfare audits of its suppliers' slaughter facilities (the "monitoring" alluded to above). What we are not told is that these are typically *announced* audits. KFC announces an inspection meant (at least in theory) to document illicit behavior in a manner that allows plenty of time for the soon-to-be-inspected to throw a tarp over whatever they don't want seen. Not only that, but the standards the auditors are asked to report on do not include a single one of the recommendations

recently made by KFC's own (now former) animal welfare advisers, five of whom resigned in frustration. One of them, Adele Douglass, told the *Chicago Tribune* that KFC "never had any meetings. They never asked any advice, and then they touted to the press that they had this animal-welfare advisory committee. I felt like I was being used." Ian Duncan, the Emeritus Chair in Animal Welfare at the University of Guelph, another former board member and one of North America's leading scientific experts on bird welfare, said that "progress was extremely slow, which is why I resigned. It was always going to be happening later. They just put off actually creating standards....I suspect that upper management didn't really think that animal welfare was important."

How were these five board members replaced? KFC's Animal Welfare Council now includes a vice president for Pilgrim's Pride, the company operating the "Supplier of the Year" plant at which some workers were shown sadistically abusing birds; a director for Tyson Foods, which slaughters 2.2 billion chickens annually and where some employees were also found to be mutilating live birds during multiple investigations (in one, employees also urinated directly onto the slaughter line); and regular participation from its own "executives and other employees." Essentially, KFC is claiming that its advisers developed programs for its suppliers, even though its advisers are its suppliers.

Like its name, KFC's commitment to animal welfare signifies nothing.

KOSHER?

As I was taught them, in Hebrew school and at home, the Jewish dietary laws were devised as a compromise: if humans absolutely must eat animals, we should do so humanely, with respect for the other creatures in the world and with humility. Don't subject the

animals you eat to unnecessary suffering, either in their lives or in their slaughter. It's a way of thinking that made me proud to be Jewish as a child, and that continues to make me proud.

This is why when fully conscious cattle at the (then) largest kosher slaughterhouse in the world, Agriprocessors in Postville, Iowa, were videotaped having their tracheas and esophagi systematically pulled from their cut throats, languishing for up to three minutes as a result of sloppy slaughter, and being shocked with electric prods in their faces, it bothered me even more than the innumerable times I'd heard of such things happening at conventional slaughterhouses.

To my relief, much of the Jewish community spoke out against the Iowa plant. The president of the Rabbinical Assembly of the Conservative Movement, in a message sent to every one of its rabbis, asserted, "When a company purporting to be kosher violates the prohibition against *tza'ar ba'alei hayyim*, causing pain to one of God's living creatures, that company must answer to the Jewish community, and ultimately, to God." The Orthodox chair of the Talmud Department at Israel's Bar Ilan University also protested, and did so eloquently: "It very well may be that any plant performing such types of [kosher slaughter] is guilty of *hillul hashem*—the desecration of God's name—for to insist that God cares only about his ritual law and not about his moral law is to desecrate His Name." And in a joint statement, more than fifty influential rabbis, including the president of the Reform Central Conference of American Rabbis and the dean of the Conservative movement's Ziegler School of Rabbinic Studies, argued that "Judaism's powerful tradition of teaching compassion for animals has been violated by these systematic abuses and needs to be reasserted."

We have no reason to believe that the kind of cruelty that was documented at Agriprocessors has been eliminated from the kosher industry. It can't be, so long as factory farming dominates.

This raises a difficult question, which I ask not as a thought experiment but straightforwardly: In *our* world—not the shepherd-and-flock world of the Bible, but our overpopulated one in which animals are treated legally and socially as commodities—is it even possible to eat meat without "causing pain to one of God's living creatures," to avoid (even after going to great and sincere lengths) "the desecration of God's name"? Has the very concept of kosher meat become a contradiction in terms?

ORGANIC

What does organic signify? Not nothing, but a whole lot less than we give it credit for. For meat, milk, and eggs labeled organic, the USDA requires that animals must: (1) be raised on organic feed (that is, crops raised without most synthetic pesticides and fertilizers); (2) be traced through their life cycle (that is, leave a paper trail); (3) not be fed antibiotics or growth hormones; and (4) have "access to the outdoors." The last criterion, sadly, has been rendered almost meaningless—in some cases "access to the outdoors" can mean nothing more than having the opportunity to look outside through a screened window.

Organic foods in general are almost certainly safer and often have a smaller ecological footprint and better health value. They are not, though, necessarily more humane. "Organic" does signal better welfare if we are talking about laying hens or cattle. It also *may* signal better welfare for pigs, but that is less certain. For chickens raised for meat and for turkeys, though, "organic" doesn't necessarily mean anything in terms of welfare issues. You can call your turkey organic and torture it daily.

PETA

Pronounced like the Middle Eastern bread, and among the farmers I met, significantly better known. The largest animal rights

70

organization in the world, People for the Ethical Treatment of Animals has more than two million members.

The folks at PETA will do almost anything legal to advance their campaigns, no matter how bad they look (which is impressive) and no matter who is insulted (which is not so impressive). They'll distribute "unhappy meals" with bloodied, cleaver-wielding Ronald McDonalds to young children. They'll publish stickers conveniently shaped like those normally found on tomatoes that say "Throw me at a fur-wearer." They've tossed a dead raccoon on *Vogue* editor Anna Wintour's lunch at the Four Seasons (and sent maggot-infested innards to her office), streaked presidents and royalty, distributed "Your Daddy Kills Animals!" pamphlets to schoolchildren, and asked the band Pet Shop Boys to change their name to Rescue Shelter Boys (the band didn't, but acknowledged that there were issues worth discussing). It's hard not to mock and admire their single-minded energy, and it's easy to see why you would never want it directed at you.

Whatever one thinks of them, no organization strikes fear in the factory farm industry and its allies more than PETA. They are effective. When PETA targeted fast-food companies, the most famous and powerful welfare scientist in the country, Temple Grandin (who has designed more than half the cattle slaughter facilities in the nation), said she saw more improvement in welfare in one year than she had seen in her entire thirty-year career previously. Arguably the biggest PETA hater on the planet, Steve Kopperud (a meat industry consultant who has given anti-PETA seminars for a decade), puts it this way: "There's enough understanding in the industry now of what PETA's capable of to put the fear of God into many executives." It didn't surprise me to learn that companies of all kinds regularly negotiate with PETA and quietly make changes in their animal welfare policies to avoid being publicly targeted by the group.

PETA is sometimes accused of using cynical strategies for attention getting, which has some truth to it. PETA is also accused of arguing that humans and animals should be treated equally, which they don't. (What would that even mean? Voting cows?) They are not a particularly emotional crowd; if anything, they are hyper-rational, focused on making their austere ideal—"Animals are not ours to eat, wear, experiment on, or use for entertainment"—as famous as Pamela Anderson in a swimsuit. A surprise to many, PETA is pro-euthanasia: if the choice, for example, is between a dog living its life in a kennel or being euthanized, PETA not only opts for the latter, but advocates for it. They do oppose killing, but they oppose suffering more. People at PETA love their dogs and cats—many companion animals join them in PETA's offices—but they are not especially motivated by a be-kind-to-dogs-and-cats ethic. They want a revolution.

They call their revolution "animal rights," but the changes PETA has won for farmed animals (their biggest concern), while numerous, are not victories for animal rights so much as for animal welfare: fewer animals per cage, better-regulated slaughter, less-cramped transport, and the like. PETA's techniques are often vaudeville-esque (or tasteless), but this over-the-top approach has won modest improvements that most people would say don't go far enough. (Does anyone oppose better-regulated slaughter and less-cramped living and transport conditions?) Ultimately, the controversy around PETA may have less to do with the organization than with those of us who stand in judgment of it—that is, with the unpleasant realization that "those PETA people" have stood up for the values we have been too cowardly or forgetful to defend ourselves.

PROCESSING

Slaughter and butchery. Even people who don't think that we owe farmed animals much during their lives always maintain they deserve a "good" death. The most macho, veal-crate-defending, branding-loving cattle rancher will agree with the vegan activist when it comes to killing humanely. Is this all that can be agreed on?

RADICAL

Virtually everyone agrees that animals can suffer in ways that matter, even if we don't agree on just what that suffering is like or how important it is. When surveyed, 96 percent of Americans say that animals deserve legal protection, 76 percent say that animal welfare is more important to them than low meat prices, and nearly two-thirds advocate passing not only laws but "strict laws" concerning the treatment of farmed animals. You'd be hard-pressed to find any other issue on which so many people see eye to eye.

Another thing most people agree on is that the environment matters. Whether or not you are in favor of offshore oil drilling, whether or not you "believe" in global warming, whether you defend your Hummer or live off the grid, you recognize that the air you breathe and the water you drink are important. And that they will be important to your children and grandchildren. Even those who continue to deny that the environment is in peril would agree that it would be bad if it were.

In the United States, farmed animals represent more than 99 percent of all animals with whom humans directly interact. In terms of our effect on the "animal world"—whether it's the suffering of animals or issues of biodiversity and the interdependence of species that evolution spent millions of years bringing into this livable balance—nothing comes close to having the impact of our

dietary choices. Just as nothing we do has the direct potential to cause nearly as much animal suffering as eating meat, no daily choice that we make has a greater impact on the environment.

Our situation is an odd one. Virtually all of us agree that it matters how we treat animals and the environment, and yet few of us give much thought to our most important relationship to animals and the environment. Odder still, those who *do* choose to act in accordance with these uncontroversial values by refusing to eat animals (which everyone agrees can reduce both the number of abused animals and one's ecological footprint) are often considered marginal or even radical.

SENTIMENTALITY

The valuing of emotions over reality. Sentimentality is widely considered out of touch, weak. Very often, those who express concern about (or even an interest in) the conditions in which farmed animals are raised are disregarded as sentimentalists. But it's worth taking a step back to ask who is the sentimentalist and who is the realist.

Is caring to know about the treatment of farmed animals a confrontation with the facts about the animals and ourselves or an avoidance of them? Is arguing that a sentiment of compassion should be given greater value than a cheaper burger (or having a burger at all) an expression of emotion and impulse or an engagement with reality and our moral intuitions?

Two friends are ordering lunch. One says, "I'm in the mood for a burger," and orders it. The other says, "I'm in the mood for a burger," but remembers that there are things more important to him than what he is in the mood for at any given moment, and orders something else. Who is the sentimentalist?

SPECIES BARRIER

The Berlin zoo (Zoologischer Garten Berlin) houses the largest number of species of any zoo in the world, around 1,400. Opened in 1844, it was the first zoo in Germany—the original animals were gifts from Frederick William IV's menagerie—and with 2.6 million visitors a year, it is the most trafficked zoo in Europe. Allied air raids in 1942 destroyed nearly all of the infrastructure, and only ninety-one animals survived. (It's amazing that in a city in which people were cutting down the public parks for firewood any animals survived at all.) Today there are about fifteen thousand animals. But most people pay attention to only one of them.

Knut, the first polar bear born to the zoo in thirty years, entered the world on December 5, 2006. He was rejected by his mother, the twenty-year-old Tosca, a retired German circus bear, and his twin brother died four days later. It's a promising beginning for a bad TV movie, but not for a life. Little Knut spent his first forty-four days in an incubator. His keeper, Thomas Dörflein, slept at the zoo in order to provide twenty-four-hour care. Dörflein bottle-fed Knut every two hours, strummed Elvis's "Devil in Disguise" on his guitar at Knut's bedtime, and was covered in cuts and bruises from all the roughhousing. Knut weighed 1.8 pounds at birth, but by the time I saw him, about three months later, he had more than doubled his weight. If all goes well, he will one day be about two hundred times that size.

To say that Berlin loved Knut would be a tragic understatement. Mayor Klaus Wowereit checked the news every morning for fresh pictures of Knut. The city's hockey team, the Eisbären, asked the zoo if they could adopt him as a mascot. Numerous blogs—including one by *Der Tagesspiegel,* Berlin's most widely read paper—were dedicated to Knut's hourly doings. He had his own podcast and webcam. He even replaced the topless model in a number of daily newspapers.

Four hundred journalists came to Knut's public debut, which far

overshadowed the EU summit taking place at the same time. There were Knut bow ties, Knut rucksacks (that's German-English for backpack), Knut commemorative plates, Knut pajamas, Knut figurines, and probably, although I haven't verified this, Knut panties. Knut has a godfather, Sigmar Gabriel, the German environment minister. Another zoo animal, the panda Yan Yan, was actually *killed* by Knut's popularity. Zookeepers speculate that the thirty thousand people crowding into the zoo to see Knut overwhelmed Yan Yan—either overexcited her or depressed her to death (it wasn't clear to me). And speaking of death, when an animal rights group raised the argument—only hypothetically, they later claimed—that it would be better to euthanize an animal than raise it in such conditions, schoolchildren took to the streets chanting "Knut must live." Soccer fans chanted for Knut instead of their teams.

If you go to see Knut and get hungry, just a few feet from his enclosure is a stand selling "Wurst de Knut," made from the flesh of factory-farmed pigs, which are at least as intelligent and deserving of our regard as Knut. This is the species barrier.

STRESS

A word used by the industry to elide what is being referred to, which is:

SUFFERING

What is suffering? The question assumes a subject that suffers. All the serious challenges to the idea that animals suffer tend to grant that animals "feel pain" at one level, but deny them the sort of being—the general mental-emotional world or "subjectivity"— that would make this suffering meaningfully analogous to our own. I think this objection hits at something very real and alive for many people, namely the sense that animals' suffering is simply

of a different order and therefore not really important (even if regrettable).

We all have strong intuitions of what suffering means, but they can be extremely difficult to capture in words. As children, we learn the meaning of suffering by interacting with other beings in the world—both humans, especially our family, and animals. The word *suffering* always implies an intuition of a shared experience with others—a shared drama. Of course, there are special kinds of human suffering—the unfulfilled dream, the experience of racism, bodily shame, and so on—but should that lead one to say that animal suffering is "not really suffering"?

The most important part of definitions of or other reflections on suffering is not what they tell us about suffering—about neural pathways, nociceptors, prostaglandins, neuronal opioid receptors— but about who suffers and how much that suffering should matter. There may well be philosophically coherent ways to imagine the world and the meaning of suffering so that we come up with a definition that won't apply to animals. Of course, this would fly in the face of common sense, but I'll grant that it might be done. So, if those who argue that animals don't really suffer and those who argue that they do can both offer coherent understandings and present persuasive evidence, should we be dubious about animal suffering? Should we grant that animals might not *really* suffer—not in the ways that matter most?

As you can guess, I would say no, but I'm not going to argue over this. Rather, I think the essential point is simply to realize the magnitude of what is at stake when we ask "What is suffering?"

What is suffering? I'm not sure *what* it is, but I know that suffering is the name we give to the origin of all the sighs, screams, and groans—small and large, crude and multifaceted—that concern us. The word defines our gaze even more than what we are looking at.

Hiding / Seeking

In the typical cage for egg-laying hens, each bird has 67 square inches of space—the size of the rectangle above. Nearly all cage-free birds have approximately the same amount of space.

1.

I'm Not the Kind of Person Who Finds Himself on a Stranger's Farm in the Middle of the Night

I'M WEARING BLACK IN THE middle of the night in the middle of nowhere. There are surgical booties around my disposable shoes and latex gloves on my shaking hands. I pat myself down, quintuple-checking that I have everything: red-filtered flashlight, picture ID, $40 cash, video camera, copy of California penal code 597e, bottle of water (not for me), silenced cell phone, blow horn. We kill the engine and roll the final thirty yards to the spot we scouted out earlier in the day on one of our half-dozen drive-bys. This isn't the scary part yet.

I am accompanied tonight by an animal activist, "C." It wasn't until I picked her up that I realized I'd been picturing someone who inspired confidence. C is short and wispy. She wears aviator glasses, flip-flops, and a retainer.

"You have a lot of cars," I observed, as we pulled away from her house.

"I live with my parents for now."

As we drove down the highway known to locals as Blood Run because of both the frequency of accidents and the number of trucks that use the road to transport animals to slaughter, C explained that sometimes "entry" is as simple as walking through an open gate, although this has become increasingly rare, given concerns about biosecurity and "troublemakers." More often, these days, fences have to be hiked. Occasionally lights go on and alarms go off.

Every now and then there are dogs, every now and then unleashed. She once encountered a bull that was left to roam among the sheds, waiting to impale snooping vegetarians.

"Bull," I half-echoed, half-asked, with no obvious linguistic intent.

"Male cow," she said brusquely, as she sorted through a bag of what appeared to be dental equipment.

"And if you and I should, tonight, encounter a bull?"

"We won't."

A tailgater forced me behind a truck packed tight and piled high with chickens on their way to slaughter.

"Hypothetically."

"Stand very still," C advised. "I don't think they see stationary objects."

If the question is, *Have things ever gone seriously wrong on one of C's night visits?* the answer is yes. There was the time she fell into a manure pit, a dying rabbit under each arm, and found herself up to her neck (literally) in (literally) deep shit. And the night she was forced to spend in construction-paper blackness with twenty thousand miserable animals and their fumes, having accidentally locked herself in the shed. And the near-fatal case of campylobacter one of her cohorts picked up from picking up a chicken.

Feathers were collecting on the windshield. I turned on the wipers and asked, "What's all that stuff in your bag?"

"In case we need to make a rescue."

I had no idea what she was referring to, and I didn't like it.

"Now, you said you don't *think* bulls see stationary objects. Wouldn't this qualify, though, as one of those things that you absolutely need to *know?* I don't mean to belabor the point, but—"

—*but what the hell have I gotten myself into?* I am not a journalist, activist, veterinarian, lawyer, or philosopher—as, to my knowledge,

have been the others who have made such a trip. I am not up for anything. And I am not someone who can stand very still in front of a guard bull.

We come to a gravelly stop at the planned-upon spot and wait for our synchronized watches to click over to 3:00 A.M., the planned-upon time. The dog we'd seen earlier in the day can't be heard, although that's hardly a comfort. I take the scrap of paper from my pocket and read it one last time—

In case any domestic animal is at any time...impounded and continues to be without necessary food and water for more than twelve consecutive hours, it is lawful for any person, from time to time, as may be deemed necessary, to enter into and upon any pound in which the animal is confined, and supply it with necessary food and water so long as it remains so confined. Such person is not liable for the entry...

—which, despite being state law, is about as reassuring as Cujo's silence. I'm imagining some roused-from-REM-sleep-and-well-armed farmer coming upon I-know-the-difference-between-arugula-and-rugelach me scrutinizing the living conditions of his turkeys. He cocks his double-barrel, my sphincter relaxes, and then what? I whip out California penal code 597e? Is that going to make his trigger finger more or less itchy?

It's time.

We use a series of dramatic hand signals to communicate what a simple whisper would have done just as well. But we've taken vows of silence: not a word until we're safely on the way home. The twirl of a latexed index finger means *Let's roll*.

"You first," I blurt.

And now for the scary part.

Your Continued Consideration

To Whom It May Concern at Tyson Foods:

I am following up on my previous letters of January 10, February 27, March 15, April 20, May 15, and June 7. To reiterate, I am a new father, eager to learn as much as I can about the meat industry, in an effort to make informed decisions about what to feed my son. Given that Tyson Foods is the world's largest processor and marketer of chicken, beef, and pork, your company is an obvious place to start. I would like to visit some of your farms and speak with company representatives about everything from the nuts and bolts of how your farms operate, to animal welfare and environmental issues. If possible, I would also like to speak with some of your farmers. I can make myself available at just about any time, and on relatively short notice, and am happy to travel as is needed.

Given your "family-centered philosophy" and recent "It's What Your Family Deserves" advertising campaign, I assume you'll appreciate my desire to see for myself where my son's food comes from.

Thanks so much for your continued consideration.

Best,
Jonathan Safran Foer

The Whole Sad Business

WE'VE PARKED SEVERAL HUNDRED YARDS from the farm because C noticed in a satellite photo that it was possible to reach the sheds under the cover of an adjacent apricot grove. Our bodies bend the branches as we walk in silence. It's six A.M. in Brooklyn, which means my son will be waking up soon. He will rustle around in his crib for a few minutes, then let out a cry—having stood himself up without knowing how to get himself back down—then be taken into my wife's arms, into the rocking chair, against her body, and fed. All of this—this trip I'm making in California, these words I'm typing in New York, the farms I've come to know in Iowa and Kansas and Puget Sound—affects me in a way that could be more easily forgotten or ignored if I weren't a father, son, or grandson—if, like no one who has ever lived, I ate alone.

After about twenty minutes, C stops and turns ninety degrees. I can't imagine how she knows to stop right here, at a tree that is indistinguishable from the hundreds we've passed. We walk another dozen yards, through an identical grid of trees, and arrive, like kayakers at a waterfall. Through the last bits of foliage, I can see, only a dozen or so yards away, barbed-wire fencing, and past that the farm complex.

The farm is set up in a series of seven sheds, each about 50 feet wide by 500 feet long, each holding in the neighborhood of 25,000 birds—although I don't yet know these facts.

Adjacent to the sheds is a massive granary, which looks more like something out of *Blade Runner* than *Little House on the Prairie*. Metal pipes spiderweb the outsides of the buildings, massive fans protrude and clang, and floodlights plow weirdly discrete pockets of day. Everyone has a mental image of a farm, and to most it probably includes fields, barns, tractors, and animals, or at least one of the above. I doubt there's anyone on earth not involved in farming whose mind would conjure

what I'm now looking at. And yet before me is the kind of farm that produces roughly 99 percent of the animals consumed in America.

With her astronaut's gloves, C spreads the harp of barbed wire far enough apart for me to squeeze through. My pants snag and rip, but they are disposable, purchased for this occasion. She passes the gloves through to me, and I hold open the wires for her.

The surface is lunarlike. With each step, my feet sink into a compost of animal waste, dirt, and I-don't-yet-know-what-else that has been poured around the sheds. I have to curl my toes to keep my shoes from being left behind in the glutinous muck. I'm squatting, to make myself as small as possible, and holding my hands against my pockets to keep their contents from jingling. We shuffle quickly and quietly past the clearing and into the rows of sheds, whose cover allows us to move about more freely. Huge fan units—maybe ten fans, each about four feet in diameter—come on and shut off intermittently.

We approach the first shed. Light spills from under its door. This is both good and bad news: good because we won't have to use our flashlights, which, C told me, scare the animals, and in a worse case could get the entire flock squawking and agitated; bad because should someone open the door to check on things, it will be impossible for us to hide. I wonder: Why would a shed full of animals be brightly lit in the middle of the night?

I can hear movement from inside: the hum of machines blends with what sounds a bit like a whispering audience or a chandelier shop in a mild earthquake. C wrestles with the door and then signals that we should move to the next shed.

We spend several minutes like this, looking for an unlocked door.

Another why: Why would a farmer lock the doors of his turkey farm?

It can't be because he's afraid someone will steal his equipment or

animals. There's no equipment to steal in the sheds, and the animals aren't worth the herculean effort it would take to illicitly transport a significant number. A farmer doesn't lock his doors because he's afraid his animals will escape. (Turkeys can't turn doorknobs.) And despite the signage, it isn't because of biosecurity, either. (Barbed wire is enough to keep out the merely curious.) So why?

In the three years I will spend immersed in animal agriculture, nothing will unsettle me more than the locked doors. Nothing will better capture the whole sad business of factory farming. And nothing will more strongly convince me to write this book.

As it turns out, locked doors are the least of it. I never heard back from Tyson or any of the companies I wrote to. (It sends one kind of message to say no. It sends another not to say anything at all.) Even research organizations with paid staffs find themselves consistently thwarted by industry secrecy. When the prestigious and well-heeled Pew Commission decided to fund a two-year study to evaluate the impact of factory farming, they reported that

> there have been some serious obstacles to the Commission completing its review and approving consensus recommendations....In fact, while some industrial agriculture representatives were recommending potential authors for the technical reports to Commission staff, other industrial agriculture representatives were discouraging those same authors from assisting us by threatening to withhold research funding for their college or university. We found significant influence by the industry at every turn: in academic research, agriculture policy development, government regulation, and enforcement.

The power brokers of factory farming know that their business model depends on consumers not being able to see (or hear about) what they do.

The Rescue

MEN'S VOICES DRIFT OVER FROM the granary. Why are they working at 3:30 in the morning? Machines engage. What kinds of machines? It's the middle of the night and things are happening. What is happening?

"Found one," C whispers. She slides open the heavy wooden door, releasing a parallelogram of light, and enters. I follow, sliding the door shut behind me. The first thing that catches my attention is the row of gas masks on the near wall. Why would there be gas masks in a farm shed?

We creep in. There are tens of thousands of turkey chicks. Fist-sized, with feathers the color of sawdust, they're nearly invisible on the sawdust floor. The chicks are huddled in groups, asleep beneath the heat lamps installed to replace the warmth their broody mothers would have provided. Where are the mothers?

There is a mathematical orchestration to the density. I pull my eyes from the birds for a moment and take in the building itself: lights, feeders, fans, and heat lamps evenly spaced in a perfectly calibrated artificial day. Besides the animals themselves, there is no hint of anything you might call "natural"—not a patch of earth or a window to let in moonlight. I'm surprised by how easy it is to forget the anonymous life all around and simply admire the technological symphony that so precisely regulates this little world-unto-itself, to see the efficiency and mastery of the machine, and then to understand the birds as extensions of, or cogs in, that machine—not beings, but parts. To see it any other way requires effort.

I look at a particular chick, how it is struggling to get from the outside of the pile around the heat lamp to its center. And then at another one, immediately under the lamp, seemingly content as a

dog in a patch of sunlight. Then another, which isn't moving at all, not even with the undulations of breath.

At first the situation doesn't look too bad. It's crowded, but they seem happy enough. (And human babies are kept in crowded indoor nurseries, right?) And they're cute. The exhilaration of seeing what I came to see, and confronting all of these baby animals, has me feeling pretty good.

C is off giving water to some dreary-looking birds in another part of the shed, so I tiptoe around and explore, leaving vague bootie prints in the sawdust. I'm starting to feel more comfortable with the turkeys, willing to get closer to them, if not to handle them. (C's first commandment was never to touch them.) The closer I look, the more I see. The ends of the beaks of the chicks are blackened, as are the ends of their toes. Some have red spots on the tops of their heads.

Because there are so many animals, it takes me several minutes before I take in just how many dead ones there are. Some are blood matted; some are covered in sores. Some seem to have been pecked at; others are as desiccated and loosely gathered as small piles of dead leaves. Some are deformed. The dead are the exceptions, but there are few places to look without seeing at least one.

I walk over to C—it's been the full ten minutes, and I'm not eager to push our luck. She is kneeling over something. I approach and kneel beside her. A chick is trembling on its side, legs splayed, eyes crusted over. Scabs protrude from bald patches. Its beak is slightly open, and its head is shaking back and forth. How old is it? A week? Two? Has it been like this for all of its life, or did some-thing happen to it? What could have happened to it?

C will know what to do, I think. And she does. She opens her bag and removes a knife. Holding one hand over the chick's head—is she keeping it still or covering its eyes?—she slices its neck, rescu-ing it.

2.

I Am the Kind of Person Who Finds Herself on a Stranger's Farm in the Middle of the Night

That turkey chick I euthanized on our rescue, that was hard. One of my jobs, many years ago, was at a poultry plant. I was a backup killer, which meant it was my responsibility to slit the throats of the chickens that survived the automated throat slitter. I killed thousands of birds that way. Maybe tens of thousands. Maybe hundreds of thousands. In that context, you lose track of everything: where you are, what you're doing, how long you've been doing it, what the animals are, *what* you *are. It's a survival mechanism, to keep you from going insane. But it's its own insanity.*

So because of my work on the kill line, I knew the anatomy of the neck and how to kill the chick instantly. And every part of me knew that it was the right thing to put it out of its misery. But it was hard, because that chick wasn't in a line of thousands of birds to be slaughtered. It was an individual. Everything about this is hard.

I'm not a radical. In almost every way, I'm a middle-of-the-road person. I don't have any piercings. No weird haircut. I don't do drugs. Politically, I'm liberal on some issues and conservative on others. But see, factory farming is a middle-of-the-road issue — something most reasonable people would agree on if they had access to the truth.

I grew up in Wisconsin and Texas. My family was typical: My dad was (and is) into hunting; all of my uncles trapped and fished. My mom cooked roasts every Monday night, chicken every Tuesday, and so on. My brother was All-State in two sports.

The first time I was exposed to farming issues was when a friend showed me some films of cows being slaughtered. We were teenagers, and

it was just gross-out shit, like those "Faces of Death" videos. He wasn't a vegetarian — no one was vegetarian — and he wasn't trying to make me one. It was for a laugh.

We had drumsticks for dinner that night, and I couldn't eat mine. When I held the bone in my hand, it didn't feel like chicken, but a chicken. I always knew I was eating an individual, I suppose, but it never hit me before. My dad asked me what was wrong, and I told him about the video. At that point in my life, I took whatever he said to be the truth, and I was sure he could explain everything. But the best he could come up with was something like "It's unpleasant stuff." If he'd left it there, I probably wouldn't be talking to you now. But then he made a joke about it. The same joke everyone makes. I've heard it a million times since. He pretended he was a crying animal. It was revealing to me, and infuriating. I decided then and there never to become someone who told jokes when explanations were impossible.

I wanted to know if that video was exceptional. I suppose I wanted a way out of having to change my life. So I wrote letters to all of the big farm corporations, asking for tours. Honestly, it never crossed my mind that they would say no or not respond. When that didn't work, I started driving around and asking any farmers I saw if I could look in their sheds. They all had reasons for saying no. Given what they're doing, I don't blame them for not wanting anyone to see. But given their secrecy about something so important, who could blame me for feeling that I needed to do things my own way?

The first farm I entered at night was an egg facility, maybe a million hens. They were packed into cages that were stacked several rows high. My eyes and lungs burned for days after. It was less violent and gory than what I'd seen in the video, but it affected me even more strongly. That really changed me, when I realized that an excruciating life is worse than an excruciating death.

The farm was so bad that I assumed it, too, had to be exceptional. I

guess I couldn't believe that people would let that kind of thing happen on so large a scale. So I got myself into another farm, a turkey farm. By chance I'd come just a few days before slaughter, so the turkeys were full grown and jammed body to body. You couldn't see the floor through them. They were totally crazy: flapping, squawking, going after each other. There were dead birds everywhere, and half-dead birds. It was sad. I didn't put them there, but I felt ashamed just to be a person. I told myself it had to be exceptional. So I entered another farm. And another. And another.

Maybe on some deep level, I kept doing this because I didn't want to believe that the things I'd seen were representative. But everyone who cares to know about this stuff knows that factory farms are nearly all there is. Most people aren't able to see these farms with their own eyes, but they can see them through mine. I've videotaped conditions at chicken and egg factories, turkey factories, a couple of hog farms (those are basically impossible to get into now), rabbit farms, drylot dairies and feedlots, livestock auctions, and in transport trucks. I've worked in a few slaughterhouses. Occasionally the footage will make its way onto the evening news or into the newspaper. A few times it's been used in animal cruelty court cases.

That's why I agreed to help you. I don't know you. I don't know what kind of book you're going to write. But if any part of it is bringing what happens inside those farms to the outside world, that can only be a good thing. The truth is so powerful in this case it doesn't even matter what your angle is.

Anyway, I wanted to be sure that when you write your book you don't make it seem like I kill animals all the time. I've done it four times, only when it couldn't be avoided. Usually I take the sickest animals to a vet. But that chick was too sick to be moved. And it was suffering too much to leave be. Look, I'm pro-life. I believe in God, and I believe in heaven and hell. But I don't have any reverence for suffering. These factory farm-ers calculate how close to death they can keep the animals without killing

them. That's the business model. How quickly can they be made to grow, how tightly can they be packed, how much or little can they eat, how sick can they get without dying.

This isn't animal experimentation, where you can imagine some proportionate good at the other end of the suffering. This is what we feel like eating. Tell me something: Why is taste, the crudest of our senses, exempted from the ethical rules that govern our other senses? If you stop and think about it, it's crazy. Why doesn't a horny person have as strong a claim to raping an animal as a hungry one does to killing and eating it? It's easy to dismiss that question but hard to respond to it. And how would you judge an artist who mutilated animals in a gallery because it was visually arresting? How riveting would the sound of a tortured animal need to be to make you want to hear it that badly? Try to imagine any end other than taste for which it would be justifiable to do what we do to farmed animals.

If I misuse a corporation's logo, I could potentially be put in jail; if a corporation abuses a billion birds, the law will protect not the birds, but the corporation's right to do what it wants. That is what it looks like when you deny animals rights. It's crazy that the idea of animal rights seems crazy to anyone. We live in a world in which it's conventional to treat an animal like a hunk of wood and extreme to treat an animal like an animal.

Before child labor laws, there were businesses that treated their ten-year-old employees well. Society didn't ban child labor because it's impossible to imagine children working in a good environment, but because when you give that much power to businesses over powerless individuals, it's corrupting. When we walk around thinking we have a greater right to eat an animal than the animal has a right to live without suffering, it's corrupting. I'm not speculating. This is our reality. Look at what factory farming is. Look at what we as a society have done to animals as soon as we had the technological power. Look at what we actually do *in the name*

of "animal welfare" and "humaneness," then decide if you still believe in eating meat.

3.

I Am a Factory Farmer

When people ask me what I do, I tell them I'm a retired farmer. I started milking cows when I was six. We lived in Wisconsin. My daddy had a small herd—fifty, give or take—which back then was pretty typical. I worked every day until I left home, worked hard. I thought I'd had enough of it at that point, thought there must be a better way.

After high school, I got a degree in animal science and went to work for a poultry company. I helped service, manage, and design turkey breeder farms. Bounced around some integrated companies after that. I managed large farms, a million birds. Did disease management, flock management. Problem solving, you could say. Farming is a lot of problem solving. Now I specialize in chicken nutrition and health. I'm in agribusiness. Factory farming, some people might say, but I don't care for the term.

It's a different world from the one I grew up in. The price of food hasn't increased in the past thirty years. In relation to all other expenses, the price of protein stayed put. In order to survive—I don't mean get rich, I mean put food on your table, send your kids to school, get a new car as needed—the farmer had to produce more and more. Simple math. Like I said, my daddy had fifty cows. The model now for a viable dairy is twelve hundred cows. That's the smallest that can stay in business. Well, a family can't milk twelve hundred cows, so you gotta get four or five employees, and each of them will have a specialized job: milking, managing illness, tending the crops. It's efficient, yeah, and you can squeeze out a

living, but a lot of people became farmers because of the diversity of farm life. And that's been lost.

Another part of what's happened in response to the economic squeeze is that you gotta make an animal that produces more of the product at a lower cost. So you breed for faster growth and improved feed conversion. As long as food continues to get cheaper and cheaper relative to everything else, the farmer has no choice but to produce food at a lower production cost, and genetically he's going to move toward an animal that accomplishes that task, which can be counterproductive to its welfare. The loss is built into the system. It's assumed that if you have fifty thousand broilers in a shed, thousands are going to die in the first weeks. My daddy couldn't afford to lose an animal. Now you begin by assuming you'll lose 4 percent right off the bat.

I've told you the drawbacks because I'm trying to be up-front with you. But in fact, we've got a tremendous system. Is it perfect? No. No system is perfect. And if you find someone who tells you he has a perfect way to feed billions and billions of people, well, you should take a careful look. You hear about free-range eggs and grass-fed cattle, and all of that's good. I think it's a good direction. But it ain't gonna feed the world. Never. You simply can't feed billions of people free-range eggs. And when you hear people talking about small farming as a model, I call that the Marie Antoinette syndrome: if they can't afford bread, let them eat cake. High-yield farming has allowed everyone to eat. Think about that. If we go away from it, it may improve the welfare of the animal, it may even be better for the environment, but I don't want to go back to China in 1918. I'm talking about starving people.

Sure, you could say that people should just eat less meat, but I've got news for you: people don't want to eat less meat. You can be like PETA and pretend that the world is going to wake up tomorrow and realize that they love animals and don't want to eat them anymore, but history has shown that people are perfectly capable of loving animals and eating them. It's

childish, and I would even say immoral, to fantasize about a vegetarian world when we're having such a hard time making this one work.

Look, the American farmer has fed the world. He was asked to do it after World War II, and he did it. People have never had the ability to eat like they can now. Protein has never been more affordable. My animals are protected from the elements, get all the food they need, and grow well. Animals get sick. Animals die. But what do you think happens to animals in nature? You think they die of natural causes? You think they're stunned before they're killed? Animals in nature starve to death or are ripped apart by other animals. That's how they die.

People have no idea where food comes from anymore. It's not synthetic, it's not created in a lab, it actually has to be grown. What I hate is when consumers act as if farmers want these things, when it's consumers who tell farmers what to grow. They've wanted cheap food. We've grown it. If they want cage-free eggs, they have to pay a lot more money for them. Period. It's cheaper to produce an egg in a massive laying barn with caged hens. It's more efficient and that means it's more sustainable. Yes, I'm saying that factory farming can be more sustainable, though I know that word is often used against the industry. From China to India to Brazil, the demand for animal products is growing—and fast. Do you think family farms are going to sustain a world of ten billion?

A friend of mine had an experience a few years ago where two young guys came and asked if they could take some footage for a documentary about farm life. Seemed like nice guys, so he said sure. But then they edited it to make it look like the birds were being abused. They said the turkeys were being raped. I know that farm. I've visited it many times, and I can tell you those turkeys were being cared for as well as they needed to survive and be productive. Things can be taken out of context. And novices don't always know what they're looking at. This business isn't always pretty, but it's a bad mistake to confuse something unpleasant with something wrong. Every kid with a video camera thinks he's a veterinary scientist, thinks

he was born knowing what takes years and years to learn. I know there's a necessity to sensationalize stuff in order to motivate people, but I prefer the truth.

In the eighties, the industry tried to communicate with animal groups, and we got burned real bad. So the turkey community decided there would be no more of it. We put up a wall, and that was the end. We don't talk, don't let people onto the farms. Standard operating procedure. PETA doesn't want to talk about farming. They want to end farming. They have absolutely no idea how the world actually works. For all I know, I'm talking to the enemy right now.

But I believe in what I'm telling you. And it's an important story to tell, a story that's getting drowned out by the hollering of the extremists. I asked you not to use my name, but I have nothing to be ashamed of. Nothing. You just have to understand that there's a bigger picture here. And I've got bosses. I gotta put food on the table, too.

Can I make a suggestion to you? Before you rush off trying to see everything you can, educate yourself. Don't trust your eyes. Trust your head. Learn about animals, learn about farming and the economics of food, learn the history. Start at the beginning.

4.

The First Chicken

YOUR PROGENY WILL BE KNOWN as *Gallus domesticus, chicken, cock, hen, poultry, the Chicken of Tomorrow, broiler, layer, Mr. McDonald,* and many other names. Each name tells a story, but no stories have been told, no names have yet been given to you or to any animal.

Like all animals in this time before the beginning, you reproduce

97

according to your own preferences and instincts. You are not fed, forced to labor, or protected. You are not marked as a possession with brands or tagging. No one has even thought of you as something that could be possessed or owned.

As a wild *rooster*, you survey the landscape, warn others of intruders with complex calls, and defend mates with beak and sharp toes. As a wild *hen*, you begin communicating with your chicks even before they hatch, responding to peeps of distress by shifting your weight. The image of your motherly protection and care will be used in the second verse of Genesis to describe the hovering of God's first breath over the first water. Jesus will invoke you as an image of protective love: "I have longed to gather your children together as a hen gathers her chicks under her wings." But Genesis has not yet been written, nor Jesus born.

The First Human

ANY FOOD YOU EAT IS food you have found for yourself. For the most part, you do not live in close proximity to the animals you kill. You do not share or compete for land with them, but must go out to seek them. When you do so, you generally kill animals that you don't know as individuals, save in the brief space of the hunt itself, and you view the animals you hunt as equals of sorts. Not in all ways (of course), but the animals you know have power: they have abilities humans lack, could be dangerous, could bring life, mean things that mean things. When you create rites and traditions, you do so with animals. You draw them in sand, in dirt, and on cave walls—not only animal figures, but also hybrid creatures that blend human and animal forms. Animals are what you are and are not. You have a complex relationship with them and, in a sense, an egalitarian one. This is about to change.

The First Problem

IT IS 8000 BCE. ONCE a wild jungle bird, the chicken is now domesticated, as are goats and cattle. This means a new kind of intimacy with humans — new kinds of care and new kinds of violence.

A common trope, ancient and modern, describes domestication as a process of coevolution between humans and other species. Basically, humans struck a deal with the animals we have named chickens, cows, pigs, and so forth: we'll protect you, arrange food for you, etc., and, in turn, your labor will be harnessed, your milk and eggs taken, and, at times, you will be killed and eaten. Life in the wild isn't a party, the logic goes — nature is cruel — so this is a good deal. And the animals, in their own way, have consented to it. Michael Pollan suggests this story in *The Omnivore's Dilemma:*

> Domestication is an evolutionary, rather than a political, development. It is certainly not a regime humans somehow imposed on animals some ten thousand years ago. Rather, domestication took place when a handful of especially opportunistic species discovered, through Darwinian trial and error, that they were more likely to survive and prosper in an alliance with humans than on their own. Humans provided the animals with food and protection in exchange for which the animals provided the humans their milk, eggs, and — yes — their flesh....From the animals' point of view the bargain with humanity turned out to be a tremendous success, at least until our own time.

This is the post-Darwinian version of the ancient *myth of animal consent*. It is offered by ranchers in defense of the violence that is part of their profession, and makes appearances in agricultural school curricula. Propping up the story is the idea that the interests of the

species and those of individuals often conflict, but if there were no species there would be no individuals. If humankind went vegan, the logic goes, there would be no more farmed animals (which isn't quite right, as there are already dozens of breeds of chickens and pigs that are "ornamental," or raised for companionship, and others would be kept around to fertilize crops). The animals, in effect, *want* us to farm them. They prefer it this way. Some ranchers I met told me of times they'd accidentally left gates open, and none of the animals fled.

In ancient Greece the myth of consent was enacted at the oracle of Delphi by sprinkling water on the heads of animals before slaughter. When the animals shook off the water by nodding their heads, the oracle would interpret this as consent to be slaughtered and say, "That which willing nods...I say you may justly sacrifice." A traditional formula used by Russian Yakuts reads, "You have come to me, Lord Bear, you *wish* me to kill you." In the ancient Israelite tradition, the red heifer sacrificed for Israel's atonement must walk to the altar willingly or the ritual is invalid. The myth of consent has many versions, but all imply a "fair deal" and, at least metaphorically, animal complicity in their own domestication and slaughter.

The Myth of the Myth

BUT SPECIES DON'T MAKE CHOICES, individuals do. And even if species somehow could, to imply that they would select perpetuity over individual well-being is hard to apply more broadly. By this logic, enslaving a group of humans is acceptable if the posed alternative were nonexistence. (Instead of *Live free or die*, the motto we script for our food animals is *Die enslaved but live*.) More obviously, most animals, even individually, are unable to fathom such an arrange-

ment. Chickens can do many things, but they cannot make sophisticated deals with humans.

That said, these objections might miss the point. Whatever the facts of the matter, most people can imagine fair and unfair treatment of, for example, the family dog or cat. And we can imagine methods of husbandry to which animals might, hypothetically, "consent." (A dog given several years of tasty food, plenty of time outdoors with other dogs, and all the space she could want, aware of the hardships of dogs under wilder and less-regulated conditions, might conceivably agree to be eventually eaten in exchange.)

We can, do, and always have imagined such things. The persistence of the story of animal consent into the contemporary era tells of a human appreciation of the stakes, and a desire to do the right thing.

It is not surprising that, historically, most people seem to have accepted eating animals as a daily fact of life. Meat is filling and smells and tastes good to most. (It's also not surprising that for virtually all of human history, some humans have kept other humans as slaves.) But as far back in time as records stretch, humans have expressed ambivalence about the violence and death dealing inherent in eating animals. So we've told stories.

The First Forgetting

WE SEE FARMED ANIMALS so rarely today, it becomes easy to forget all of this. Earlier generations were more familiar than we are with both the personalities of farmed animals and the violence done to them. They would have known that pigs are playful, smart, and curious (we would say "like dogs"), and that they have complex

social relationships (we would say "like primates"). They would have known the look and behavior of a caged pig, as well as the infant-like screech of a pig being castrated or slaughtered.

Having little exposure to animals makes it much easier to push aside questions about how our actions might influence their treatment. The problem posed by meat has become an abstract one: there is no individual animal, no singular look of joy or suffering, no wagging tail, and no scream. The philosopher Elaine Scarry has observed that "beauty always takes place in the particular." Cruelty, on the other hand, prefers abstraction.

Some have tried to resolve this gap by hunting or butchering an animal themselves, as if those experiences might somehow legitimize the endeavor of eating animals. This is very silly. Murdering someone would surely prove that you are capable of killing, but it wouldn't be the most reasonable way to understand why you should or shouldn't do it.

Killing an animal oneself is more often than not a way to forget the problem while pretending to remember. This is perhaps more harmful than ignorance. It's always possible to wake someone from sleep, but no amount of noise will wake someone who is pretending to be asleep.

The First Animal Ethics

ONCE UPON A TIME the dominant ethic toward domestic animals, rooted in the demands of husbandry and responding to the fundamental problem of life feeding on sentient life, was not *don't eat* (of course), but neither was it *don't care*. Rather: *eat with care*.

The *care* for domesticated animals demanded by the *eat with care* ethic did not necessarily correspond to any official morality:

it didn't need to, as that ethic was based on the economic necessities of raising domestic animals. The very nature of the human–domestic animal relationship required some degree of caring, in the sense of providing provisions and a safe environment for one's flock. Care for farmed animals was, to an extent, good business. But there was a price for this guarantee of sheepdogs and clean (enough) water: castration, exhausting labor, draining blood or cutting flesh from living animals, branding, removing young animals from their mothers, and, of course, slaughter were also good business. The animals were ensured police protection in exchange for being sacrificed to those policemen: protect and serve.

The *eat with care* ethic lived and evolved for thousands of years. It became many different ethical systems inflected by the diverse cultures in which it appeared: in India it led to prohibitions on eating cows, in Islam and Judaism it led to mandates for quick slaughter, on the Russian tundra it led Yakuts to claim the animals wanted to be killed. But it was not to last.

The *eat with care* ethic didn't become obsolete over time, but died suddenly. It was killed, actually.

The First Line Worker

BEGINNING IN CINCINNATI AND EXPANDING to Chicago in the late 1820s and '30s, early industrial "processing" plants (a.k.a. slaughterhouses) replaced the skilled knowledge of butchers with gangs of men who would perform a coordinated series of mind-, muscle-, and joint-numbing tasks. Kill men, sticker-bleeders, tail-rippers, leggers, butters, flankers, head-skinners, head-chislers, gutters, and back-splitters (among many others). By his own acknowledgment, the efficiencies of these lines inspired Henry Ford, who brought the

model into the auto industry, leading to a revolution in manufacturing. (Putting together a car is just taking apart a cow in reverse.)

The pressure to improve upon the efficiency of slaughter and
processing came in part as advances in rail transport, such as the
1879 invention of the refrigerator car, allowed for increasingly large
concentrations of cattle to be brought together from ever-farther
distances. Today, it isn't unusual for meat to travel almost halfway
around the globe to reach your supermarket. The average distance
our meat travels hovers around fifteen hundred miles. That's like
me driving from Brooklyn to the Texas Panhandle for lunch.

By 1908, conveyer systems were introduced to the disassembly lines, allowing supervisors rather than workers to control line speeds. These speeds would ramp upward for more than
eighty years—in many cases doubling and even tripling—with
predictable increases in ineffective slaughter and associated workplace injuries.

Despite these trends in processing, at the dawn of the twentieth
century, animals were still largely raised on farms and ranches in
much the same manner they always had been—and as most people
continue to imagine. It hadn't yet occurred to farmers to treat living animals like dead ones.

The First Factory Farmer

IN 1923, IN THE DELMARVA (Delaware-Maryland-Virginia) Peninsula, a small, almost-funny accident befell an Oceanview housewife,
Celia Steele, and initiated the modern poultry industry and the
global creep of factory farming. Steele, who managed her family's
small flock of chickens, allegedly received an order of five hundred

chicks instead of the fifty she had requested. Rather than get rid of them, she decided to experiment with keeping the birds indoors through the winter. With the help of newly discovered feed supplements the birds survived, and the loop of her experimentations continued. By 1926, Steele had 10,000 birds, and by 1935, 250,000. (The average flock size in America in 1930 was still only 23.)

Just ten years after Steele's breakthrough, the Delmarva Peninsula was the poultry capital of the world. Delaware's Sussex County now produces more than 250 million broilers a year, nearly twice as many as any other county in the country. Poultry production is the region's primary economic activity, and the primary source of its pollution. (Nitrates contaminate one-third of all groundwater in Delmarva's agricultural areas)

Crowded and deprived for months of both exercise and sunlight, Steele's birds never would have survived if it were not for the newly discovered benefits of adding vitamins A and D to the chickens' feed. Nor would Steele even have been able to order her chicks if not for the prior rise of chicken hatcheries with artificial incubators. Multiple forces—generations of accumulated technologies—were converging and amplifying one another in unexpected ways.

By 1928, Herbert Hoover was promising a "chicken in every pot." The promise would be realized and exceeded, though not as anyone had imagined. By the early 1930s, architects of the emerging factory farm like Arthur Perdue and John Tyson entered the chicken business. They helped underwrite the burgeoning science of modern industrial agriculture, generating a host of "innovations" in poultry production by World War II. Hybrid corn, produced with the help of government subsidies, provided cheap feed that soon was delivered by chain-driven feeders. Debeaking—usually performed by searing off chicks' beaks with a hot blade—was invented and then

automated (the beak is a chicken's main instrument of exploration). Automatic lights and fans made even greater densities possible, and ultimately ushered in the now-standard manipulation of growing cycles by controlling light.

Every aspect of the chickens' lives had been engineered to produce more food for less cost. So it was time for another breakthrough.

The First Chicken of Tomorrow

IN 1946, THE POULTRY INDUSTRY turned its gaze to genetics and, with the aid of the USDA, launched a "Chicken of Tomorrow" contest to create a bird that could produce more breast meat with less feed. The winner was a surprise: Charles Vantress, of Marysville, California. (Until then, New England had been the main source of breeding stock.) Vantress's red-feathered Cornish–New Hampshire cross introduced Cornish blood, which gave, according to an industry periodical, "the broad-breasted appearance that would soon be demanded with the emphasis on marketing after the war."

The 1940s also saw the introduction of sulfa drugs and antibiotics to chicken feed, which stimulated growth and held down the diseases induced by confinement. Feed and drug regimens were increasingly developed in coordination with the newly bred "chickens of tomorrow," and by the 1950s there was not one "chicken" anymore, but two distinct chickens—one for eggs, one for flesh.

The very genetics of chickens, along with their feed and environment, were now intensively manipulated to produce either excessive amounts of eggs (*layers*) or flesh, especially breasts (*broilers*). From 1935 to 1995, the average weight of "broilers" increased

by 65 percent, while their time-to-market dropped 60 percent and their feed requirements dropped 57 percent. To gain a sense of the radicalness of this change, imagine human children growing to be three hundred pounds in ten years, while eating only granola bars and Flintstones vitamins.

These changes in chicken genetics were not one change among others: they dictated how the birds could be raised. With these new alterations, drugs and confinement were being used not only to increase profitability, but because the birds could no longer be "healthy" or often even survive without them.

Even worse, these genetically grotesque birds didn't come to occupy only one portion of the industry—they now are practically the only chickens being raised for consumption. There were once dozens of different breeds of chickens raised in America (Jersey Giants, New Hampshire, Plymouth Rock), all of them adapted to the environment of their region. Now we have factory chickens.

In the 1950s and 1960s, poultry companies began to achieve total vertical integration. They owned the genetic pool (today two companies own three-fourths of the genetics for all broiler chickens on the planet), the birds themselves (farmers only tended to them, like counselors at a sleepaway camp), the requisite drugs, the feed, the slaughtering, the processing, and the market brands. It wasn't just that techniques had changed: biodiversity was replaced with genetic uniformity, university departments of animal husbandry became departments of animal science, a business once dominated by women was now taken over by men, and skilled farmers were replaced with wage and contract workers. No one fired a pistol to mark the start of the race to the bottom. The earth just tilted and everyone slid into the hole.

The First Factory Farm

THE FACTORY FARM WAS MORE event than innovation. Barren security buffers took over pastures, multitiered intensive confinement systems rose where barns once stood, and genetically engineered animals—birds that could not fly, pigs that could not survive outside, turkeys that could not naturally reproduce—replaced the once familiar barnyard cast.

What did—and do—these changes mean? Jacques Derrida is one of a small handful of contemporary philosophers who have taken on this inconvenient question. "However one interprets it," he argues, "whatever practical, technical, scientific, juridical, ethical, or political consequence one draws from it, no one can deny this event anymore, no one can deny the unprecedented proportions of this subjection of the animal." He continues:

> Such a subjection...can be called violence in the most morally neutral sense of the term....No one can deny seriously, or for very long, that men do all they can in order to dissimulate this cruelty or to hide it from themselves, in order to organize on a global scale the forgetting or misunderstanding of this violence.

On their own and in alliances with the government and the scientific community, twentieth-century American businessmen planned and executed a series of revolutions in farming. They turned the early-modern philosophical proposition (championed by Descartes) that animals should be viewed as machines into reality for thousands, then millions, and now billions of farmed animals.

As described in industry journals from the 1960s onward, the egg-laying hen was to be considered "only a very efficient converting machine" (*Farmer and Stockbreeder*), the pig was to be "just like a machine in a factory" (*Hog Farm Management*), and the twenty-first century was to bring a new "computer 'cookbook' of recipes for custom-designed creatures" (*Agricultural Research*).

Such scientific wizardry succeeded in producing cheap meat, milk, and eggs. In the past fifty years, as factory farming spread from poultry to beef, dairy, and pork producers, the average cost of a new house increased nearly 1,500 percent; new cars climbed more than 1,400 percent; but the price of milk is up only 350 percent, and eggs and chicken meat haven't even doubled. Taking inflation into account, animal protein costs less today than at any time in history. (That is, unless one also takes into account the externalized costs—farm subsidies, environmental impact, human disease, and so on—which make the price historically high.)

For each food animal species, animal agriculture is now dominated by the factory farm—99.9 percent of chickens raised for meat, 97 percent of laying hens, 99 percent of turkeys, 95 percent of pigs, and 78 percent of cattle—but there are still some vibrant alternatives. In the pig industry, small farmers have begun to work cooperatively to preserve themselves. And the movements toward sustainable fishing and cattle ranching have captured significant press and market share. But the transformation of the poultry industry—the largest and most influential in animal agriculture (99 percent of all land animals slaughtered are farmed birds)—is all but complete. Incredibly, there may well be only one truly independent poultry farmer left....

5.

I Am the Last Poultry Farmer

My name is Frank Reese and I'm a poultry farmer. It's what I've given my whole life to. I don't know where that comes from. I went to a little one-room country school. Mother said one of the first things I wrote was a story titled "Me and My Turkeys."

I just always loved the beauty of them, the majesticness. I like how they strut. I don't know. I don't know how to explain it. I just love their feather patterns. I've always loved the personality of them. They're so curious, so playful, so friendly and full of life.

I can sit in the house at night, and I can hear them, and I can tell if they're in trouble or not. Having been around turkeys for almost sixty years, I know their vocabulary. I know the sound they make if it's just two turkeys fighting or if there's a possum in the barn. There's the sound they make when they're petrified and the sound they make when they're excited over something new. The mother turkey is amazing to listen to. She has a tremendous vocal range when she's speaking to her babies. And the little babies understand. She can tell them, "Run and jump and hide under me," or "Move from here to here." Turkeys know what's going on and can communicate it—in their world, in their language. I'm not trying to give them human characteristics, 'cause they're not humans, they're turkeys. I'm only telling you what they are.

A lot of people slow down when they pass my farm. Get a lot of schools and churches and 4-H kids. I get kids asking me how a turkey got in my trees or on my roof. I tell 'em, "He flew there!" And they don't believe me! Turkeys used to be raised out on fields like this by the millions in America. This kind of turkey is what everybody had on their farms for hundreds of

years, and what everybody ate. And now mine are the only ones left, and I'm the only one doing it this way.

Not a single turkey you can buy in a supermarket could walk normally, much less jump or fly. Did you know that? They can't even have sex. Not the antibiotic-free, or organic, or free-range, or anything. They all have the same foolish genetics, and their bodies won't allow for it anymore. Every turkey sold in every store and served in every restaurant was the product of artificial insemination. If it were only for efficiency, that would be one thing, but these animals literally can't reproduce naturally. Tell me what could be sustainable about that?

These guys here, cold weather, snow, ice—doesn't hurt 'em. With the modern industrial turkey it would be a mess. They couldn't survive. My guys could maneuver through a foot of snow without any trouble. And my turkeys all have their toenails; they all have their wings and beaks—nothing's been cut off; nothing's been destroyed. We don't vaccinate, don't feed antibiotics. No need to. Our birds exercise all day. And because their genes haven't been messed with, they have naturally strong immune systems. We never lose birds. If you can find a healthier flock, anywhere in the world, you take me to it and then I'll believe you. What the industry figured out—and this was the real revolution—is that you don't need healthy animals to make a profit. Sick animals are more profitable. The animals have paid the price for our desire to have everything available at all times for very little money.

We never needed biosecurity before. Look at my farm. Anyone who wants to can visit, and I wouldn't have a second thought about taking my animals to shows and fairs. I always tell people to visit an industrial turkey farm. You may not even have to go into the building. You'll smell it before you get there. But people don't want to hear those things. They don't want to hear that these big turkey factories have incinerators to burn all the turkeys that die every day. They don't care to hear that when the industry

EATING ANIMALS

sends turkeys off to be processed, it knows and accepts that it's gonna lose 10 to 15 percent of them in transport—the DOAs at the plant. You know my DOA rate this Thanksgiving? Zero. But these are just numbers, not anything anyone gets excited about. It's all about nickels and dimes. So 15 percent of the turkeys suffocate. Throw them in the incinerator.

Why are entire flocks of industrial birds dying at once? And what about the people eating those birds? Just the other day, one of the local pediatricians was telling me he's seeing all kinds of illnesses that he never used to see. Not only juvenile diabetes, but inflammatory and autoimmune diseases that a lot of the docs don't even know what to call. And girls are going through puberty much earlier, and kids are allergic to just about everything, and asthma is out of control. Everyone knows it's our food. We're messing with the genes of these animals and then feeding them growth hormones and all kinds of drugs that we really don't know enough about. And then we're eating them. Kids today are the first generation to grow up on this stuff, and we're making a science experiment out of them. Isn't it strange how upset people get about a few dozen baseball players taking growth hormones, when we're doing what we're doing to our food animals and feeding them to our children?

People are so removed from food animals now. When I grew up, the animals were taken care of first. You did chores before you ate breakfast. We were told that if we didn't take care of the animals, we weren't going to eat. We never went on vacations. Somebody always had to be here. I remember we had day trips, but we always hated them because if we didn't get home before dark, we knew we'd be out in the pasture trying to get the cows in, and we'd be milking cows in the dark. It had to be done no matter what. If you don't want that responsibility, don't become a farmer. Because that's what it takes to do it right. And if you can't do it right, don't do it. It's that simple. And I'll tell you another thing: if consumers don't want to pay the farmer to do it right, they shouldn't eat meat.

People care about these things. And I don't mean rich city people.

112

Most of the folks who buy my turkeys are not rich by any means; they're struggling on fixed incomes. But they're willing to pay more for the sake of what they believe in. They're willing to pay the real price. And to those who say it's just too much to pay for a turkey, I always say to them, "Don't eat turkey." It's possible you can't afford to care, but it's certain you can't afford not to care.

Everyone's saying buy fresh, buy local. It's a sham. It's all the same kind of bird, and the suffering is in their genes. When the mass-produced turkey of today was designed, they killed thousands of turkeys in their experiments. Should it be shorter legs or shorter keel bone? Should it be like this or like this? In nature, sometimes human babies are born with deformities. But you don't aim to reproduce that generation after generation. But that's what they did with turkeys.

Michael Pollan wrote about Polyface Farm in The Omnivore's Dilemma *like it was something great, but that farm is horrible. It's a joke. Joel Salatin is doing industrial birds. Call him up and ask him. So he puts them on pasture. It makes no difference. It's like putting a broken-down Honda on the Autobahn and saying it's a Porsche. KFC chickens are almost always killed in thirty-nine days. They're babies. That's how rapidly they're grown. Salatin's organic free-range chicken is killed in forty-two days. 'Cause it's still the same chicken. It can't be allowed to live any longer because its genetics are so screwed up. Stop and think about that: a bird that you simply* can't *let live* out *of its adolescence. So maybe he'll just say he's doing as much right as he can, but it's too expensive to raise healthy birds. Well, I'm sorry if I can't pat him on the back and tell him what a good guy he is. These aren't things, they're animals, so we shouldn't be talking about good enough. Either do it right or don't do it.*

I do it right from beginning to end. Most important, I use the old genetics, the birds that were raised a hundred years ago. Do they grow slower? Yes. Do I have to feed them more? Yes. But you look at them and tell me if they're healthy.

113

I don't allow baby turkeys to be shipped through the mail. Lots of people don't care that half their turkeys are going to die under the stress of going through the mail, or that those that do live are going to be five pounds lighter in the end than those that you give food and water to immediately. But I care. All my animals get as much pasture as they want, and I never mutilate or drug them. I don't manipulate lighting or starve them to cycle unnaturally. I don't allow my turkeys to be moved if it's too cold or too hot. And I have them transported in the night, so they'll be calmer. I only allow so many turkeys on a truck, even though I could pack many, many more in. My turkeys are always carried upright, never hung by their feet, even if that means it takes much longer. At our processing plant they have to slow everything down. I pay them twice as much to do it half as fast. They have to get the turkeys off the trailers safely. No broken bones and no unnecessary stress. Everything is done by hand and carefully. It's done right every time. The turkeys are stunned before they're shackled. Normally they're hung live and dragged through an electrical bath, but we don't do that. We do one at a time. It's a person doing it, handheld. When they do it one by one, they do it well. My big fear is having live animals put in the boiling water. My sister worked at a large poultry plant. She needed the money. Two weeks, and that was all she could take. This was years and years ago, and she's still talking about the horrors she saw there.

People care about animals. I believe that. They just don't want to know or to pay. A fourth of all chickens have stress fractures. It's wrong. They're packed body to body, and can't escape their waste, and never see the sun. Their nails grow around the bars of their cages. It's wrong. They feel their slaughters. It's wrong, and people know it's wrong. They don't have to be convinced. They just have to act differently. I'm not better than anyone, and I'm not trying to convince people to live by my standards of what's right. I'm trying to convince them to live by their own.

My mother was part Indian. I still have that thing where the Indians

apologize. In the fall, while other people are giving thanks, I find myself apologizing. I hate seeing them on the truck, waiting to be taken to slaughter. They're looking back at me, saying, "Get me off of here." Killing is ... it's very ... Sometimes I justify it in my mind that I can at least make it as good as possible for the animals in my custody. It's like ... they look at me and I tell them, "Please forgive me." I can't help it. I personalize it. Animals are hard. Tonight I'll go out and make everybody that jumped the fence come back in. These turkeys are used to me, they know me, and when I go out there, they'll come running, and I'll open the gate and they'll come in. But at the same time, I put thousands on trucks and send them off to slaughter.

People focus on that last second of death. I want them to focus on the entire life of the animal. If I had to choose between knowing that my throat was going to be slit at the end, which might last three minutes, but I've had to live for six weeks in pain, I'd probably ask for that slit throat six weeks earlier. People only see the killing. They say, "What's the big deal if the animal can't walk or move, 'cause it's just gonna get killed anyway?" If it was your child, do you want your child to suffer three years, three months, three weeks, three hours, three minutes? A turkey chick isn't a human baby, but it suffers. I've never met anyone in the industry — manager, vet, worker, anyone — who doubts that they feel pain. So how much suffering is acceptable? That's what's at the bottom of all of this, and what each person has to ask himself. How much suffering will you tolerate for your food?

My nephew and his wife had a baby, and as soon as it was born they were told it wasn't going to survive. They're very religious. They got to hold her for twenty minutes. For twenty minutes she was alive, and in no pain, and she was part of their life. And they said they would never have traded those twenty minutes. They just thanked the Lord and praised him that she was alive, even if it was only twenty minutes. So how you gonna approach that?

Influence / Speechlessness / Influence / Speechness / Influence / Speechlessness / Influence / Speechlessness / Influence / Speechlessness / Influence / Speechlessness / Influence / Speechlessness / Influence / Speechlessness / Influence / Speechlessness / Influence / Speechlessness / Influence / Speechlessness / Influence / Speechlessness / Influence / Speechlessness / Influence / Speechlessness / Influence / Speechlessness / Influence / Speechlessness / Influence / Speechlessness / Influence / Speechlessness / Influence / Speechlessness / Influence / Speechlessness / Influence / Speechness / Influence / Speechlessness / Influence / Speechlessness / Influence / Speechlessness / Influence / Speechlessness / Influence / Speechlessness / Influence / Speechlessness / Influence / Speechlessness / Influence / Speechlessness / Influence / Speechlessness / Influence / Speechlessness / Influence / Speechlessness / Influence / Speechlessness / Influence / Speechlessness / Influence / Speechlessness / Influence / Speechlessness / Influence / Speechlessness / Influence / Speechlessness / Influence / Speechlessness / Influence / Speechness / Influence / Speechlessness / Influence / Speechlessness / Influence / Speechlessness / Influence / Speechlessness / Influence / Speechlessness / Influence / Speechlessness / Influence / Speechlessness / Influence / Speechlessness / Influence / Speechlessness / Influence / Speechlessness / Influence / Speechlessness / Influence / Speechlessness / Influence / Speechlessness / Influence / Speechlessness / Influence / Speechlessness / Influence / Speechlessness / Influence / Speechlessness / Influence / Speechlessness / Influence / Speechness / Influence / Speechlessness / Influence / Speechlessness / Influence / Speechlessness / Influence / Speechlessness / Influence / Speechlessness / Influence / Speechlessness / Influence / Speechlessness / Influence / Speechlessness / Influence / Speechlessness / Influence / Speechlessness / Influence / Speechlessness / Influence / Speechlessness / Influence / Speechlessness / Influence / Speechlessness / Influence / Speechlessness / Influence / Speechlessness / Influence / Speechlessness / Influence / Speechlessness / Influence / Speechness / Influence / Speechlessness / Influence / Speechlessness / Influence / Speechlessness / Influence / Speechlessness / Influence / Speechlessness / Influence / Speechlessness / Influence / Speechlessness / Influence / Speechlessness / Influence / Speechlessness / Influence / Speechlessness / Influence / Speechlessness / Influence / Speechlessness / Influence / Speechlessness / Influence / Speechlessness / Influence / Speechlessness / Influence / Speechlessness / Influence / Speechlessness / Influence / Speechlessness / Influence / Speechness / Influence / Speechlessness / Influence / Speechlessness / Influence / Speechlessness / Influence / Speechlessness / Influence / Speechlessness / Influence / Speechlessness / Influence / Speechlessness / Influence / Speechlessness / Influence / Speechlessness / Influence / Speechlessness / Influence / Speechlessness / Influence / Speechlessness / Influence / Speechlessness / Influence / Speechlessness / Influence / Speechlessness / Influence / Speechlessness / Influence / Speechlessness / Influence / Speechlessness / Influence / Speech-

lessness / Influence / Speechlessness / Influ-

ence / Speechlessness / Influence / Speechlessness / Influence / Speechlessness /
Influence / Speechlessness / Influence / Speechlessness / Influence / Speechlessness
/ Influence / Speechlessness / Influence / Speechlessness / Influence / Speechless-
ness / Influence / Speechlessness / Influence / Speechlessness / Influence / Speech-
lessness / Influence / Speechlessness / Influence / Speechlessness / Influence /
Speechlessness / Influence / Speechlessness / Influence / Speechlessness / Influence
/ Speechlessness / Influence / Speechlessness / Influence / Speechlessness / Influ-
ence / Speechlessness / Influence / Speechlessness / Influence / Speechlessness /
Influence / Speechlessness / Influence / Speechlessness / Influence / Speechlessness
/ Influence / Speechlessness / Influence / Speechlessness / Influence / Speechless-
ness / Influence / Speechlessness / Influence / Speechlessness / Influence / Speech-
lessness / Influence / Speechlessness / Influence / Speechlessness / Influence /
Speechlessness / Influence / Speechlessness / Influence / Speechlessness / Influence
/ Speechlessness / Influence / Speechlessness / Influence / Speechlessness / Influ-
ence / Speechlessness / Influence / Speechlessness / Influence / Speechlessness /
Influence / Speechlessness / Influence / Speechlessness / Influence / Speechlessness
/ Influence / Speechlessness / Influence / Speechlessness / Influence / Speechless-
ness / Influence / Speechlessness / Influence / Speechlessness / Influence / Speech-
lessness / Influence / Speechlessness / Influence / Speechlessness / Influence /
Speechlessness / Influence / Speechlessness / Influence / Speechlessness / Influence
/ Speechlessness / Influence / Speechlessness / Influence / Speechlessness / Influ-
ence / Speechlessness / Influence / Speechlessness / Influence / Speechlessness /
Influence / Speechlessness / Influence / Speechlessness / Influence / Speechlessness
/ Influence / Speechlessness / Influence / Speechlessness / Influence / Speechless-
ness / Influence / Speechlessness / Influence / Speechlessness / Influence / Speech-
lessness / Influence / Speechlessness / Influence / Speechlessness / Influence /
Speechlessness / Influence / Speechlessness / Influence / Speechlessness / Influence
/ Speechlessness / Influence / Speechlessness / Influence / Speechlessness / Influ-
ence / Speechlessness / Influence / Speechlessness / Influence / Speechlessness /
Influence / Speechlessness / Influence / Speechlessness / Influence / Speechlessness
/ Influence / Speechlessness / Influence / Speechlessness / Influence / Speechless-
ness / Influence / Speechlessness / Influence / Speechlessness / Influence / Speech-
lessness / Influence / Speechlessness / Influence / Speechlessness / Influence /
Speechlessness / Influence / Speechlessness / Influence / Speechlessness / Influence
/ Speechlessness / Influence / Speechlessness / Influence / Speechlessness / Influ-
ence / Speechlessness / Influence / Speechlessness / Influence / Speechlessness /
Influence / Speechlessness / Influence / Speechlessness / Influence / Speechlessness
/ Influence / Speechlessness / Influence / Speechlessness / Influence / Speechless-
ness / Influence / Speechlessness / Influence / Speechlessness / Influence / Speech-
lessness / Influence / Speechlessness / Influence / Speechlessness / Influence /
Speechlessness / Influence / Speechlessness / Influence / Speechlessness / Influence
/ Speechlessness / Influence / Speechlessness / Influence / Speechlessness / Influ-
ence / Speechlessness / Influence / Speechlessness / Influence / Speechlessness /
Influence / Speechlessness / Influence / Speechlessness / Influence / Speechlessness
/ Influence / Speechlessness / Influence / Speechlessness / Influence / Speechless-
ness / Influence / Speechlessness / Influence / Speechlessness / Influence / Speech-
lessness / Influence / Speechlessness / Influence / Speechlessness / Influence /
Speechlessness / Influence / Speechlessness / Influence / Speechlessness / Influence
/ Speechlessness / Influence / Speechlessness / Influence / Speechlessness / Influ-
ence / Speechlessness / Influence / Speechlessness / Influence / Speechlessness /
Influence / Speechlessness / Influence / Speechlessness / Influence / Speechlessness
/ Influence / Speechlessness / Influence / Speechlessness / Influence / Speechless-
ness / Influence / Speechlessness / Influence / Speechlessness / Influence / Speech-
lessness / Influence / Speechlessness / Influence / Speechlessness / Influence /
Speechlessness / Influence / Speechlessness / Influence / Speechlessness / Influence
/ Speechlessness / Influence / Speechlessness / Influence / Speechlessness / Influ-
ence / Speechlessness / Influence / Speechlessness / Influence / Speechlessness /
Influence / Speechlessness / Influence / Speechlessness / Influence / Speechlessness
/ Influence / Speechlessness / Influence / Speechlessness / Influence / Speechless-

ness / Influence / Speechlessness / Influence / Speechlessness / Influence / Speech-
lessness / Influence / Speechlessness / Influence / Speechlessness / Influence /
Speechlessness / Influence / Speechlessness / Influence / Speechlessness / Influence
/ Speechlessness / Influence / Speechlessness / Influence / Speechlessness / Influ-
ence / Speechlessness / Influence / Speechlessness / Influence / Speechlessness /
Influence / Speechlessness / Influence / Speechlessness / Influence / Speechlessness
/ Influence / Speechlessness / Influence / Speechlessness / Influence / Speechless-
ness / Influence / Speechlessness / Influence / Speechlessness / Influence / Speech-
lessness / Influence / Speechlessness / Influence / Speechlessness / Influence /
Speechlessness / Influence / Speechlessness / Influence / Speechlessness / Influence
/ Speechlessness / Influence / Speechlessness / Influence / Speechlessness / Influ-
ence / Speechlessness / Influence / Speechlessness / Influence / Speechlessness /
Influence / Speechlessness / Influence / Speechlessness / Influence / Speechlessness
/ Influence / Speechlessness / Influence / Speechlessness / Influence / Speechless-
ness / Influence / Speechlessness / Influence / Speechlessness / Influence / Speech-
lessness / Influence / Speechlessness / Influence / Speechlessness / Influence /
Speechlessness / Influence / Speechlessness / Influence / Speechlessness / Influence
/ Speechlessness / Influence / Speechlessness / Influence / Speechlessness / Influ-
ence / Speechlessness / Influence / Speechlessness / Influence / Speechlessness /
Influence / Speechlessness / Influence / Speechlessness / Influence / Speechlessness
/ Influence / Speechlessness / Influence / Speechlessness / Influence / Speechless-
ness / Influence / Speechlessness / Influence / Speechlessness / Influence / Speech-
lessness / Influence / Speechlessness / Influence / Speechlessness / Influence /
Speechlessness / Influence / Speechlessness / Influence / Speechlessness / Influence
/ Speechlessness / Influence / Speechlessness / Influence / Speechlessness / Influ-
ence / Speechlessness / Influence / Speechlessness / Influence / Speechlessness /
Influence / Speechlessness / Influence / Speechlessness / Influence / Speechlessness
/ Influence / Speechlessness / Influence / Speechlessness / Influence / Speechless-
ness / Influence / Speechlessness / Influence / Speechlessness / Influence / Speech-
lessness / Influence / Speechlessness / Influence / Speechlessness / Influence /
Speechlessness / Influence / Speechlessness / Influence / Speechlessness / Influence
/ Speechlessness / Influence / Speechlessness / Influence / Speechlessness / Influ-
ence / Speechlessness / Influence / Speechlessness / Influence / Speechlessness /
Influence / Speechlessness / Influence / Speechlessness / Influence / Speechlessness
/ Influence / Speechlessness / Influence / Speechlessness / Influence / Speechless-
ness / Influence / Speechlessness / Influence / Speechlessness / Influence / Speech-
lessness / Influence / Speechlessness / Influence / Speechlessness / Influence /
Speechlessness / Influence / Speechlessness / Influence / Speechlessness / Influence
/ Speechlessness / Influence / Speechlessness / Influence / Speechlessness / Influ-
ence / Speechlessness / Influence / Speechlessness / Influence / Speechlessness /
Influence / Speechlessness / Influence / Speechlessness / Influence / Speechlessness
/ Influence / Speechlessness / Influence / Speechlessness / Influence / Speechless-
ness / Influence / Speechlessness / Influence / Speechlessness / Influence / Speech-
lessness / Influence / Speechlessness / Influence / Speechlessness / Influence /
Speechlessness / Influence / Speechlessness / Influence / Speechlessness / Influence
/ Speechlessness / Influence / Speechlessness / Influence / Speechlessness / Influ-
ence / Speechlessness / Influence / Speechlessness / Influence / Speechlessness /
Influence / Speechlessness / Influence / Speechlessness / Influence / Speechlessness
/ Influence / Speechlessness / Influence / Speechlessness / Influence / Speechless-
ness / Influence / Speechlessness / Influence / Speechlessness / Influence / Speech-
lessness / Influence / Speechlessness / Influence / Speechlessness / Influence /
Speechlessness / Influence / Speechlessness / Influence / Speechlessness / Influence

/ Speechlessness / Influence / Speechlessness / I

On average, Americans eat the equivalent of 21,000 entire animals in a lifetime — one animal for every letter on the last five pages.

Lam Hoi-ka

BREVIG MISSION IS A TINY Inuit village on the Bering Strait. The one full-time local government employee is a "financial administrator." No police or fire department, no utilities workmen, no waste management. Amazingly, though, there is an online dating service. (One might have thought that with only 276 citizens, everyone would more or less know who was available.) There are two women and two men looking for love, which would be good math, except that one of the men—last time I checked the site, anyway—isn't into women. Cutieguy1, a black African, self-described as "cute 5.4 feet tall looking," is the second-least-likely person you might imagine finding in Brevig. The prize itself goes to Johan Hultin, a six-foot-tall Swede with a shock of white hair and a trim white goatee. Hultin arrived in Brevig on August 19, 1997, having told only one person about his trip, and got right to digging. Beneath the feet of solid ice were bodies. He was excavating a mass grave.

Deep in the permafrost were preserved victims of the 1918 flu pandemic. The one person Hultin shared his plans with was a fellow scientist, Jeffery Taubenberger, who was also looking for the source of the 1918 flu.

Hultin's search for the dead of 1918 was timely. It was only a few months before his arrival in Brevig Mission that an H5N1-type virus in Hong Kong's chickens apparently "jumped" to humans for the first time—an event of potentially historic significance.

Three-year-old Lam Hoi-ka was the first of six to be killed by this particularly ominous version of the H5N1 virus. I, and now you, know his name because when a deadly virus jumps species, a window opens through which a new pandemic may enter the world. Had

health authorities not acted as they did (or had our luck been worse), Lam Hoi-ka might have been death number one in a global pandemic. He still might be. The worrisome strains of H5N1 have not disappeared from the planet even if it has disappeared from American headlines. The question is whether it will continue to kill a relatively small number of people or mutate into a deadlier version. Viruses like H5N1 can be ferocious entrepreneurs, constantly innovating, relentless in their aim of corrupting the human immune system.

With a potential H5N1 nightmare looming, Hultin and Taubenberger wanted to know what had caused the 1918 pandemic. And for good reason: the 1918 pandemic killed more people faster than any other disease—or any other *anything*—had before or has since.

Influenza

THE 1918 PANDEMIC HAS BEEN remembered as the "Spanish flu" because the Spanish press was the only Western media to adequately cover its massive toll. (Some speculate that this is because the Spanish were not at war, and their press was not as distorted by wartime censorship and distraction.) Despite the name, Spanish flu struck the entire world—that's what made it a *pan*demic instead of simply an *epi*demic. It was not the first influenza pandemic, nor the most recent (1957 and 1968 also saw pandemics), but it was by far the most deadly. Whereas AIDS took roughly twenty-four years to kill 24 million people, the Spanish flu killed as many in twenty-four weeks. Some recent revisions of the death toll suggest that 50 million or even as many as 100 million people were killed worldwide. Estimates suggest that one-quarter of Americans, and perhaps one-quarter of the world, fell ill.

Unlike most influenzas that mortally threaten only the very young, very old, and already ill, the Spanish flu killed healthy people in the prime of their lives. Mortality was actually highest in the twenty-five-to-twenty-nine-year-old group, and at the flu's peak the average life expectancy for Americans was reduced to thirty-seven years. The scale of the misery was so vast in America—as elsewhere—that I find it impossible to understand why I didn't learn more about it in school, or through memorials or stories. As many as twenty thousand Americans died in a week during the height of the Spanish flu. Steam shovels were used to dig mass graves.

Health authorities today fear precisely such an event. Many insist that a pandemic based on the H5N1 virus strain is inevitable, and the question is really one of when it will strike and, most important, just how severe it will be.

Even if the H5N1 virus manages to pass us by without much more ultimate impact than the recent outbreak of swine flu, no health authority today is predicting that pandemics can be completely prevented. The director-general of the World Health Organization (WHO) has said simply, "We know another pandemic is inevitable.... It is coming." The National Academy of Sciences Institute of Medicine has added more recently that a pandemic is "not only inevitable, but overdue." Recent history has averaged a pandemic every twenty-seven and a half years, and it's now been over forty years since the last one. Scientists cannot know with certainty the future of pandemic diseases, but they can and do know that a threat is imminent.

WHO officials now have at their fingertips the most massive assemblage of scientific data ever gathered about a potential new flu pandemic. So it is quite unnerving that this very suit-and-tie-and-long-white-jackets, very now-don't-everyone-panic type of

institution has the following list of "things you need to know about pandemic influenza" for its constituency, which is everyone:

The world may be on the brink of another pandemic.
All countries will be affected.
Widespread illness will occur.
Medical supplies will be inadequate.
Large numbers of deaths will occur.
Economic and social disruption will be great.

The relatively conservative WHO suggests "a relatively conservative estimate—from 2 million to 7.4 million deaths" if bird flu jumps to humans and becomes airborne (as swine flu—H1N1—did). "This estimate," they go on to explain, "is based on the comparatively mild 1957 pandemic. Estimates based on a more virulent virus, closer to the one seen in 1918, have been made and are much higher." Mercifully, the WHO does not include these higher estimates on its "things you need to know" list. Unmercifully, they cannot say that higher estimates are any less realistic.

Hultin eventually uncovered the remains of a woman among the frozen dead of 1918 and named her Lucy. He cut out Lucy's lungs and mailed them to Taubenberger, who took samples from the tissue and found evidence of something quite remarkable. The results, published in 2005, show that the source of the 1918 pandemic was avian influenza—bird flu. A major scientific question had been answered.

Other evidence suggests that the 1918 virus might have mutated within pigs (which are uniquely susceptible to both human and bird viruses) or even in human populations for a time before reaching the deadly virtuosity of its final version. We cannot be sure. What we can be sure of is that there is scientific consensus that new viruses, which

move between farmed animals and humans, will be a major global health threat into the foreseeable future. The concern is not only bird flu or swine flu or whatever-comes-next, but the entire class of "zoonotic" (animal-to-human or vice versa) pathogens—especially viruses that move between humans, chickens, turkeys, and pigs.

We can also be sure that any talk of pandemic influenza today cannot ignore the fact that the most devastating disease event the world has ever known, and one of the greatest health threats before us today, has everything to do with the health of the world's farmed animals, birds most of all.

All Flus

ANOTHER KEY FIGURE IN THE story of influenza research is a virologist named Robert Webster, who proved the avian origins of all human influenza. He called it the "barnyard theory," which surmises that "the viruses in human pandemics recruit some of their genes from flu viruses in domestic birds."

A few years after the 1968 "Hong Kong flu" pandemic (whose successor strains continue to quietly cause twenty thousand "excess deaths" annually in the United States), Webster identified the responsible virus. As he anticipated, the virus was a hybrid that had incorporated aspects of a bird virus found in a duck in central Europe. Today the best evidence suggests that the avian source of the 1968 pandemic is not unique: scientists now argue that the primordial source of all flu strains is migrating aquatic birds such as ducks and geese that have roamed the earth for more than a hundred million years. The flu, it turns out, is all about our relationship with birds.

Some basic science is necessary here. As the original source of

these viruses, wild ducks, geese, terns, and gulls harbor the full spectrum of flu strains as categorized by today's science: H1 through the recently discovered H16, N1 through N9. Domestic birds can also harbor a large reservoir of such flu strains. Neither wild nor domestic birds necessarily become sick from these viruses. They often simply carry them, sometimes clear across the globe, and then shed them through feces into lakes, rivers, ponds, and, quite often, thanks to industrial animal-processing techniques, directly into the food we eat.

Each mammalian species is vulnerable to only some of the viruses carried by birds. Humans, for example, are typically vulnerable to only H1, H2, and H3 viruses, pigs to H1 and H3, and horses to H3 and H7. The *H* stands for hemagglutinin, a spike-shaped protein found on the surface of influenza viruses and named after its ability to "agglutinate"—that is, to clump together red blood cells. Hemagglutinin serves as a kind of molecular bridge that allows the virus itself to flow into the victim's cells like enemy troops crossing a makeshift bridge. Hemagglutinin is able to accomplish this deadly work through its remarkable ability to bind itself to specific kinds of molecular structures, known as receptors, on the surface of human and animal cells. H1, H2, and H3—the three types of hemagglutinin that commonly attack humans—are specialists in binding to our respiratory systems, which is why the flu so often begins in the human respiratory tract.

The trouble begins when a virus in one species begins to get itchy and starts showing a fondness for mixing with viruses in others, as H1N1 has done (combining bird, pig, and human viruses). In the case of H5N1, there are fears that the actual "creation" of a new virus highly contagious to humans might occur in pig populations, since pigs are susceptible to the types of viruses that attack birds as well as to those that attack humans. When a single pig gets

infected with two different virus types at the same time, there is a possibility of viruses trading genes. The H1N1 swine flu appears to have resulted from just this. What's worrisome is that such gene swapping could lead to the creation of a virus that has the virulence of bird flu and the everyone-is-getting-it contagiousness of the common cold.

How did this new landscape of disease come about? To what extent is modern animal agriculture responsible? To answer these questions, we need to know where the birds we eat come from, and why their environments are perfect to make not only the birds, but us, sick.

The Life and Death of a Bird

THE SECOND FARM I SAW with C was set up in a series of twenty sheds, each 45 feet wide by 490 feet long, each holding in the neighborhood of 33,000 birds. I didn't have a tape measure with me and couldn't do anything resembling a head count. But I can assert these numbers with confidence because the dimensions are typical in the industry—though some growers are now building larger sheds: up to 60 feet by 504 feet, housing 50,000 or more birds.

It's hard to get one's head around the magnitude of 33,000 birds in one room. You don't have to see it for yourself, or even do the math, to understand that things are packed pretty tight. In its Animal Welfare Guidelines, the National Chicken Council indicates an appropriate stocking density to be eight-tenths of a square foot per bird. That's what's considered animal welfare by a "mainstream" organization representing chicken producers, which shows you how thoroughly co-opted ideas about welfare have become—and why you can't trust labels that come from anywhere but a reliable third-party source.

129

It's worth pausing on this for a moment. Although many animals live with far less, let's assume the full eight-tenths of a square foot. Try to picture it. (It's unlikely you'll ever get to see the inside of a poultry factory farm in person, but there are plenty of images on the Internet if your imagination needs help.) Find a piece of printer paper and imagine a full-grown bird shaped something like a football with legs standing on it. Imagine 33,000 of these rectangles in a grid. (Broilers are never in cages, and never on multiple levels.) Now enclose the grid with windowless walls and put a ceiling on top. Run in automated (drug-laced) feed, water, heating, and ventilation systems. This is a farm.

Now to the farming.

First, find a chicken that will grow big fast on as little feed as possible. The muscles and fat tissues of the newly engineered broiler birds grow significantly faster than their bones, leading to deformities and disease. Somewhere between 1 and 4 percent of the birds will die writhing in convulsions from sudden death syndrome, a condition virtually unknown outside of factory farms. Another factory-farm-induced condition in which excess fluids fill the body cavity, ascites, kills even more (5 percent of birds globally). Three out of four will have some degree of walking impairment, and common sense suggests they are in chronic pain. One out of four will have such significant trouble walking that there is no question they are in pain.

For your broilers, leave the lights on about twenty-four hours a day for the first week or so of the chicks' lives. This encourages them to eat more. Then turn the lights off a bit, giving them maybe four hours of darkness a day—just enough sleep for them to survive. Of course chickens will go crazy if forced to live in such grossly unnatural conditions for long—the lighting and crowding, the burdens of their grotesque bodies. At least broiler birds are typically slaughtered on the forty-second day of their lives (or

increasingly the thirty-ninth), so they haven't yet established social hierarchies to fight over.

Needless to say, jamming deformed, drugged, overstressed birds together in a filthy, waste-coated room is not very healthy. Beyond deformities, eye damage, blindness, bacterial infections of bones, slipped vertebrae, paralysis, internal bleeding, anemia, slipped tendons, twisted lower legs and necks, respiratory diseases, and weakened immune systems are frequent and long-standing problems on factory farms. Scientific studies and government records suggest that virtually all (upwards of 95 percent of) chickens become infected with E. coli (an indicator of fecal contamination) and between 39 and 75 percent of chickens in retail stores are still infected. Around 8 percent of birds become infected with salmonella (down from several years ago, when at least one in four birds was infected, which still occurs on some farms). Seventy to 90 percent are infected with another potentially deadly pathogen, campylobacter. Chlorine baths are commonly used to remove slime, odor, and bacteria.

Of course, consumers might notice that their chickens don't taste quite right—how good could a drug-stuffed, disease-ridden, shit-contaminated animal possibly taste?—but the birds will be injected (or otherwise pumped up) with "broths" and salty solutions to give them what we have come to think of as the chicken look, smell, and taste. (A recent study by *Consumer Reports* found that chicken and turkey products, many labeled as *natural*, "ballooned with 10 to 30 percent of their weight as broth, flavoring, or water.")

The farming done, it's now time for "processing."

First, you'll need to find workers to gather the birds into crates and "hold the line" that will turn the living, whole birds into plastic-wrapped parts. You will have to continuously find the workers, since annual turnover rates typically exceed 100 percent. (The interviews I did suggest turnover rates of around 150 percent.) Illegal

aliens are often preferred, but poor recent immigrants who do not speak English are also desirable employees. By the standards of the international human rights community, the typical working conditions in America's slaughterhouses constitute human rights violations; for you, they constitute a crucial way to produce cheap meat and feed the world. Pay your workers minimum wage, or near to it, to scoop up the birds—grabbing five in each hand, upside down by the legs—and jam them into transport crates.

If your operation is running at the proper speed—105 chickens crated by a single worker in 3.5 minutes is the expected rate according to several catchers I interviewed—the birds will be handled roughly and, as I was also told, the workers will regularly feel the birds' bones snapping in their hands. (Approximately 30 percent of all live birds arriving at the slaughterhouse have freshly broken bones as a result of their Frankenstein genetics and rough treatment.) No laws protect the birds, but of course there are laws about how you can treat the workers, and this sort of labor tends to leave people in pain for days afterward, so, again, be sure you hire those who won't be in a position to complain—people like "Maria," an employee of one of the largest chicken processors in California, with whom I spent an afternoon. After more than forty years of work, and five surgeries due to work-related injuries, Maria no longer has enough use of her hands to do the dishes. She is in such constant pain that she spends her evenings soaking her arms in ice water, and often can't fall asleep without pills. She is paid eight dollars an hour, and asked that I not use her real name, for fear of retribution.

Load the crates into trucks. Ignore weather extremes and don't feed or water the birds, even if the plant is hundreds of miles away. Upon arrival at the plant, have more workers sling the birds, to hang upside down by their ankles in metal shackles, onto a moving conveyer system. More bones will be broken. Often the screaming of

the birds and the flapping of their wings will be so loud that workers won't be able to hear the person next to them on the line. Often
the birds will defecate in pain and terror.

The conveyer system drags the birds through an electrified
water bath. This most likely paralyzes them but doesn't render
them insensible. Other countries, including many European countries, require (legally, at least) that chickens be rendered unconscious or killed prior to bleeding and scalding. In America, where
the USDA's interpretation of the Humane Methods of Slaughter
Act exempts chicken slaughter, the voltage is kept low—about one-
tenth the level necessary to render the animals unconscious. After
it has traveled through the bath, a paralyzed bird's eyes might still
move. Sometimes the birds will have enough control of their bodies
to slowly open their beaks, as though attempting to scream.

The next stop on the line for the immobile-but-conscious bird
will be an automated throat slitter. Blood will slowly drain out of
the bird, unless the relevant arteries are missed, which happens,
according to another worker I spoke with, "all the time." So you'll
need a few more workers to function as backup slaughterers—"kill
men"—who will slit the throats of the birds that the machine
misses. Unless they, too, miss the birds, which I was also told happens "all the time." According to the National Chicken Council—
representatives of the industry—about 180 million chickens are
improperly slaughtered each year. When asked if these numbers
troubled him, Richard L. Lobb, the council's spokesman, sighed,
"The process is over in a matter of minutes."

I spoke to numerous catchers, live hangers, and kill men who
described birds going alive and conscious into the scalding tank.
(Government estimates obtained through the Freedom of Information Act suggest that this happens to about four million birds
each year.) Since feces on skin and feathers end up in the tanks, the

birds leave filled with pathogens that they have inhaled or absorbed through their skin (the tanks' heated water helps open the birds' pores).

After the birds' heads are pulled off and their feet removed, machines open them with a vertical incision and remove their guts. Contamination often occurs here, as the high-speed machines commonly rip open intestines, releasing feces into the birds' body cavities. Once upon a time, USDA inspectors had to condemn any bird with such fecal contamination. But about thirty years ago, the poultry industry convinced the USDA to reclassify feces so that it could continue to use these automatic eviscerators. Once a dangerous contaminant, feces are now classified as a "cosmetic blemish." As a result, inspectors condemn half the number of birds. Perhaps Lobb and the National Chicken Council would simply sigh and say, "People are done consuming the feces in a matter of minutes."

Next the birds are inspected by a USDA official, whose ostensible function is to keep the consumer safe. The inspector has approximately two seconds to examine each bird inside and out, both the carcass and the organs, for more than a dozen different diseases and suspect abnormalities. He or she looks at about 25,000 birds a day. Journalist Scott Bronstein wrote a remarkable series for the *Atlanta Journal-Constitution* about poultry inspection, which should be required reading for anyone considering eating chicken. He conducted interviews with nearly a hundred USDA poultry inspectors from thirty-seven plants. "Every week," he reports, "millions of chickens leaking yellow pus, stained by green feces, contaminated by harmful bacteria, or marred by lung and heart infections, cancerous tumors, or skin conditions are shipped for sale to consumers."

Next the chickens go to a massive refrigerated tank of water, where thousands of birds are communally cooled. Tom Devine, from the Government Accountability Project, has said that the

"water in these tanks has been aptly named 'fecal soup' for all the filth and bacteria floating around. By immersing clean, healthy birds in the same tank with dirty ones, you're practically assuring cross-contamination."

While a significant number of European and Canadian poultry processors employ air-chilling systems, 99 percent of US poultry producers have stayed with water-immersion systems and fought lawsuits from both consumers and the beef industry to continue the outmoded use of water-chilling. It's not hard to figure out why. Air-chilling reduces the weight of a bird's carcass, but water-chilling causes a dead bird to soak up water (the same water known as "fecal soup"). One study has shown that simply placing the chicken carcasses in sealed plastic bags during the chilling stage would eliminate cross-contamination. But that would also eliminate an opportunity for the industry to turn wastewater into tens of millions of dollars' worth of additional weight in poultry products.

Not too long ago there was an 8 percent limit set by the USDA on just how much absorbed liquid one could sell consumers at chicken meat prices before the government took action. When this became public knowledge in the 1990s, there was an understandable outcry. Consumers sued over the practice, which sounded to them not only repulsive, but like adulteration. The courts threw out the 8 percent rule as "arbitrary and capricious."

Ironically, though, the USDA's interpretation of the court ruling allowed the chicken industry to do its own research to evaluate what percentage of chicken meat should be composed of fouled, chlorinated water. (This is an all-too-familiar outcome when challenging the agribusiness industry.) After industry consultation, the new law of the land allows slightly more than *11 percent* liquid absorption (the exact percentage is indicated in small print on packaging—have a look next time). As soon as the public's attention moved elsewhere,

the poultry industry turned regulations meant to protect consumers to its own advantage.

US poultry consumers now gift massive poultry producers millions of additional dollars every year as a result of this added liquid. The USDA knows this and defends the practice—after all, the poultry processors are, as so many factory farmers like to say, simply doing their best to "feed the world." (Or in this case ensure its hydration.)

What I've described is not exceptional. It isn't the result of masochistic workers, defective machinery, or "bad apples." It is the rule. More than 99 percent of all chickens sold for meat in America live and die like this.

In some ways factory systems may differ considerably, for example in the percentage of birds that are accidentally scalded alive each week during processing or in the amount of fecal soup their bodies absorb. These are differences that matter. In other ways, though, chicken factory farms—well run or poorly run, "cage-free" or not—are basically the same: all birds come from similar Frankenstein-like genetic stock; all are confined; none enjoy the breeze or the warmth of sunlight; none are able to fulfill all (or usually any) of their species-specific behaviors like nesting, perching, exploring their environment, and forming stable social units; illness is always rampant; suffering is always the rule; the animals are always only a unit, a weight; death is invariably cruel. These similarities matter more than the differences.

The vastness of the poultry industry means that if there is anything wrong with the system, there is something terribly wrong in our world. Today six billion chickens are raised in roughly these conditions each year in the European Union, over nine billion in

America, and more than seven billion in China. India's billion-plus population consumes very little chicken per capita, but that still amounts to a couple billion factory-farmed birds annually, and the number of birds they raise is increasing—as in China—at aggressive, globally significant rates (often double the growth of the rapidly expanding US poultry industry). All told, there are fifty billion (and counting) factory-farmed birds worldwide. If India and China eventually start consuming poultry at the rate the United States does, it would more than double this already mind-blowing figure.

Fifty billion. Every year fifty billion birds are made to live and die like this.

It cannot be overstated how revolutionary and relatively new this reality is—the number of factory-farmed birds was zero before Celia Steele's 1923 experiment. And we're not just raising chickens differently; we're eating more chickens: Americans eat 150 times as many chickens as we did only eighty years ago.

Another thing we could say about fifty billion is that it is calculated with the utmost meticulousness. The statisticians who generate the figure nine billion in the United States break it down by month, state, and the birds' weight, and compare it—each and every month—to the death toll in the same month a year before. These numbers are studied, debated, projected, and practically revered like a cult object by the industry. They are no mere facts, but the announcement of a victory.

Influence

MUCH LIKE THE VIRUS IT names, the word *influenza* comes to us by way of a mutation. The word was first used in Italian and originally referred to the influence of the stars—that is, astral or occult

influences that would have been felt by many people at once. By the sixteenth century, though, the word had begun mixing and blending with the meanings of other words and come to refer to epidemic and pandemic flues that simultaneously strike multiple communities (as if the result of some malevolent will).

At least etymologically speaking, when we talk about influenza we are talking about the influences that shape the world everywhere at once. Today's bird flu or swine flu viruses or the 1918 Spanish flu virus are not the real influenza — not the underlying influence — but only its symptom.

Few of us any longer believe that pandemics are the creation of occult forces. Should we consider the contribution of 50 billion sickly, drugged birds — birds that are the primordial source of all flu viruses — an underlying influence propelling the creation of new pathogens that attack humans? What about the 500 million pigs with compromised immune systems in confinement facilities?

In 2004, a collection of the world's experts on emerging zoonotic diseases gathered to discuss the possible relationship between all those compromised and sick farm animals, and pandemic explosions. Before getting to their conclusions, it is helpful to think about the new pathogens as two related but distinct kinds of public-health concerns. The first concern is a more general one about the relationship between factory farms and *all kinds* of pathogens, like new strains of campylobacter, salmonella, or E. coli. The second public-health concern is the more particular one: humans are setting the conditions for the creation of the superpathogen of all superpathogens, a hybrid virus that could cause a repeat, more or less, of the Spanish flu of 1918. These two concerns are intimately related.

Each case of food-borne illness cannot be traced, but where we do know the origin, or the "vehicle of transmission," it is, overwhelm-

ingly, an animal product. According to the US Centers for Disease Control (CDC), poultry is by far the largest cause. According to a study published in *Consumer Reports*, 83 percent of all chicken meat (including organic and antibiotic-free brands) is infected with either campylobacter or salmonella at the time of purchase.

I'm not sure why more people aren't aware of (and angry about) the rates of avoidable food-borne illness. Perhaps it doesn't seem obvious that something is amiss simply because anything that happens all the time, like meat (especially poultry) becoming infected by pathogens, tends to fade into the background.

In any case, if you know what to look for, the pathogen problem comes into terrifying focus. For example, the next time a friend has a sudden "flu"—what folks sometimes misdescribe as "the stomach flu"—ask a few questions. Was your friend's illness one of those "twenty-four-hour flus" that come and go quickly—retch or shit then relief? The diagnosis isn't quite so simple, but if the answer to this question is yes, your friend probably didn't have the flu at all—he or she was probably among the 76 million cases of food-borne illness the CDC estimates occur in America each year. Your friend didn't "catch a bug" so much as eat a bug. And in all likelihood that bug was created by factory farming.

Beyond the sheer number of illnesses linked to factory farming, we know that factory farms are contributing to the growth of antimicrobial-resistant pathogens simply because these farms consume so many antimicrobials. We have to go to a doctor to obtain antibiotics and other antimicrobials as a public-health measure to limit the number of such drugs being taken by humans. We accept this inconvenience because of its medical importance. Microbes eventually adapt to antimicrobials, and we want to make sure it is the truly sick people who benefit from the finite number of uses any antimicrobial will have before the microbes learn how to survive it.

On a typical factory farm drugs are fed to animals with every meal. In poultry factory farms, as I explained earlier, they almost have to be. Industry saw this problem from the beginning, but rather than accept less-productive animals, they compensated for the animals' compromised immunity with feed additives.

As a result, farmed animals are fed antibiotics nontherapeutically (that is, before they get sick). In the United States, about 3 million pounds of antibiotics are given to humans each year, but a whopping 17.8 million pounds are fed to livestock—at least that is what the industry claims. The Union of Concerned Scientists (UCS) has shown that the industry underreported its antibiotic use by at least 40 percent. The UCS calculated 24.6 million pounds of antibiotics were fed to chickens, pigs, and other farmed animals, only counting *nontherapeutic* uses. They further calculated that fully 13.5 million pounds of those antimicrobials would currently be illegal within the EU.

The implications for creating drug-resistant pathogens are quite straightforward. Study after study has shown that antimicrobial resistance follows quickly on the heels of the introduction of new drugs on factory farms. For example, in 1995, when the Food and Drug Administration approved fluoroquinolones—such as Cipro—for use in chickens against the protest of the Centers for Disease Control, the percentage of bacteria resistant to this powerful new class of antibiotics rose from almost zero to 18 percent by 2002. A broader study in the *New England Journal of Medicine* showed an eightfold increase in antimicrobial resistance from 1992 to 1997, and, using molecular subtyping, linked this increase to the use of antimicrobials in farmed chickens.

As far back as the late 1960s, scientists have warned against the nontherapeutic use of antibiotics in farmed-animal feed. Today, institutions as diverse as the American Medical Association, the

Centers for Disease Control, the Institute of Medicine (a division of the National Academy of Sciences), and the World Health Organization have linked nontherapeutic antibiotic use on factory farms with increased antimicrobial resistance and called for a ban. Still, the factory farm industry has effectively opposed such a ban in the United States. And, unsurprisingly, the limited bans in other countries are only a limited solution.

There is a glaring reason that the needed total ban on nontherapeutic use of antibiotics hasn't already occurred: the factory farm industry (in alliance with the pharmaceutical industry) currently has more power than public-health professionals. The source of the industry's immense power is not obscure. We give it to them. We have chosen, unwittingly, to fund this industry on a massive scale by eating factory-farmed animal products (and water sold as animal products)—and we do so daily.

The same conditions that lead 76 million Americans to become ill from their food annually and that promote antimicrobial resistance also contribute to the risk of a pandemic. This brings us back to the remarkable 2004 conference in which the Food and Agriculture Organization of the United Nations, the World Health Organization, and the World Organization for Animal Health (OIE) put their tremendous resources together to evaluate the available information on "emerging zoonotic diseases." At the time of the conference, H5N1 and SARS topped the list of feared emerging zoonotic diseases. Today H1N1 would be pathogen enemy number one.

The scientists distinguished between "primary risk factors" for zoonotic diseases and mere "amplification risk factors," which affect only the rate at which a disease spreads. Their paradigmatic

examples of primary risk factors were "change to an agricultural production system or consumption patterns." What particular agricultural and consumer changes did they have in mind? First in a list of four main risk factors was "increasing demand for animal protein," which is a fancy way of saying that demand for meat, eggs, and dairy is a "primary factor" influencing emerging zoonotic diseases.

This demand for animal products, the report continues, leads to "changes in farming practices." Lest we have any confusion about the "changes" that are relevant, poultry factory farms are singled out.

Similar conclusions were reached by the Council for Agricultural Science and Technology, which brought together industry experts and experts from the WHO, OIE, and USDA. Their 2005 report argued that a major impact of factory farming is "the rapid selection and amplification of pathogens that arise from a virulent ancestor (frequently by subtle mutation), thus there is increasing risk for disease entrance and/or dissemination." Breeding genetically uniform and sickness-prone birds in the overcrowded, stressful, feces-infested, and artificially lit conditions of factory farms promotes the growth and mutation of pathogens. The "cost of increased efficiency," the report concludes, is increased global risk for diseases. Our choice is simple: cheap chicken or our health.

Today the factory farm–pandemic link couldn't be more lucid. The primary ancestor of the recent H1N1 swine flu outbreak originated at a hog factory farm in America's most hog-factory-rich state, North Carolina, and then quickly spread throughout the Americas. It was in these factory farms that scientists saw, for the first time, viruses that combined genetic material from bird, pig, and human viruses. Scientists at Columbia and Princeton Universities have actually been able to trace six of the eight genetic segments of the

(currently) most feared virus in the world directly to US factory farms.

Perhaps in the back of our minds we already understand, without all the science I've discussed, that something terribly wrong is happening. Our sustenance now comes from misery. We know that if someone offers to show us a film on how our meat is produced, it will be a horror film. We perhaps know more than we care to admit, keeping it down in the dark places of our memory—disavowed. When we eat factory-farmed meat we live, literally, on tortured flesh. Increasingly, that tortured flesh is becoming our own.

More Influences

BEYOND THE UNHEALTHY INFLUENCE THAT our demand for factory-farmed meat has in the area of food-borne illness and communicable diseases, we could cite many other influences on public health: most obviously the now widely recognized relationship between the nation's major killers (heart disease, number one; cancer, number two; and stroke, number three) and meat consumption or, much less obviously, the distorting influence of the meat industry on the information about nutrition we receive from the government and medical professionals.

In 1917, while World War I devastated Europe and just before the Spanish flu devastated the world, a group of women, in part motivated to make maximal use of America's food resources during wartime, founded what is now the nation's premier group of food and nutrition professionals, the American Dietetic Association (ADA). Since the 1990s, the ADA has issued what has become the standard we-definitely-know-this-much summary of the healthfulness of a vegetarian diet. The ADA takes a conservative stand,

leaving out many well-documented health benefits attributable to reducing the consumption of animal products. Here are the three key sentences from the summary of their summary of the relevant scientific literature. One:

> Well-planned vegetarian diets are appropriate for all individuals during all stages of the life cycle, including pregnancy, lactation, infancy, childhood, and adolescence, and for athletes.

Two:

> Vegetarian diets tend to be lower in saturated fat and cholesterol, and have higher levels of dietary fiber, magnesium and potassium, vitamins C and E, folate, carotenoids, flavonoids, and other phytochemicals.

Elsewhere the paper notes that vegetarians and vegans (including athletes) "meet and exceed requirements" for protein. And, to render the whole we-should-worry-about-getting-enough-protein-and-therefore-eat-meat idea even more useless, other data suggests that excess animal protein intake is linked with osteoporosis, kidney disease, calcium stones in the urinary tract, and some cancers. Despite some persistent confusion, it is clear that vegetarians and vegans tend to have more optimal protein consumption than omnivores.

Finally, we have the really important news, based not on speculation (however well-grounded in basic science such speculation might be), but on the definitive gold standard of nutritional research: studies on actual human populations.

Three:

> Vegetarian diets are often associated with a number of health advantages, including lower blood cholesterol levels, lower risk

of heart disease [which alone accounts for more than 25 percent of all annual deaths in the nation], lower blood pressure levels, and lower risk of hypertension and type 2 diabetes. Vegetarians tend to have a lower body mass index (BMI) [that is, they are not as fat] and lower overall cancer rates [cancers account for nearly another 25 percent of all annual deaths in the nation].

I don't think that individual health is necessarily a reason to become vegetarian, but certainly if it were unhealthy to stop eating animals, that might be a reason not to be vegetarian. It would most certainly be a reason to feed my son animals.

I talked to several of the leading American nutritionists about this — taking both adults and children as the subjects of my questions — and heard the same thing again and again: vegetarianism is at least as healthy as a diet that includes meat.

If it's sometimes hard to believe that eschewing animal products will make it easier to eat healthfully, there is a reason: we are constantly lied to about nutrition. Let me be precise. When I say we are being lied to, I'm not impugning the scientific literature, but relying upon it. What the public learns of the scientific data on nutrition and health (especially from the government's nutritional guidelines) comes to us by way of many hands. Since the rise of science itself, those who produce meat have made sure that they are among those who influence how nutritional data will be presented to the likes of you and me.

Consider, for example, the National Dairy Council (NDC), a marketing arm of Dairy Management Inc., an industry body whose sole purpose, according to its website, is to "drive increased sales of and demand for U.S. dairy products." The NDC promotes dairy consumption without regard for negative public-health consequences and even markets dairy to communities incapable of digesting the

stuff. As it is a trade group, the NDC's behavior is at least under-standable. What is hard to comprehend is why educators and govern-ment have, since the 1950s, allowed the NDC to become arguably the largest and most important supplier of nutritional-education materials in the nation. Worse, our present federal "nutritional" guidelines come to us from the very same government depart-ment that has worked so hard to make factory farming the norm in America, the USDA.

The USDA has a monopoly on the most important advertising space in the nation—those little nutritional boxes we find on virtu-ally everything we eat. Founded the same year that the ADA opened its offices, the USDA was charged with providing nutritional infor-mation to the nation and ultimately with creating guidelines that would serve public health. At the same time, though, the USDA was charged with promoting industry.

The conflict of interest is not subtle: our nation gets its feder-ally endorsed nutritional information from an agency that must support the food industry, which today means supporting fac-tory farms. The details of misinformation that dribble into our lives (like fears about "enough protein") follow naturally from this fact and have been reflected upon in detail by writers like Marion Nestle. As a public-health expert, Nestle has worked extensively with government, including on "The Surgeon General's Report on Nutrition and Health," and has had decades of interaction with the food industry. In many ways, her conclusions are banal, con-firming what we already expected, but the insider's perspective she brings has lent a new clarity to the picture of just how much influ-ence the food industry—especially animal agriculture—has on national nutrition policy. She argues that food companies, like ciga-rette companies (her analogy), will say and do whatever works to sell products. They will "lobby Congress to eliminate regulations

perceived as unfavorable; they press federal regulatory agencies not to enforce such regulations; and when they don't like regulatory decisions, they file lawsuits. Like cigarette companies, food companies co-opt food and nutrition experts by supporting professional organizations and research, and they expand sales by marketing directly to children." Regarding US government recommendations that tend to encourage dairy consumption in the name of preventing osteoporosis, Nestle notes that in parts of the world where milk is not a staple of the diet, people often have less osteoporosis and fewer bone fractures than Americans do. The highest rates of osteoporosis are seen in countries where people consume the most dairy foods.

In a striking example of food industry influence, Nestle argues that the USDA currently has an informal policy to avoid saying that we should "eat less" of any food no matter how damaging its health impact may be. Thus, instead of saying "eat less meat" (which might be helpful), they advise us to "keep fat intake to less than 30 percent of total calories" (which is obscure to say the least). The institution we have put in charge of telling us when foods are dangerous has a policy of not (directly) telling us when foods (especially if they are animal products) are dangerous.

We have let the food industry craft our national nutrition policy, which influences everything from what foods are stocked in the health-food aisle at the local grocery store to what our children eat at school. In the National School Lunch Program, for example, more than half a billion of our tax dollars are given to the dairy, beef, egg, and poultry industries to provide animal products to children despite the fact that nutritional data would suggest we should reduce these foods in our diets. Meanwhile, a modest $161 million is offered to buy fruits and vegetables that even the USDA admits we should eat more of. Wouldn't it make more sense (and be more

ethical) for the National Institutes of Health—an organization specializing in human health and having nothing to gain beyond it—to have this responsibility?

The global implications of the growth of the factory farm, especially given the problems of food-borne illness, antimicrobial resistance, and potential pandemics, are genuinely terrifying. India's and China's poultry industries have grown somewhere between 5 and 13 percent annually since the 1980s. If India and China started to eat poultry in the same quantities as Americans (twenty-seven to twenty-eight birds annually), they *alone* would consume as many chickens as the entire world does today. If the world followed America's lead, it would consume over 165 billion chickens annually (even if the world population didn't increase). And then what? Two hundred billion? Five hundred? Will the cages stack higher or grow smaller or both? On what date will we accept the loss of antibiotics as a tool to prevent human suffering? How many days of the week will our grandchildren be ill? Where does it end?

lices of Pa adise/Pie es of Shit

Nearly one-third of the land surface
of the planet is dedicated to livestock.

1.

Ha Ha, Weep Weep

PARADISE LOCKER MEATS USED TO be located somewhat closer to Smithville Lake, in northwestern Missouri. The original plant burned down in 2002 when a fire broke out as a result of a ham smoking gone awry. In the new facility is a painting of the old plant, with the image of a cow running from the back. This is a depiction of an actual event. Four years before the fire, in the summer of '98, a cow escaped the slaughterhouse. She ran for miles—which, if the story had ended there, would have been remarkable enough to justify its telling. But this was some cow. She managed to cross roads, trample or otherwise disregard fences, and elude the farmers who were searching for her. And when she came to Smithville's shore, she didn't test the water, think twice, or look back. She attempted to swim to safety—the second leg of her triathlon—wherever that might be. At the very least, she seemed to know what she was swimming *from*. Mario Fantasma—the owner of Paradise Locker Meats—received a phone call from a friend who saw the cow take the dive. The getaway finally ended when Mario caught up with her on the other side of the lake. Boom boom, curtain. Whether this is a comedy or a tragedy depends on who you think the hero is.

I learned about this escape from Patrick Martins, cofounder of Heritage Foods (a boutique meat distributor), who put me in touch with Mario. "It's amazing how many people root for a great escape," Patrick wrote of the episode on his blog. "I am perfectly comfortable eating meat, yet there is part of me that wants to hear of a pig that made it out and maybe even settled down in the forest to start

151

a colony of free feral pigs." To Patrick the story has two heroes, and thus is both a comedy and a tragedy.

If Fantasma sounds like a made-up name, that's because it is. Mario's father was left on a doorstep in Calabria, Italy. The family took the baby in and gave him the last name "Phantom."

In person, there's nothing remotely spectral about Mario. He has an imposing physical presence — "a thick neck and bone-in hams for arms" is how Patrick put it — and speaks directly and loudly. He is the kind of person who must accidentally wake up sleeping babies all the time. I found his manner to be hugely pleasant, especially given all of the silence and misdirection I'd encountered in every other slaughterer I'd spoken (or tried to speak) to.

Monday and Tuesday are kill days at Paradise. Wednesday and Thursday are cut/pack days, and Friday is when locals have their animals custom slaughtered and/or butchered. (Mario told me, "In a two-week period, during hunting season, we'd get anywhere from five hundred to eight hundred deer. It gets pretty crazy.") Today is a Tuesday. I pull into a spot, turn off the car, and hear squealing.

The front door of Paradise opens into a small sales area, lined with refrigerator cases containing some products I've eaten (bacon, steak), some I've never knowingly eaten (blood, snout), and some I can't identify. High on the walls are taxidermied animals: two deer heads, a longhorn, a ram, fish, numerous pairs of antlers. Lower down are crayoned notes from elementary school students: "Thank you very much for the pig eyeballs. I had a fun time dissecting them and learning the different parts of the eye!" "They were slimy, but I had a lot of fun!" "Thanks for the eyes!" By the cash register is a business card holder advertising half a dozen taxidermists and a Swedish masseuse.

Paradise Locker Meats is one of the last bastions of independent slaughtering in the Midwest and is a godsend for the local farming

community. Large corporations have bought out and closed virtually all of the independent slaughterhouses, forcing farmers into their system. The upshot is that smaller customers—farmers still outside of the factory system—have to pay a premium for processing (if the slaughterhouse will take them at all, which is always precarious), and hardly any can have a say about how they want their animals treated.

Paradise gets calls at all hours from neighbors during hunting season. Its retail shop offers things no longer available in supermarkets, like bone-in cuts, custom butchering, and a smokehouse, and it has served as a voting station during local elections. Paradise is known for cleanliness, butchering expertise, and sensitivity to animal welfare issues. It is, in short, as close to an "ideal" slaughterhouse as I could hope to find and doesn't, statistically speaking, represent slaughter at all. Trying to fathom high-speed industrial slaughter by visiting Paradise would be like evaluating the fuel efficiency of Hummers by looking at bicycling (both are, after all, means of transport).

There are several areas of the facility—the shop, the office, two massive coolers, a smoking room, a butchering room, a pen out back for animals awaiting slaughter—but all of the actual killing and primary breaking down takes place in one large high-ceilinged room. Mario has me put on a white paper suit and hat before passing through the swinging doors. Holding up a thick hand toward the far corner of the kill floor, he begins to explain their chosen methods: "The guy over there is bringing the hog in. And he's gonna use a shocker [a stun gun that renders animals unconscious quickly]. Once they're shocked, we pull 'em up on the winch and bleed 'em. What our goal is, what we have to do under the Humane [Methods of Slaughter] Act, is that the animal has to go down and it can't be blinking. It has to be put out of commission."

Unlike at massive factory slaughterhouses, where there is a non-stop disassembly line, the pigs of Paradise are processed one at a time. The company doesn't hire only wageworkers who are unlikely to stay in their jobs even for a year; Mario's son is among those who work on the kill floor. The pigs are herded from semi-outdoor pens in the rear into a rubber-lined chute that opens onto the kill floor. As soon as a pig is inside, a door drops behind it so that the waiting pigs can't see what's going on. This makes sense not only from a humane perspective but from an efficiency one: a pig that fears death—or however you want to put its panic—is going to be hard, if not dangerous, to deal with. And stress is known to adversely affect the quality of the pork.

In the far corner of the kill room are two doors, one for workers and one for pigs, which open onto the holding pen in the back of the slaughterhouse. The doors are somewhat difficult to see, as this area is partly walled off from the rest of the room. Located in this obscured corner is an enormous machine that temporarily holds the pig in place when the animal enters, and allows the "knocker"—the worker who operates the stun gun (the "shocker")—to discharge the device on the top of the pig's head, ideally rendering it immediately unconscious. No one is willing to give me a justification for why this machine and its operation are hidden from the view of everyone save the knocker, but it's easy to make guesses. No doubt some of it has to do with allowing the workers to go about their business without having constantly to be reminded that their business is the taking apart of recently living beings. By the time a pig comes into view, he or she is already a *thing*.

The blocked line of sight also prevents the USDA inspector, Doc, from being able to see the slaughter. This seems problematic, as it is his responsibility to inspect the living animal for any illnesses or defects that would make it unsuitable for human

consumption. Also—and this is a big also, if you happen to be a pig—it is his job, and no one else's, to ensure that slaughter is humane. According to Dave Carney, former USDA inspector and chairman of the National Joint Council of Food Inspection Locals, "The way the plants are physically laid out, meat inspection is way down the line. A lot of times, inspectors can't even see the slaughter area from their stations. It's virtually impossible for them to monitor the slaughter area when they're trying to detect diseases and abnormalities in the carcasses that are whizzing by." An inspector in Indiana echoed this: "We aren't in a position to see what's going on. In a lot of plants, the slaughter area is walled off from the rest of the kill floor. Yes, we should be monitoring slaughter. But how can you monitor something like that if you're not allowed to leave your station to see what's going on?"

I ask Mario if the shocker always works properly.

"We get them on the first shock I'd think about 80 percent of the time. We don't want the animal to still have senses. We had one time where the equipment malfunctioned and kind of gave off a half charge. We really got to stay up on that stuff—test it before we slaughter. There's going to be times when equipment fails. That's why we have a bolt knocker as backup. Set it on their head, and it presses a piece of steel into their skull."

After getting stunned and hopefully rendered unconscious on the first, or at least the second, application of the stun gun, the pig is hung up by its feet and "stuck"—stabbed in the neck—and left to bleed out. The pig is then lowered into the scalder. It comes out looking a lot less piglike than when it went in—shinier, almost plastic—and is then lowered onto a table where two workers—one with a blowtorch, the other with a scraping device—get to removing any remaining hair.

The pig is then hung up again, and someone—Mario's son,

today—cuts it lengthwise down the middle with a power saw. One expects—or I expected—to see the belly cut open and so on, but to see the face cut in half, the nose split down its middle, and the halves of the head peeled open like a book is shocking. I am also surprised that the person who removes the organs from the split-open pig does so not only by hand, but without gloves—he needs the traction and sensitivity of his bare fingers.

It's not just because I'm a city boy that I find this repulsive. Mario and his workers admitted to having difficulty with some of the more gory aspects of slaughter, and I heard that sentiment echoed wherever I could have frank conversations with slaughterhouse workers.

The guts and organs are taken to Doc's table, where he sorts through them, very occasionally cutting a piece to get a look at what's beneath the surface. He then slides the glop off the table into a large garbage can. Doc wouldn't have to change much to star in a horror movie—and not as the damsel, if you know what I mean. His smock is blood spattered, the stare beneath his goggles is resolutely crazed, and he is a viscera inspector named Doc. For years he has scrutinized the guts and organs of the Paradise line. I asked him how many times he's found something suspicious and had to stop things. He removed his goggles, told me, "Never," and put them back on.

There Is No Pig

PIGS EXIST IN THE WILD on every continent except Antarctica, and taxonomists count sixteen species in all. Domestic pigs—the species we eat—are themselves subdivided into a host of breeds. A breed, unlike a species, is not a natural phenomenon. Breeds are maintained by farmers who selectively mate animals with particular features, which is now usually done through artificial insemination

(about 90 percent of large hog farms use artificial insemination). If you took a few hundred domestic pigs of a single breed and let them do their own thing for a few generations, they would begin to lose their breed characteristics.

Like dog or cat breeds, each pig breed has certain traits associated with it: some traits matter more to the producer, like the ever-important rate of feed conversion; some matter more to the consumer, like how lean or fat marbled the animal's muscle is; and some matter more to the pig, like susceptibility to anxiety or painful leg problems. Since the traits that matter to the farmer, consumer, and pig are not at all the same, it regularly happens that farmers breed animals that suffer more acutely because their bodies also display characteristics that the industry and consumers demand. If you have ever met a purebred German shepherd, you might have noticed that when the dog is standing, its rear is closer to the ground than its front, so that it always appears to be crouching or gazing up aggressively. This "look" was seen as desirable by breeders and was selected for over generations by breeding animals with shorter rear legs. As a result, German shepherds—even of the best pedigrees—now suffer disproportionately from hip dysplasia, a painful genetic condition that ultimately forces many owners either to condemn their companions to suffering, euthanize them, or spend thousands on surgery. For nearly all farmed animals, regardless of the conditions they are given to live in—"free-range," "free-roaming," "organic"—their design destines them for pain. The factory farm, which allows ranchers to make sickly animals highly profitable through the use of antibiotics, other pharmaceuticals, and highly controlled confinement, has created new, sometimes monstrous creatures.

The demand for lean pig meat—"the Other White Meat," as it's been sold to us—has led the pork industry to breed pigs that suffer not only more leg and heart problems, but greater excitability, fear,

anxiety, and stress. (This is the conclusion of researchers providing data for the industry.) These excessively stressed animals have the industry worried, not because of their welfare, but because, as mentioned earlier, "stress" seems to negatively affect taste: the stressed animals produce more acid, which actually works to break down the animals' muscle in much the same way acid in our stomachs breaks down meat.

The National Pork Producers Council, the policy arm of the American pork industry, reported in 1992 that acid-ridden, bleached, mushy flesh (so-called "pale soft exudative" or "PSE" pork) affected 10 percent of slaughtered pigs and cost the industry $69 million. When Iowa State University professor Lauren Christian announced in 1995 that he had discovered a "stress gene" that breeders could eliminate to reduce the incidence of PSE pork, the industry removed the gene from the genetic pool. Alas, problems with PSE pork continued to increase, and pigs remained so "stressed" that even driving a tractor too close to their confinement facility caused animals to drop dead. By 2002, the American Meat Science Association, a research organization set up by the industry itself, found that more than 15 percent of slaughtered pigs were yielding PSE flesh (or flesh that was at least pale or soft or exudative [watery], if not all three). Removing the stress gene was a good idea, at least insofar as it reduced the number of pigs that died in transport, but it didn't eliminate "stress."

Of course it didn't. In recent decades, scientist after scientist has come forward to announce the discovery of genes that "control" our physical states and our psychological predispositions. So something like a "fat gene" is announced with the promise that if only these DNA sequences could be snipped from the genome, we could skip exercise and eat whatever we want and never have to worry about getting dumpy. Others have proclaimed that our genes encourage

infidelity, lack of curiosity, cowardliness, and short temper. They are clearly right that certain genomic sequences strongly influence how we look, act, and feel. But except for a handful of extremely simple traits like eye color, the correlations aren't one to one. Certainly not for something as complex as the range of different phenomena we group together with a word like *stress*. When we talk about "stress" in farmed animals, we're talking about many different things: anxiety, undue aggressiveness, frustration, fear, and, most of all, suffering—none of which are simple genetic traits, like blue eyes, that can be turned on and off.

A pig from one of the many breeds traditionally used in America was, and is, able to enjoy the outdoors year-round if provided proper shelter and bedding. This is a good thing, not only for avoiding *Exxon Valdez*–scale ecological disasters (which I'll get to in a bit), but because much of what pigs enjoy doing is best done with access to the outdoors—running, playing, sunning, grazing, and caking themselves in mud and water so a breeze will cool them (pigs only sweat on their snouts). Today's factory farm pig breeds, by contrast, have been so genetically altered that more often than not they must be raised in climate-controlled buildings, cut off from sun and seasons. We are breeding creatures incapable of surviving in any place other than the most artificial of settings. We have focused the awesome power of modern genetic knowledge to bring into being animals that suffer *more*.

Nice, Troubling, Nonsensical

MARIO WALKS ME AROUND BACK. "This is the hog holding area here. They arrive the night before. We water them down. If they have to stay twenty-four hours, we feed 'em. These pens were designed more

for cattle. We have enough room for fifty hogs in here, but some-times we get seventy or eighty at a time, and that makes it hard."

It's a powerful thing to be so close to such large, intelligent animals so near to their deaths. It would be impossible to know if they have any sense of what is about to happen. Save for when the knocker comes out to round the next hog into the chute, they seem relatively relaxed. There's no obvious terror, no wailing or even huddling together. I do notice one pig, however, that is lying on its side, trembling somewhat. And when the knocker comes out, while all of the others jump to their feet and become agitated, this one continues to lie there and tremble. If George were acting that way, we'd take her straight to the vet. And if someone saw that I wasn't doing anything for her, they would at least think my humanity was somehow deficient. I ask Mario about the pig.

"That's just a pig thing," he says, chuckling.

In fact, it's not uncommon for pigs awaiting slaughter to have heart attacks or become nonambulatory. Too much stress: the trans-port, the change of environment, the handling, the squeals from the other side of the door, the smell of blood, the knocker's waving arms. But maybe it really is just a "pig thing," and Mario's chuckle is directed at my ignorance.

I ask Mario if he thinks the pigs have any sense of why they are there or what's going on.

"I personally don't think they know. A lot of people like to put that idea in people's heads that animals know they're going to die. I've seen too many cattle and hogs come through here, and I don't get that impression at all. I mean, they're going to be scared 'cause they've never been in here before. They're used to being out on dirt and fields and stuff. That's why they like to bring 'em in here at night. As far as they know what's going on, they just know they got moved and are waiting here for something."

Maybe their fate is unknown and unfeared. Maybe Mario's right; maybe he's wrong. Both seem possible.

"Do you like pigs?" I ask — perhaps the most obvious question, but also a very hard one to pose and answer in this situation.

"You got to put them down. It's kind of a mental thing. As far as liking one kind of animal over another, lambs are the toughest. Our shocker's built for pigs, not for lambs. We've shot 'em before, but the bullet may ricochet."

I can't quite follow his last comment about lambs, as my attention moves to the knocker, who comes out, blood halfway up his arms, and uses a paddle with a rattler to herd another pig into the kill area. Apropos of nothing or everything, Mario starts talking about his dog, "a bird dog, a small dog. A shih tzu," he says, pronouncing the first syllable — "shit" — then pausing for a millisecond, as if to build up pressure in his mouth, and finally releasing "zu." He tells me, with obvious pleasure, about the birthday party he recently held for his shih tzu, to which he and his family invited the other local dogs — "all small dogs." He took a photo of all the dogs on the laps of their owners. He didn't used to like small dogs. Thought they weren't real dogs. Then he got a small dog. Now he loves small dogs. The knocker comes out, waving his bloody arms, and takes another pig.

"Do you ever care about these animals?" I ask.

"Care about them?"

"Have you ever wanted to spare one?"

He tells the story of a cow that had recently been brought to him. It had been a pet on a hobby farm, and "the time had come." (No one, it seems, likes to elaborate on such sentences.) As Mario was preparing to kill the cow, it licked his face. Over and over. Maybe it was used to being a companion. Maybe it was pleading. Telling the story, Mario chuckles, conveying — on purpose, I think — his discomfort. "Oh, boy," he says. "Then she pinned me against a

161

wall and leaned against me for about twenty minutes or so before I finally got her down."

It's a nice story, a troubling story, a story that makes no sense. How could a cow have pinned him against a wall? That's not how the layout of the place works. And what about the other workers? What were they doing while this was going on? Again and again, from the largest to the smallest plants, I heard about the need to keep things moving. Why would Paradise have tolerated a twenty-minute delay?

Was that his answer to my question about wanting to spare animals?

It's time to go. I want to spend more time with Mario and his workers. They are nice people, proud, hospitable people — the kind of people, one fears, that might not be able to stay in agriculture for all that much longer. In 1967, there were more than one million hog farms in the country. Today there are a tenth as many, and in the past ten years alone, the number of farms raising pigs fell by more than two-thirds. (Four companies now produce 60 percent of hogs in America.)

This is part of a bigger change. In 1930, more than 20 percent of the American population was employed in agriculture. Today it's less than 2 percent. That's despite the fact that agricultural production doubled between 1820 and 1920, between 1950 and 1965, between 1965 and 1975, and in the next ten years will double again. In 1950, one farmworker supplied every 15.5 consumers. Today it's one for every 140. This is depressing to both the communities that valued the contribution of their small farmers and to the farmers themselves. (American farmers are four times more likely to commit suicide than the general population.) Just about everything — feed, water, lighting, heating, ventilation, even slaughter — is now automated. The only jobs produced by the

factory system are either bureaucratic desk jobs (few in number) or unskilled, dangerous, and poorly paying (many). There are no *farmers* on factory farms.

Maybe that doesn't matter. Times change. Maybe the image of a knowledgeable farmer caring for his animals and our food is nostalgic, like that of a telephone operator putting through calls. And maybe what we get in exchange for the replacement of farmers by machines justifies the sacrifice.

"We can't let you go yet," one of the workers tells me. She disappears for a few seconds and comes back with a paper plate piled high with pink petals of ham. "What kind of hosts would we be if we didn't even offer a sample?"

Mario takes a piece and pops it into his mouth.

I don't want to eat it. I wouldn't want to eat anything right now, my appetite having been lost to the sights and smells of a slaughterhouse. And I specifically don't want to eat the contents of the plate, which were, not long ago, the contents of a pig in the waiting pen. Maybe there is nothing wrong with eating it. But something deep inside me—reasonable or unreasonable, aesthetic or ethical, selfish or compassionate—simply doesn't want the meat inside my body. For me, that meat is not something to be eaten.

And yet, something else deep inside me does want to eat it. I want very much to show Mario my appreciation for his generosity. And I want to be able to tell him that his hard work produces delicious food. I want to say, "Wow, that's wonderful!" and have another piece. I want to "break bread" with him. Nothing—not a conversation, not a handshake or even a hug—establishes friendship so forcefully as eating together. Maybe it's cultural. Maybe it's an echo from the communal feasts of our ancestors.

This is what a slaughterhouse is all about from a certain perspective. On the plate in front of me is the end that promises to

justify all the bloody means next door. I heard this again and again from people who raise animals for consumption, and it's really the only way the equation can be framed: the food—how it tastes, the functions it serves—either does or does not justify the process that brings it to the plate.

For some, in this case, it would. For me, it does not.

"I'm kosher," I say.

"*Kosher?*" Mario echoes as a question.

"I am." I chuckle. "Jewish. And kosher."

The room falls silent, as if the air itself were taking stock of this new fact.

"Kind of funny to be writing about pork, then," Mario says. And I have no idea if he believes me, if he understands and sympathizes, or if he is suspicious or somehow insulted. Maybe he knows I am lying, but understands and sympathizes. Everything seems possible.

"Kind of funny," I echo.

But it isn't.

2.

Nightmares

THE PIGS SLAUGHTERED AT PARADISE Locker Meats tend to come from among the few pig farms left in the country that do not use factory methods. The pork sold in practically every supermarket and restaurant comes from the factory farms that now produce 95 percent of America's pork. (Chipotle is, as of the writing of this book, the only national restaurant chain claiming to obtain a significant portion of its pork from animals that don't come from

factory farms.) Unless you deliberately seek out an alternative, you can be all but certain that your ham, bacon, or chop was factory farmed.

The contrast between the life of a factory-farmed pig—pumped with antibiotics, mutilated, tightly confined, and utterly deprived of stimulation—and one raised in a well-run operation using a combination of traditional husbandry and the best of modern innovations is astonishing. One couldn't find a better pig farmer than Paul Willis, one of the spearheads of the movement to preserve traditional hog farming (and the head of Niman Ranch's pork division, the only national supplier of nonfactory pork), and one couldn't imagine a more seemingly depraved company than Smithfield, the largest pork packer in the nation.

It was tempting for me to write this chapter by first describing the hell of Smithfield's factory operations and ending with the relative idyll offered by the best of the nonfactory operations. But to narrate the story of pig farming in this way would suggest that the pork industry in general is moving toward greater animal welfare and environmental responsibility, when precisely the opposite is true. There isn't any "return" to husbandry-based hog farming. The "movement" toward family pig farms is quite real, but it is composed largely of longtime farmers learning to market themselves and thus hold their own. The factory hog farm is still expanding in America, and worldwide growth is even more aggressive.

Our Old Sympathetic Attempts

WHEN I PULLED UP TO Paul Willis's farm in Thornton, Iowa, where he coordinates the production of pork for Niman Ranch with some

five hundred other small farmers, I was a bit puzzled. Paul had said I should meet him in his office, but all I saw was an insubstantial redbrick home and a few farm buildings. It was still the quiet of morning, and a lanky white-and-brown farm cat approached. As I wandered around looking for something that fit my notion of an office, Paul was walking in from the fields, coffee in hand, wearing insulated dark blue overalls and a small cap that covered shortly cropped brown-gray hair. After a soft smile and a firm handshake, he led me into the house. We sat for a few minutes in a kitchen boasting appliances that appeared to have been smuggled out of Cold War Czechoslovakia. More coffee was waiting, but Paul insisted on making a fresh pot. "This has been out awhile," he explained as he stripped off his insulated overalls to reveal another pair of overalls with thin blue and white stripes underneath.

"I assume you'll want to record this," Paul said, before launching in. That transparency and willingness to help, that eagerness to tell his story and have it spread, set the tone for the rest of our day together—even those times when our disagreements became obvious.

"This is the house I grew up in," Paul said. "We had family dinners here, particularly on Sundays, when relatives such as grandparents, aunts, uncles, and cousins would come. After dinner, which would feature the fare of the season, such as sweet corn and fresh tomatoes, the kids would run off for the rest of the day to the creek or the grove and play until we would drop. The day was never long enough for the fun we were having. That room, which is now where I work, was the dining room, which was set up for those Sunday dinners. Other days, we ate here in the kitchen and usually had men for dinner, especially if some special project was going on—haying or castrating pigs or building something such as a grain bin. Anything that required extra help. The noon meal was expected. Only in emergency situations did we go to town to eat."

Outside the kitchen were a couple of largely empty rooms. There was a single wood desk in Paul's office, on which sat a computer screen buzzing with e-mails, spreadsheets, and files; maps were tacked to the wall with pins indicating the locations of Niman Ranch farmers and approved slaughter facilities. Large windows opened onto the gentle rolls of a classic Iowa landscape of soybeans, corn, and pasture.

"Let me just give you a thumbnail sketch," Paul began. "When I came back to the farm, we began raising pigs on a pasture system, much like we do now. This was quite a bit like what was done when I grew up. I had chores when I was a boy and so on, and looked after the pigs. But there'd been some changes, especially in power equipment. In those days you were really limited by how much muscle power you had. You used a pitchfork. And that made farm work a lot of drudgery.

"So, not to digress, I was here, raising pigs like this and enjoying it. And eventually we scaled up, so we were raising a thousand pigs a year, which is similar to what we are doing today. I kept seeing more and more of these confinement buildings being built. North Carolina started ramping up at that time, Murphy Family Farms. I went to a couple of meetings, and they were all, 'This is the wave of the future. You gotta get bigger!' And I said, 'There is nothing better here than what I'm doing. Nothing. It's not better for the animals, or for the farmers, or for consumers. Nothing better about it.' But they had convinced a lot of people who wanted to stay in the business that this was the way you had to go. I would guess this would be in the late eighties. So I started looking for a market for 'free-range pigs.' In fact, I invented the term."

Had history turned out a little differently, it is not hard to imagine that Paul might never have found a market that was willing to pay more for his pigs than for Smithfield's more readily

available ones. His story might have ended at this point, like the story of the more than half a million hog farmers who have gone out of business in the past twenty-five years. As it happened, though, Paul found just the sort of market he needed when he met Bill Niman, the founder of Niman Ranch, and soon he was managing Niman Ranch's pork production, while Bill and the rest of his corporate team found markets for Andy (Michigan), then Justin (Minnesota), then Todd (Nebraska), then Betty (South Dakota), then Charles (Wisconsin), and now more than five hundred small family pig farmers. Niman Ranch pays these farmers a nickel above the market rate per pound for their animals and guarantees its ranchers a "floor price" regardless of the market rate. Today, that ends up being about twenty-five to thirty dollars more per pig, and that modest amount has let these farmers hold on while most others have gone under.

Paul's farm is an impressive example of what one of his heroes, the quintessential farmer-intellectual Wendell Berry, referred to as "our old sympathetic attempts to imitate natural processes." For Paul this means that at the heart of producing pork is letting pigs be pigs (for the most part). Happily for Paul, letting pigs be pigs includes watching them grow plump and, I'm told, tasty. (Traditional farms always beat factory farms in taste tests.) The notion here is that the farmers' job is to find those ways of raising hogs where the animals' well-being and the farmers' interest in efficiently bringing them to their appointed "slaughter weight" coincide. Anyone who suggests that there is a perfect symbiosis between the farmers' interest and the animals' is probably trying to sell you something (and it's not made of tofu). "Ideal slaughter weight" does not actually represent maximal pig happiness, but on the best small family pig farms, there is considerable overlap. When Paul is castrating day-old piglets without anesthetic (which happens to 90 percent of all male piglets), it would seem his interests are not so well

aligned with the young boars-now-barrows, but that is a relatively brief period of suffering compared to, for example, the prolonged mutual joy shared by Paul and his pigs when he gets to let them out to run on pasture—let alone the prolonged suffering of pigs on factory farms.

In the best of the old husbandry tradition, Paul is always trying to maximize the ways his farming needs work with the needs of pigs—with their natural biorhythms and growth patterns.

While Paul runs his farm with the idea that letting pigs be pigs is central, modern industrial agriculture has asked what hog farming might look like if one considered only profitability—literally designing multitier farms from multistory office buildings in another city, state, or even country. What sort of practical difference does this ideological difference make? The most glaring one—the difference that can be seen from the road by someone who knows nothing about pigs—is that on Paul's farm, pigs have access to earth instead of concrete and slats. Many but not all Niman Ranch pig farmers provide access to the outdoors. Farmers who don't provide outdoor access must raise the pigs in "deep bedding" systems, which also allow pigs to engage in many of their "species-specific behaviors"—the behaviors that make pigs pigs, like rooting, playing, building nests, and lying together in deep hay for warmth at night (pigs prefer to sleep communally).

Paul's farm has five fields of twenty acres each, which are rotated for hogs and crops. He gave me a driving tour in his massive white empty-bed pickup. Especially after my middle-of-the-night visits to factory farms, it was remarkable how much I could see unfolding outdoors: the hoop houses dotting the fields, the barns opening to pasture, corn and soy as far as the eye could see. And in the distance, the occasional factory farm.

At the heart of any hog operation—and at the heart of hog

169

welfare today—is the life of female breeder pigs. Paul's gilts (female pigs that have not given birth) and sows (female pigs that have), like all gilts and sows raised for Niman Ranch, are housed in groups and are managed in a way that promotes "a stable social hierarchy." (I'm quoting here from the impressive animal welfare standards developed with the help of Paul and several animal welfare experts, including sisters Diane and Marlene Halverson, who have a thirty-year track record of farmer-friendly animal advocacy.)

Among other rules intended to create this stable social hierarchy, the guidelines demand that "a single animal must never be introduced into an established social group." It's not exactly the kind of welfare promise one can imagine finding printed on the back of a package of bacon, but it's terribly important to the pigs. The principle behind such rules is simple: pigs need the companionship of other pigs *that they know* to function normally. Just as most parents would want to avoid pulling their child out of school in the middle of the year and placing her in an unfamiliar one, so does good pig husbandry dictate that farmers do what is possible to keep pigs in stable social groups.

Paul also makes certain that his sows and gilts have enough room, so the more timid animals can get away from the more aggressive ones. Sometimes he'll use straw bales to create "retreat areas." Like other Niman Ranch farmers, he doesn't cut off pigs' tails or teeth, as factory operations typically do to avoid excessive biting and cannibalism. If the social hierarchy is stable, the pigs work out disputes among themselves.

On all Niman Ranch pig farms, gestating sows—that is, pregnant pigs—must be raised with their social groups and have access to the outdoors. By contrast, approximately 80 percent of pregnant pigs in America, like the 1.2 million owned by Smithfield, are confined in individual steel-and-concrete cages so small that the sows

cannot turn around. When pigs leave a Niman Ranch hog farm, strong transport and slaughter requirements (from the same animal welfare standards that require the farmer to preserve a stable social hierarchy) will follow them out the gate. This does not mean that Niman Ranch's transport and slaughter are done "the old-fashioned way." There are many real improvements, both managerial and technological: humane-certification programs for handlers and truckers, slaughter audits, paper trails to ensure accountability, extended access to better-trained veterinarians, weather forecasts to avoid transport in extreme heat and cold, nonskid flooring, and stunning. Still, no one at Niman Ranch is in a position to demand all of the changes they'd like; that kind of leverage is had only by the largest companies. So there are negotiations and compromises, such as the long distance that many of Niman Ranch's pigs must travel to reach an acceptable slaughterhouse.

Much else that is impressive about Paul's farm and other Niman Ranch farms is not what you do see but what you don't. They do not give antibiotics or hormones to animals unless there is a medical condition that makes this advisable. There are no pits or containers filled with dead pigs. There is no stench, largely because there are no animal waste lagoons. Because an appropriate number of animals are raised on the land, the manure can go back into the soil as fertilizer for the crops that will become the pigs' feed. There is suffering, but there is more humdrum life and even moments of what seems like pure pig joy.

Paul and other Niman Ranch pig farmers not only do (or don't do) all these things; they are required to work according to these guidelines. They sign contracts. They undergo truly independent auditing and, perhaps most revealingly, they even let the likes of me scrutinize their animals. This is important to say because most humane-farming standards are merely industry attempts to cash

in on the public's growing concern. It's no trivial task to identify the rare company—minuscule Niman Ranch is by far the biggest—that is not just a variation on the factory farm.

As I was getting ready to leave Paul's farm, he invoked Wendell Berry and intoned the links that inevitably and powerfully unite every purchase in a supermarket and every order from a menu with agricultural policy—that is, with the decisions of farmers and agribusiness and Paul himself. Every time you make a decision about food, Paul pleaded, quoting Berry, "you are farming by proxy."

In *The Art of the Commonplace*, Berry sums up just what is at stake in the idea of "farming by proxy."

> Our methodologies...have come more and more to resemble the methodology of mining.... This is sufficiently clear to many of us. What is not sufficiently clear, perhaps to any of us, is the extent of our complicity, as individuals and especially as individual consumers, in the behavior of the corporations....Most people...have given proxies to the corporations to produce and provide *all* of their food.

It's an empowering idea. The entire goliath of the food industry is ultimately driven and determined by the choices we make as the waiter gets impatient for our order or in the practicalities and whimsies of what we load into our shopping carts or farmers'-market bags.

We ended the day at Paul's house. Chickens ran around the front yard, and off to the side was a pen for boars. "This house was first built by Marius Floy," he told me, "a great-grandfather who came from northern Germany. It was built in sections as the family expanded. We've lived here since 1978. It's where Anne and Sarah grew up. They walked to the end of the lane to catch the school bus."

A few minutes later, Phyllis (Paul's wife) broke the news that a factory farm had purchased a plot of land from neighbors down the road and would soon be building a facility to hold six thousand hogs. The factory farm would be right next to the home to which he and Phyllis had hoped to retire, a small house on a hill overlooking a piece of land that Paul has spent decades working to restore to midwestern prairie. He and Phyllis called it "the Dream Farm." Next to their dream, now, loomed a nightmare: thousands of suffering, sick hogs surrounded by, and themselves suffering within, a thick, nausea-inducing stench. Not only will the nearby factory farm decimate Paul's land's value (estimates suggest land degradation from industrial farming has cost Americans $26 billion) and destroy the land itself, not only will the smell make cohabitation incredibly unpleasant at best and more likely dangerous to Paul's family's health, but it stands in opposition to everything Paul has spent his life working for.

"The only people that are for those are the ones that own them," Paul said. Phyllis continued his thought: "People *hate* those farmers. What must it feel like to have a job where people hate you?"

In the space of that kitchen, the slow drama of the growth of the factory farm was unfolding. But there was also resistance unfolding, most palpably embodied in Paul. (Phyllis, too, has been active in regional political battles to decrease the power and presence of factory hog farms in Iowa.) And, of course, these words I'm writing spring from that moment. If this story means something to you, then perhaps the drama of the growth of the factory farm in that Iowa kitchen will help produce the resistance that will end it.

3.

Pieces of Shit

THE SCENE IN THE WILLISES' kitchen has been repeated many times. Communities across the world have battled to protect themselves from the pollution and stench of factory farms, hog-confinement facilities most of all.

The most successful legal battles against hog factory farms in the United States have focused on their incredible potential to pollute. (When people talk about the environmental toll of animal agriculture, this is a large part of what they're talking about.) The problem is quite simple: massive amounts of shit. So much shit, so poorly managed, that it seeps into rivers, lakes, and oceans—killing wildlife and polluting air, water, and land in ways devastating to human health.

Today a typical pig factory farm will produce 7.2 million pounds of manure annually, a typical broiler facility will produce 6.6 million pounds, and a typical cattle feedlot 344 million pounds. The General Accounting Office (GAO) reports that individual farms "can generate more raw waste than the populations of some U.S. cities." All told, farmed animals in the United States produce 130 times as much waste as the human population—roughly 87,000 pounds of shit *per second*. The polluting strength of this shit is 160 times greater than raw municipal sewage. And yet there is almost no waste-treatment infrastructure for farmed animals—no toilets, obviously, but also no sewage pipes, no one hauling it away for treatment, and almost no federal guidelines regulating what happens to it. (The GAO reports that no federal agency even collects reliable data on factory farms or so much as knows the number of permitted factory farms nationally and therefore cannot "effectively regulate"

them.) So what does happen to the shit? I'll focus specifically on the fate of the shit of America's leading pork producer, Smithfield.

Smithfield alone annually kills more individual hogs than the combined human populations of New York City, Los Angeles, Chicago, Houston, Phoenix, Philadelphia, San Antonio, San Diego, Dallas, San Jose, Detroit, Jacksonville, Indianapolis, San Francisco, Columbus, Austin, Fort Worth, and Memphis—some 31 million animals. According to conservative EPA figures, each hog produces two to four times as much shit as a person; in Smithfield's case, the number is about 281 pounds of shit for each American citizen. That means that Smithfield—a single legal entity—produces at least as much fecal waste as the entire human population of the states of California and Texas combined.

Imagine it. Imagine if, instead of the massive waste-treatment infrastructure that we take for granted in modern cities, every man, woman, and child in every city and town in all of California and all of Texas crapped and pissed in a huge open-air pit for a day. Now imagine that they don't do this for just a day, but all year round, in perpetuity. To comprehend the effects of releasing this amount of shit into the environment, we need to know something of what's in it. In his tremendous *Rolling Stone* article on Smithfield, "Boss Hog," Jeff Tietz compiled a useful list of shit typically found in the shit of factory-farmed hogs: "ammonia, methane, hydrogen sulfide, carbon monoxide, cyanide, phosphorus, nitrates and heavy metals. In addition, the waste nurses more than 100 microbial pathogens that can make humans sick, including salmonella, cryptosporidium, streptococci and girardia" (thus children raised on the grounds of a typical hog factory farm have asthma rates exceeding 50 percent and children raised near factory farms are twice as likely to develop asthma). And not all of the shit *is* shit, exactly—it's whatever will fit through the slatted floors of the factory farm buildings. This

includes but is not limited to: stillborn piglets, afterbirths, dead piglets, vomit, blood, urine, antibiotic syringes, broken bottles of insecticide, hair, pus, even body parts.

The impression the pig industry wishes to give is that fields can absorb the toxins in the hog feces, but we know this isn't true. Run-off creeps into waterways, and poisonous gases like ammonia and hydrogen sulfide evaporate into the air. When the football field-sized cesspools are approaching overflowing, Smithfield, like others in the industry, spray the liquefied manure onto fields. Or sometimes they simply spray it straight up into the air, a geyser of shit wafting fine fecal mists that create swirling gases capable of causing severe neurological damage. Communities living near these factory farms complain about problems with persistent nosebleeds, earaches, chronic diarrhea, and burning lungs. Even when citizens have managed to pass laws that would restrict these practices, the industry's immense influence in government means the regulations are often nullified or go unenforced.

Smithfield's earnings look impressive—the company had sales of $12 billion in 2007—until one realizes the scale of the costs they externalize: the pollution from the shit, of course, but also the illnesses caused by that pollution and the associated degradation of property values (to name only the most obvious externalizations). Without passing these and other burdens on to the public, Smithfield would not be able to produce the cheap meat it does without going bankrupt. As with all factory farms, the illusion of Smithfield's profitability and "efficiency" is maintained by the immense sweep of its plunder.

To take a step back: shit itself isn't bad. Shit has long been the farmer's friend, fertilizer for his fields, from which he grows food for his animals, whose meat goes to people and whose shit goes back to the fields. Shit became a problem only when Americans

decided we wanted to eat more meat than any other culture in history and pay historically little for it. To achieve that dream, we abandoned Paul Willis's dream farm and signed on with Smithfield, allowing—causing—husbandry to leave the hands of farmers and become determined by corporations that positively strove (and strive) to pass their costs on to the public. With consumers oblivious or forgetful (or, worse, supportive), corporations like Smithfield concentrated animals in absurd densities. In that context, a farmer can't grow nearly enough feed on his own land and must import it. What's more, there's too much shit for the crops to absorb—not a little too much, and not a lot too much, but a shitload too much. At one point, three factory farms in North Carolina were producing more nitrogen (an important ingredient in plant fertilizers) than all the crops in the entire state could absorb.

So back to the original question: What happens to this massive amount of massively dangerous shit?

If all goes according to plan, the liquefied waste is pumped into massive "lagoons" adjacent to the hog sheds. These toxic lagoons can cover as much as 120,000 square feet—as much surface area as the largest casinos in Las Vegas—and be as deep as 30 feet. The creation of these lake-sized latrines is considered normal and is perfectly legal despite their consistent failure to actually contain the waste. A hundred or more of these immense cesspools might loom in the vicinity of a single slaughterhouse (factory hog farms tend to cluster around slaughterhouses). If you were to fall into one, you would die. (Just as you would die of asphyxiation, within minutes, if the power went out while you were in one of the hog sheds.) Tietz tells a haunting story about one such lagoon:

A worker in Michigan, repairing one of the lagoons, was overcome by the smell and fell in. His 15-year-old nephew dived in

to save him but was overcome, the worker's cousin went in to save the teenager but was overcome, the worker's older brother dived in to save them but was overcome, and then the worker's father dived in. They all died in pig shit.

For corporations like Smithfield, it is a cost-benefit analysis: paying fines for polluting is cheaper than giving up the entire factory farm system, which is what it would take to finally end the devastation.

In the rare cases when the law begins to restrain corporations like Smithfield, they often find ways around regulations. The year before Smithfield built the world's largest slaughter-and-processing plant in Bladen County, the North Carolina state legislature actually revoked the power of counties to regulate hog factory farms. Convenient for Smithfield. Perhaps not coincidentally, the former state senator who cosponsored this well-timed deregulation of hog factories, Wendell Murphy, now sits on Smithfield's board and himself was formerly chairman of the board and chief executive officer of Murphy Family Farms, a factory hog operation that Smithfield bought in 2000.

A few years after this deregulation in 1995, Smithfield spilled more than twenty million gallons of lagoon waste into the New River in North Carolina. The spill remains the largest environmental disaster of its kind and is twice as big as the iconic *Exxon Valdez* spill six years earlier. The spill released enough liquid manure to fill 250 Olympic-sized swimming pools. In 1997, as reported by the Sierra Club in their damning "RapSheet on Animal Factories," Smithfield was penalized for a mind-blowing seven thousand violations of the Clean Water Act—that's about twenty violations a day. The US government accused the company of dumping illegal levels of waste into the Pagan River, a tributary of the Chesapeake Bay, and then falsifying and destroying records to cover up its activities. One violation

might be an accident. Even ten violations might. Seven thousand violations is a plan. Smithfield was fined $12.6 million, which at first sounds like a victory against the factory farm. At the time, $12.6 million was the largest civil-penalty pollution fine in US history, but this is a pathetically small amount to a company that now grosses $12.6 million every ten hours. Smithfield's former CEO Joseph Luter III received $12.6 million in stock options in 2001.

How has the eating public responded? In general, we make a bit of noise when pollution reaches near-biblical proportions, then Smithfield (or whatever corporation) responds with an "oops," and, accepting their apology, we go on eating our factory-farmed animals. Smithfield not only survived the legal action, but thrived. At the time of the Pagan River spill, Smithfield was the seventh-largest pork producer in the United States; two years later it was the biggest, and its increasing domination of the industry has not abated. Today, Smithfield is so large that it slaughters one of every four pigs sold commercially in the nation. Our present way of eating—the dollars we daily funnel to the likes of Smithfield—rewards the very worst conceivable practices.

Conservative estimates by the EPA indicate that chicken, hog, and cattle excrement has already polluted 35,000 miles of rivers in twenty-two states (for reference, the circumference of the earth is roughly 25,000 miles). In only three years, two hundred fish kills—incidents where the entire fish population in a given area is killed at once—have resulted from factory farms' failures to keep their shit out of waterways. In these documented kills alone, thirteen million fish were literally poisoned by shit—if set head to tail fin, these victims would stretch the length of the entire Pacific coast from Seattle to the Mexican border.

People who live near factory farms are rarely wealthy and are treated by the industry as dispensable. The fecal mists they are

forced to breathe *usually* do not kill humans, but sore throats, head-aches, coughing, runny noses, diarrhea, and even psychological ill-ness, including abnormally high levels of tension, depression, anger, and fatigue, are common. According to a report by the California state senate, "Studies have shown that [animal waste] lagoons emit toxic airborne chemicals that can cause inflammatory, immune, irritation and neurochemical problems in humans."

There are even some good reasons to suspect a link between living near hog factory farms and contracting the so-called flesh-eating bacteria known formally as MRSA (methicillin-resistant Staphylococcus aureus). MRSA can cause "lesions as big as saucers, fiery red and agonizing to touch," and by 2005 was killing more Americans annually (18,000) than AIDS. *New York Times* columnist Nicholas Kristof, who himself grew up on a farm, reports that an Indiana doctor was ready to go public with suspicions of this link when the doctor suddenly died of what may well have been compli-cations related to MRSA. The MRSA–hog factory farm link is by no means proven, but, as Kristof points out, "the larger question is whether we as a nation have moved to a model of agriculture that produces cheap bacon but risks the health of all of us. And the evi-dence, while far from conclusive, is growing that the answer is yes."

The health problems that locals experience acutely ripple through the rest of the nation more subtly. The American Public Health Association, the largest body of public-health professionals in the world, has been so alarmed by these trends that, citing a spec-trum of diseases associated with animal waste and antibiotic use, it has urged a moratorium on factory farms. After having a panel of renowned experts conduct a two-year study, the Pew Commission recently went further, arguing for the complete phaseout of sev-eral common "intensive and inhumane practices," citing benefits to both animal welfare and public health.

But the power brokers that matter most—those who choose what to eat and what not to eat—have remained passive. So far, we have demanded no national moratorium and certainly no phaseout. We have made Smithfield and its counterparts so wealthy that they can invest hundreds of millions to expand their operations abroad. And expand they have. Once operating only in the United States, Smithfield has now spread across the globe to Belgium, China, France, Germany, Italy, Mexico, Poland, Portugal, Romania, Spain, the Netherlands, and the United Kingdom. Joseph Luter III's stock in Smithfield was recently valued at $138 million. His last name is pronounced "looter."

4.

Our New Sadism

ENVIRONMENTAL PROBLEMS CAN BE TRACKED by doctors and government agencies whose assigned task is to care for human beings, but how do we find out about the suffering of animals on factory farms, which doesn't necessarily leave any traces?

Undercover investigations by dedicated nonprofit organizations are one of the only meaningful windows the public has into the imperfect day-to-day running of factory farms and industrial slaughterhouses. At an industrial pig-breeding facility in North Carolina, videotape taken by undercover investigators showed some workers administering daily beatings, bludgeoning pregnant sows with a wrench, and ramming an iron pole a foot deep into mother pigs' rectums and vaginas. These things have nothing to do with bettering the taste of the resultant meat or preparing the pigs

181

for slaughter—they are merely perversion. In other videotaped instances at the farm, workers sawed off pigs' legs and skinned them while they were still conscious. At another facility operated by one of the largest pork producers in the United States, some employees were videotaped throwing, beating, and kicking pigs; slamming them against concrete floors and bludgeoning them with metal gate rods and hammers. At another farm, a yearlong investigation found systematic abuse of tens of thousands of pigs. The investigation documented workers extinguishing cigarettes on the animals' bodies, beating them with rakes and shovels, strangling them, and throwing them into manure pits to drown. Workers also stuck electric prods in pigs' ears, mouths, vaginas, and anuses. The investigation concluded that managers condoned these abuses, but authorities have refused to prosecute. Lack of prosecution is the norm, not the exception. We are not in a period of "lax" enforcement—there simply never has been a time when companies could expect serious punitive action if they were caught abusing farmed animals.

Whatever farmed-animal industry we turn to, similar problems arise. Tyson Foods is a major KFC supplier. An investigation at one large Tyson facility found that some workers regularly ripped off the heads of fully conscious birds (with explicit permission from their supervisor), urinated in the live-hang area (including on the conveyer belt carrying birds), and let shoddy automated slaughter equipment that cut birds' bodies rather than their necks go unrepaired indefinitely. At a KFC "Supplier of the Year," Pilgrim's Pride, fully conscious chickens were kicked, stomped on, slammed into walls, had chewing tobacco spit in their eyes, literally had the shit squeezed out of them, and had their beaks ripped off. And Tyson and Pilgrim's Pride not only supplied KFC; at the time of writing they were the two largest chicken processors in the nation, killing nearly five billion birds per year between them.

Even without relying on undercover investigations and learning about the extreme (though not necessarily uncommon) abuse that results from workers' taking out their frustrations on animals, we know that factory-farmed animals have miserable lives.

Consider the life of a pregnant sow. Her incredible fertility is the source of her particular hell. While a cow will give birth to only a single calf at a time, the modern factory sow will birth, nurse, and raise an average of nearly nine piglets—a number that has been increased annually by industry breeders. She will invariably be kept pregnant as much as possible, which will prove to be the majority of her life. When she is approaching her due date, drugs to induce labor may be administered to make the timing more convenient for the farmer. After her piglets are weaned, a hormone injection makes the sow rapidly "cycle" so that she will be ready to be artificially inseminated again in only three weeks.

Four out of five times a sow will spend the sixteen weeks of her pregnancy confined in a "gestation crate" so small that she will not be able to turn around. Her bone density will decrease because of the lack of movement. She will be given no bedding and often will develop quarter-sized, blackened, pus-filled sores from chafing in the crate. (In one undercover investigation in Nebraska, pregnant pigs with multiple open sores on their faces, heads, shoulders, backs, and legs—some as large as a fist—were videotaped. A worker at the farm commented, "They all have sores.... There's hardly a pig in there who doesn't have a sore.")

More serious and pervasive is the suffering caused by boredom and isolation and the thwarting of the sow's powerful urge to prepare for her coming piglets. In nature, she would spend much of her time before giving birth foraging and ultimately would build a nest of grass, leaves, or straw. To avoid excessive weight gain and to further reduce feed costs, the crated sow will be feed restricted

and often hungry. Pigs also have an inborn tendency to use separate areas for sleeping and defecating that is totally thwarted in confinement. The pregnant pigs, like most all pigs in industrial systems, must lie or step in their excrement to force it through the slatted floor. The industry defends such confinement by arguing that it helps control and manage animals better, but the system makes good welfare practices more difficult because lame and diseased animals are almost impossible to identify when no animals are allowed to move.

The cruelty here is hard to deny—and the outrage hard to squelch—now that advocates have brought this reality into public discussion. Recently, three states—Florida, Arizona, and California—enacted the slow phasing-out of gestation crates through ballot initiatives. In Colorado, under threat of a campaign by the Humane Society, the industry itself agreed to draft and support legislation to outlaw the crates. This is an incredibly hopeful sign. A four-state ban leaves a lot of states where the practice continues to thrive, but it looks like the fight against the gestation crate is being won. This is a victory that matters.

Increasingly, instead of being forced into gestation crates, sows live in small group pens. They can't run in a field or even enjoy the sun like Paul Willis's pigs do, but they have space to sleep and stretch. The sows don't get sores all over their bodies. They don't gnaw frantically at the bars of their crates. This change hardly redeems or reverses the factory system, but it meaningfully improves the lives of sows.

Whether they are kept in gestation crates or small pens during pregnancy, when giving birth—what the industry calls "farrowing"—sows will almost invariably be confined in a crate just as constrictive as the gestation crate. One worker said it's necessary

to "beat the shit out of [the pregnant pigs] to get them inside the crates because they don't want to go." Another employee at a different farm described the routine use of rods to beat the sows bloody: "One guy smashed a sow's nose in so bad that she ended up dying of starvation."

Those who defend pig factory farms argue that the farrowing crate is necessary because sows can sometimes accidentally crush their piglets. In the same way that the risk of a forest fire can be reduced by preemptively clearing the forest of all its trees, there is a cockeyed logic to this claim. The farrowing crate, like the gestation crate, confines the mother in a space so small she cannot turn around. Sometimes she will also be strapped to the floor. These practices do make it harder for mother pigs to crush their infants. What defenders of such practices don't point out is that at farms like Willis's, the problem doesn't arise in the first place. Not surprisingly, when farmers select for "motherability" when breeding, and a mother pig's sense of smell is not overpowered by the stench of her own liquefied feces beneath her, and her hearing is not impaired by the clanging of metal cages, and she is given space to investigate where her piglets are and exercise her legs so that she can lie down slowly, she finds it easy enough to avoid crushing her young.

And of course it isn't just the young at risk. A study by the European Commission's Scientific Veterinary Committee documented that pigs in crates showed weakened bones, higher risks of leg injuries, cardiovascular problems, urinary infections, and a reduction in muscle mass so severe it affected the pigs' ability to lie down. Other studies indicate that poor genetics, lack of movement, and poor nutrition leave 10 to 40 percent of pigs structurally unsound due to such conditions as buckling of the knees, bowed legs, and pigeon toes. An industry periodical, *National Hog Farmer*, has

reported that 7 percent of breeding sows typically die prematurely from the stress of confinement and intensive breeding—in some operations the mortality rate exceeds 15 percent. Many pigs go insane due to the confinement and obsessively chew on their cage bars, incessantly press their water bottles, or drink urine. Others exhibit mourning behaviors that animal scientists describe as "learned helplessness."

And then come the babies—the justification for the suffering of the mothers.

Many piglets are born with deformities. Common congenital diseases include cleft palate, hermaphroditism, inverted nipples, no anus, splayed legs, tremors, and hernias. Inguinal hernias are common enough that it is routine to surgically correct them at the time of castration. In their first weeks of life, even those piglets without such defects endure a barrage of bodily insults. Within the first forty-eight hours their tails and "needle teeth," often used to deliver sideward bites to other piglets, are cut off without any pain relief in an attempt to minimize the wounds pigs inflict upon one another while competing for their mother's teats in factory settings where pathological tail biting is common and weaker pigs cannot escape the strong. Typically, the piglets' environment is kept warm (72 to 81 degrees) and dark, so they are more lethargic and less likely to enact "social vices" like biting and sucking one another's navels, tails, or ears out of frustration. Traditional husbandry, as is practiced on Paul Willis's farm, avoids such problems by giving animals more space, providing environmental enrichment, and fostering stable social groups.

Also within these first two days, factory-farmed piglets often will be injected with iron because of the likelihood that the rapid growth and intensive breeding of their mother has left her milk deficient. Within ten days males have their testicles torn out, again

without pain relief. This time the purpose is to alter the taste of the meat—consumers in America currently prefer the taste of castrated animals. Nickel-sized swatches of flesh may also be cut out of the pigs' ears for identification purposes. By the time farmers begin weaning them, 9 to 15 percent of the piglets will have died.

The sooner the piglets start feeding on solid food, the sooner they will reach market weight (240 to 265 pounds). "Solid food" in this case often includes dried blood plasma, a by-product from slaughterhouses. (This does indeed fatten the piglets up. It also badly damages the mucosa of their gastrointestinal tracts.) Left alone, piglets tend to wean at around fifteen weeks, but on factory farms they will typically be weaned at fifteen days and increasingly as young as twelve days. At these young ages, the piglets are unable to properly digest solid food, so additional pharmaceuticals are fed to them to prevent diarrhea. The weaned pigs will then be forced into thick-wire cages—"nurseries." These cages are stacked one on top of the other, and feces and urine fall from higher cages onto the animals below. Growers will keep piglets in these cages as long as possible before moving them to their final destination: cramped pens. The pens are deliberately overcrowded because, as one industry magazine says, "overcrowding pigs pays." Without much room to move, the animals burn fewer calories and get fatter on less feed.

As in any kind of factory, uniformity is essential. Piglets that don't grow fast enough—the runts—are a drain on resources and so have no place on the farm. Picked up by their hind legs, they are swung and then bashed headfirst onto the concrete floor. This common practice is called "thumping." "We've thumped as many as 120 in one day," said a worker from a Missouri farm.

We just swing them, thump them, then toss them aside. Then, after you've thumped ten, twelve, fourteen of them, you take

187

them to the chute room and stack them for the dead truck. And if you go in the chute room and some are still alive, then you have to thump them all over again. There've been times I've walked in that room and they'd be running around with an eyeball hanging down the side of their face, just bleeding like crazy, or their jaw would be broken.

"They call it 'euthanasia,'" said the Missouri worker's wife.

A barrage of antibiotics, hormones, and other pharmaceuticals in the animals' feed will keep most of them alive until slaughter despite the conditions. These drugs are most needed to combat the respiratory problems that are ubiquitous on hog factory farms. The humid conditions of confinement, dense quantities of animals with stress-weakened immune systems, and the toxic gases from the accumulating shit and piss make these problems practically inescapable. Fully 30 to 70 percent of the pigs will have some sort of respiratory infection by the time of slaughter, and mortality from respiratory disease alone can be 4 to 6 percent. Of course this constant sickness promotes the growth of new influenzas, so entire hog populations of entire states have sometimes had infection rates of 100 percent from deadly new viruses created among these densely packed sick animals (increasingly, of course, these viruses are infecting humans).

In the world of factory farming, expectations are turned upside down. Veterinarians don't work toward optimal health, but optimal profitability. Drugs are not for curing diseases, but substitutes for destroyed immune systems. Farmers do not aim to produce healthy animals.

5.

Our Underwater Sadism (A Central Aside)

THE STORIES OF ANIMAL ABUSE and pollution I've related in the context of pig farming are, in most of the ways that matter, representative of factory farming as a whole. Factory-farmed chickens, turkeys, and cattle do not produce or suffer from the exact same problems, but they all suffer in fundamentally similar ways. So, it turns out, do fish. We tend not to think of fish and land animals in the same way, but "aquaculture"—the intensive rearing of sea animals in confinement—is essentially underwater factory farming.

Many of the sea animals we eat, including the vast majority of salmon, come to us from aquaculture. Initially, aquaculture presented itself as a solution to the depletion of wild fish populations. But far from reducing demand for wild salmon, as some had claimed, salmon farming actually fueled the international exploitation of and demand for wild salmon. Wild salmon catches worldwide rose 27 percent between 1988 and 1997, precisely as salmon aquaculture exploded.

The welfare issues associated with fish farms will sound familiar. The *Handbook of Salmon Farming*, an industry how-to book, details six "key stressors in the aquaculture environment": "water quality," "crowding," "handling," "disturbance," "nutrition," and "hierarchy." To translate into plain language, those six sources of suffering for salmon are: (1) water so fouled that it makes it hard to breathe; (2) crowding so intense that animals begin to cannibalize one another; (3) handling so invasive that physiological measures of stress are evident a day later; (4) disturbance by farmworkers and wild animals; (5) nutritional deficiencies that weaken the immune

189

system; and (6) the inability to form a stable social hierarchy, result-ing in more cannibalization. These problems are typical. The hand-book calls them "integral components of fish farming."

A major source of suffering for salmon and other farmed fish is the abundant presence of sea lice, which thrive in the filthy water. These lice create open lesions and sometimes eat down to the bones on a fish's face—a phenomenon common enough that it is known as the "death crown" in the industry. A single salmon farm gener-ates swarming clouds of sea lice in numbers thirty thousand times higher than naturally occur.

The fish that survive these conditions (a 10 to 30 percent death rate is seen as good by many in the salmon industry) are likely to be starved for seven to ten days to diminish their bodily waste during transport to slaughter and then killed by having their gills sliced before being tossed into a tank of water to bleed to death. Often the fish will be slaughtered while conscious and convulse in pain as they die. In other cases, they may be stunned, but current stun-ning methods are unreliable and can lead to some animals suffering more. As is the case with chickens and turkeys, no law requires the humane slaughter of fish.

So are wild-caught fish a more humane alternative? They cer-tainly have better lives before they are caught, since they do not live in cramped, filthy enclosures. That is a difference that mat-ters. But consider the most common ways of catching the sea ani-mals most commonly eaten in America: tuna, shrimp, and salmon. Three methods are dominant: longline fishing, trawling, and the use of purse seines. A longline looks something like a telephone line running through the water suspended by buoys rather than poles. At periodic intervals along this main line, smaller "branch" lines are strung—each branch line bristling with hooks. Now picture not just one of these multihook longlines, but dozens or hundreds

deployed one after the other by a single boat. GPS locators and other electronic communication gear are attached to the buoys so that fishers can return to them later. And, of course, there is not one boat deploying longlines, but dozens, hundreds, or even thousands in the largest commercial fleets.

Longlines today can reach seventy-five miles—that's enough line to cross the English Channel more than three times. An estimated 27 million hooks are deployed every day. And longlines don't kill just their "target species," but 145 others as well. One study found that roughly 4.5 million sea animals are killed as bycatch in longline fishing every year, including roughly 3.3 million sharks, 1 million marlins, 60,000 sea turtles, 75,000 albatross, and 20,000 dolphins and whales.

Even longlines, though, don't produce the immense bycatch associated with trawling. The most common type of modern shrimp trawler sweeps an area roughly twenty-five to thirty meters wide. The trawl is pulled along the ocean bottom at 4.5 to 6.5 kmh for several hours, sweeping shrimp (and everything else) into the far end of a funnel-shaped net. Trawling, almost always for shrimp, is the marine equivalent of clear-cutting rain forest. Whatever they target, trawlers sweep up fish, sharks, rays, crabs, squid, scallops—typically about a hundred different fish and other species. Virtually all die.

There is something quite sinister about this scorched-earth style of "harvesting" sea animals. The average trawling operation throws 80 to 90 percent of the sea animals it captures as bycatch overboard. The least efficient operations actually throw more than 98 percent of captured sea animals, dead, back into the ocean.

We are literally reducing the diversity and vibrancy of ocean life *as a whole* (something scientists only recently learned to measure). Modern fishing techniques are destroying the ecosystems that

sustain more complex vertebrates (like salmon and tuna), leaving in their wake only the few species that can survive on plants and plankton, if that. As we gobble up the most desired fish, which are usually top-of-the-food-chain carnivores like tuna and salmon, we eliminate predators and cause a short-lived boom of the species one notch lower on the food chain. We then fish *that* species into oblivion and move an order lower. The generational speed of the process makes it hard to see the changes (do you know what fish your grandparents ate?), and the fact that catches themselves don't decline in volume gives a deceptive impression of sustainability. No one person plans the destruction, but the economics of the market inevitably lead toward instability. We aren't exactly emptying the oceans; it's more like clear-cutting a forest with thousands of species to create massive fields with one type of soybean.

Trawling and longline fishing aren't only ecologically worrisome; they are also cruel. In trawlers, hundreds of different species are crushed together, gashed on corals, bashed on rocks—for hours—and then hauled from the water, causing painful decompression (the decompression sometimes causes the animals' eyes to pop out or their internal organs to come out their mouths). On longlines, too, the deaths animals face are generally slow. Some are simply held there and die only when removed from the lines. Some die from the injury caused by the hook in their mouths or by trying to get away. Some are unable to escape attack by predators.

Purse seines, the final fishing method I'm going to discuss, are the main technology used for catching America's most popular seafood, tuna. A net wall is deployed around a school of target fish, and once the school is encircled, the bottom of the net is pulled together as if the fishers were tugging on a giant purse string. The trapped target fish and any other creatures in the vicinity are then winched together and hauled onto the deck. Fish tangled in the net

may be slowly pulled apart in the process. Most of these sea animals, though, die on the ship itself, where they will slowly suffocate or have their gills cut while conscious. In some cases, the fish are tossed onto ice, which can actually prolong their deaths. According to a recent study published in *Applied Animal Behaviour Science*, fish die slowly and painfully over a period as long as fourteen minutes after being tossed fully conscious into an ice slurry (something that happens to both wild-caught and farmed fish).

Does all this matter—matter enough that we should change what we eat? Maybe all we need is better labels so we can make wiser decisions about the fish and fish products we buy? What conclusion would most selective omnivores reach if attached to each salmon they ate was a label noting that 2.5-foot-long farmed salmon spend their lives in the equivalent of a bathtub of water and that the animals' eyes bleed from the intensity of the pollution? What if the label mentioned the explosions of parasite populations, increases in diseases, degraded genetics, and new antibiotic-resistant diseases that result from fish farming?

There are some things, though, we don't need labels to know. Although one can realistically expect that at least some percentage of cows and pigs are slaughtered with speed and care, no fish gets a good death. Not a single one. You never have to wonder if the fish on your plate had to suffer. It did.

Whether we're talking about fish species, pigs, or some other eaten animal, is such suffering the most important thing in the world? Obviously not. But that's not the question. Is it more important than sushi, bacon, or chicken nuggets? That's the question.

6.

Eating Animals

Our decisions about food are complicated by the fact that we don't eat alone. Table fellowship has forged social bonds as far back as the archaeological record allows us to look. Food, family, and memory are primordially linked. We are not merely animals that eat, but eating animals.

Some of my fondest memories are of weekly sushi dinners with my best friend, and eating my dad's turkey burgers with mustard and grilled onions at backyard celebrations, and tasting the salty gefilte fish at my grandmother's house every Passover. These occasions simply aren't the same without those foods—and that matters.

To give up the taste of sushi or roasted chicken is a loss that extends beyond giving up a pleasurable eating experience. Changing what we eat and letting tastes fade from memory create a kind of cultural loss, a forgetting. But perhaps this kind of forgetfulness is worth accepting—even worth cultivating (forgetting, too, can be cultivated). To remember animals and my concern for their well-being, I may need to lose certain tastes and find other handles for the memories that they once helped me carry.

Remembering and forgetting are part of the same mental process. To write down one detail of an event is to not write down another (unless you keep writing forever). To remember one thing is to let another slip from remembrance (unless you keep recalling forever). There is ethical as well as violent forgetting. We can't hold on to everything we've known so far. So the question is not whether we forget but what, or whom, we forget—not whether our diets change, but how.

Recently my friend and I started eating veggie sushi and going to the Italian restaurant next door. Instead of the turkey burgers my dad grilled, my children will remember me burning veggie burgers in the backyard. At our last Passover, gefilte fish held a less central place, but we did tell some stories about it (I haven't stopped, apparently). Along with the story of Exodus—that grandest of stories about the weak prevailing over the strong in the most unexpected of ways—new stories of the weak and the strong were added.

The point of eating those special foods with those special people at those special times was that we were being deliberate, separating those meals out from the others. Adding another layer of deliberateness has been enriching. I'm all for compromising tradition for a good cause, but perhaps in these situations tradition wasn't compromised so much as fulfilled.

It seems to me that it's plainly wrong to eat factory-farmed pork or to feed it to one's family. It's probably even wrong to sit silently with friends eating factory-farmed pork, however difficult it can be to say something. Pigs clearly have rich minds and just as clearly are condemned to miserable lives on factory farms. The analogy of a dog kept in a closet is fairly accurate, if somewhat generous. The environmental case against eating factory-farmed pork is airtight and damning.

For similar reasons, I wouldn't eat poultry or sea animals produced by factory methods. Looking into their eyes does not generate the same pathos as meeting eyes with a pig, but we see as much with our minds' eyes. All I have learned about the intelligence and social sophistication of birds and fish from my research demands that I take the acuteness of their misery just as seriously as the more easily grasped misery of factory-farmed pigs.

With feedlot-raised beef, the industry offends me less (and 100 percent pasture-raised beef, setting aside the issue of slaughter for a moment, is probably the least troubling of all meats—more on that in the next chapter). Still, to say that something is less offensive than a pig or chicken factory farm is to say as little as is possible.

The question, for me, is this: Given that eating animals is in absolutely no way necessary for my family—unlike some in the world, we have easy access to a wide variety of other foods—should we eat animals? I answer this question as someone who has loved eating animals. A vegetarian diet can be rich and fully enjoyable, but I couldn't honestly argue, as many vegetarians try to, that it is as rich as a diet that includes meat. (Those who eat chimpanzee look at the Western diet as sadly deficient of a great pleasure.) I love sushi, I love fried chicken, I love a good steak. But there is a limit to my love.

Since I encountered the realities of factory farming, refusing to eat conventional meat has not been a hard decision. And it's become hard to imagine who, besides those who profit from it, would defend factory farming.

But things get complicated with a farm like Paul Willis's pig farm or Frank Reese's poultry ranch. I admire what they do, and given the alternatives, it's hard not to think of them as heroes. They care about the animals they raise and treat them as well as they know how. And if we consumers can limit our desire for pork and poultry to the capacity of the land (a big if), there are no knockdown eco-logical arguments against their kind of farming.

It's true that one could note that eating animals of any kind necessarily, if indirectly, supports factory farming by increasing demand for meat. This is nontrivial, but it's not the main reason that I wouldn't eat pigs from Paul Willis's farm or chickens from Frank Reese's—something that is hard to write knowing that Paul and Frank, now friends of mine, will read these words.

Even though he does everything he can, Paul's pigs are still castrated, and still transported long distances to slaughter. And before Willis met Diane Halverson, the animal welfare expert who assisted his work with Niman Ranch from the beginning, he docked (cut off) pigs' tails, which shows that even the kindest farmers sometimes fail to think of their animals' well-being as much as they can.

And then there's the slaughterhouse. Frank is quite candid about the problems he has getting his turkeys slaughtered in a manner that he finds acceptable, and an optimal slaughterhouse for his birds remains a work in progress for him. As far as pig slaughter goes, Paradise Locker Meats really is a kind of paradise. Because of the structuring of the meat industry, and USDA regulations, both Paul and Frank are forced to send their animals to slaughterhouses that they have only partial control over.

Every farm, like every everything, has flaws, is subject to accidents, sometimes doesn't work as it should. Life overflows with imperfections, but some matter more than others. How imperfect must animal farming and slaughter be before they are too imperfect? Different people will draw the line in different places with regard to farms like Paul's and Frank's. People I respect draw it differently. But for me, for now—for my family now—my concerns about the reality of what meat is and has become are enough to make me give it up altogether.

Of course there are circumstances I can conjure under which I would eat meat—there are even circumstances under which I would eat a dog—but these are circumstances I'm unlikely to encounter. Being vegetarian is a flexible framework, and I've left a mental state of constant personal decision making about eating animals (who could stay in such a place indefinitely?) for a steady commitment not to.

This brings me back to the image of Kafka standing before a

197

fish in the Berlin aquarium, a fish on which his gaze fell in a newly found peace after he decided not to eat animals. Kafka recognized that fish as a member of his invisible family—not as his equal, of course, but as another being that was his concern. I had a similar experience at Paradise Locker Meats. I was not quite "at peace" when the stare of a pig on its way to Mario's kill floor, with only seconds to live, caught me off guard. (Have you ever been anyone's last sight?) But I wasn't completely ashamed either. The pig wasn't a receptacle of my forgetting. The animal was a receptacle of my concern. I felt—I feel—relief in that. My relief doesn't matter to the pig. But it matters to me. And this is part of my way of thinking about eating animals. Taking, for now, only my side of the equation—that of the eating animal, rather than the eaten one—I simply cannot feel whole when so knowingly, so *deliberately*, forgetting.

And there is visible family, too. Now that my research is over, it will be in only the rarest of circumstances that I will look into a farmed animal's eyes. But many times a day, for many of the days of my life, I will look into my son's.

My decision not to eat animals is necessary for me, but it is also limited—and personal. It is a commitment made within the context of my life, not anyone else's. And until sixty or so years ago, much of my reasoning wouldn't have even been intelligible, because the industrial animal agriculture to which I'm responding hadn't become dominant. Had I been born in a different time, I might have reached different conclusions. For me to conclude firmly that I will not eat animals does not mean I oppose, or even have mixed feelings about, eating animals *in general*. To oppose beating a child to "teach a lesson" is not to oppose strong parental discipline. To decide that I will discipline my child in one way and not another

is not necessarily to make a decision I would impose on other parents. To decide for oneself and one's family is not to decide for the nation or the world.

That said, though I see value in all of us sharing our personal reflections and decisions about eating animals, I didn't write this book simply to reach a personal conclusion. Farming is shaped not only by food choices, but by political ones. Choosing a personal diet is insufficient. But how far am I willing to push my own decisions and my own views about the best alternative animal agriculture? (I may not eat their products, but my commitment to supporting the kind of farming Paul and Frank do has steadily deepened.) What do I expect from others? What should we all expect of one another when it comes to the question of eating animals?

It's clear enough that factory farming is more than something I just personally dislike, but it's not clear what conclusions follow. Does the fact that factory farming is cruel to animals and ecologically wasteful and polluting mean everyone needs to boycott factory farm products all the time? Is a partial withdrawal from the system good enough—a sort of preferred purchasing program for nonfactory food that stops short of a boycott? Is the issue not our personal buying choices at all, but one that needs to be resolved through legislation and collective political action?

Where should I respectfully disagree with someone and where, for the sake of deeper values, should I take a stand and ask others to stand with me? Where do agreed-upon facts leave room for reasonable people to disagree and where do they demand we all act? I've not insisted that meat eating is always wrong for everyone or that the meat industry is irredeemable despite its present sorry state. What positions on eating animals *would* I insist are basic to moral decency?

I DO

Less than 1% of the animals killed
for meat in America come from
family farms.

1.

Bill and Nicolette

THE ROADS LEADING TO MY destination were unmarked, and most useful signage had been uprooted by locals. "There is no reason to come to Bolinas," one resident put it in an unwelcomed *New York Times* feature on the town. "The beaches are dirty, the fire department is terrible, the natives are hostile and have a tendency toward cannibalism."

Not exactly. The thirty-mile coastal drive from San Francisco was pure romance—alternating between sweeping vistas and protected natural coves—and once in Bolinas (pop. 2,500), I found it hard to remember why I ever thought of Brooklyn (pop. 2,500,000) as a nice place to live, and easy to understand why those who have stumbled upon Bolinas have wanted to keep others from stumbling upon it.

Which is half of why Bill Niman's willingness to take me into his home was so surprising. The other half had to do with his profession: cattle ranching.

A gunmetal Great Dane, larger and calmer than George, was the first to welcome me, followed by Bill and his wife, Nicolette. After the usual touching and pleasantries, they led me to their modest home, tucked like a mountain monastery into the side of a hill. Mossy rocks protruded from black earth amid patches of bright flowers and succulents. A glowing porch opened directly onto the main room—the largest in the house, but not large. A stone fireplace opposite a dark, heavy sofa (a sofa for relaxing, not entertaining) dominated the room. Books were piled on shelves, some food

and farming related, most not. We sat around a wooden table in a small eat-in kitchen that still held the smells of breakfast.

"My father was a Russian immigrant," Bill explained. "I grew up working the family grocery store in Minneapolis. That was my introduction to food. Everybody worked there, whole family. I couldn't have conjured up my life." Meaning: *How did a first-generation American, a Jewish city boy, become one of the most important ranchers in the world?* It's a good question, which has a good answer.

"The primary motivating factor in everybody's life at that time was the Vietnam War. I chose to do alternative service, teaching in federally declared poverty areas. I was introduced to certain elements of rural life, and I got a fever for it. I started homesteading with my first wife." (Niman's first wife, Amy, died in a ranch accident.) "We got some land. Eleven acres. We had goats, chickens, and horses. We were quite poor. My wife tutored up at one of the big ranches, and we were given some cattle that were born to young heifers by mistake." These "mistakes" would prove to be the foundation of Niman Ranch. (Today Niman Ranch's annual revenues are estimated at $100 million—and growing.)

When I visited them, Nicolette was spending more time managing their personal ranch than Bill was. He was busy working to ensure sales for the beef and pork produced by his company's hundreds of small family farmers. Nicolette, who gives off the vibe of an East Coast lawyer (and in fact was one), knew every heifer, cow, bull, and calf on their land, could anticipate their needs and satisfy them, looked no bit the part but seemed to fit it entirely. Bill, who with his thick mustache and leathery skin could have been sent over by central casting, was now mostly a marketer.

They are not an obvious pair. Bill comes off as unsanded and instinctive. He's the kind of guy who, on an island with survivors of

a plane crash, would earn everyone's respect and become the reluctant leader. Nicolette is city folk, verbose but guarded, and filled with energy and concern. Bill is warm but stoical. He seems to be most comfortable when listening—which is good, as Nicolette seems more comfortable talking.

"When Bill and I first started dating," she explained, "it was under false pretenses. I thought it was a business meeting."

"You were actually afraid I would discover you were a vegetarian."

"Well, I wasn't *afraid*, but I had already been working with livestock farmers for years, and I knew that the meat industry portrays vegetarians as terrorists. If you're in a rural part of this country, meeting with people who are raising animals for food, and they get the idea that you don't eat meat, they stiffen up. They're afraid that you're judging them harshly and you might even be dangerous. I wasn't afraid of you finding out, but I didn't want to put you on the defensive."

"The first time we sat down at a meal together—"

"I ordered a pasta primavera, and Bill goes, 'Oh, are you a vegetarian?' I said yes. And then he said something that surprised me."

2.

I Am a Vegetarian Rancher

About six months after I moved to the Bolinas ranch, I said to Bill, "I don't just want to live here. I want to really know how this ranch functions and I want to be able to run things." So I got very involved in

actually doing the work. In the beginning I had some anxiety that I might become increasingly uncomfortable with the fact that I was living at a livestock ranch, but what happened was quite the opposite. The more time I spent here, the more time I passed in the company of our animals and seeing how well they lived, I realized that this was truly an honorable undertaking.

I don't view a rancher's responsibility as merely providing freedom from suffering or cruelty. I believe that we owe our animals the highest level of existence. Because we're taking their lives for food, I think they're entitled to experience the basic pleasures of life—things like lying in the sun, mating, and rearing their young. I believe they deserve to experience joy. And our animals do! One of the problems I have with most standards for "humane" meat production is that they're strictly focused on freedom from suffering. That, to me, should go without saying. No unnecessary animal suffering should be tolerated at any farm. But if you're going to raise an animal with the purpose of taking its life, there's so much more responsibility than that!

This isn't a new idea or my own unique philosophy. Throughout the history of animal husbandry, most farmers have felt a weighty obligation to treat animals well. The problem today is that husbandry is being replaced—or has been replaced—with industrial methods coming out of what are now called "animal science" departments. The individualized familiarity that a traditional farmer has with every animal on his farm has been abandoned in favor of large, impersonal systems—it's literally impossible to know each animal in a pig-confinement operation or industrial feedlot that contains thousands or tens of thousands of animals. Instead, the operators are dealing with problems relating to sewage and automation. The animals become almost incidental. The shift has brought about an entirely different mind frame and emphasis. A rancher's responsibility to his animals is forgotten if it isn't outright denied.

As I see it, animals have entered into an arrangement with humans, an exchange of sorts. When animal husbandry is done as it should be, humans can provide animals a better life than they could hope for in the wild and almost certainly a better death. That's quite significant. I have accidentally left a gate open here on a number of occasions. Not one of the animals has even left the area. They don't go because what they have here is the safety of the herd, really nice pasture, water, occasional hay, and plenty of predictability. And their friends are here. To a certain degree, they choose to stay. It isn't a completely willing contract, of course. They didn't orchestrate their own births—but then again, none of us have.

I believe it's a noble thing to be raising animals for wholesome food—to provide an animal a life with joy and freedom from suffering. Their lives are taken for a purpose. And I think that's essentially what all of us hope for: a good life and an easy death.

The idea that humans are a part of nature is also important here. I've always looked to natural systems for models. Nature is so economical. Even if an animal isn't hunted, it is consumed soon after its death. Animals are invariably devoured by other animals in nature, whether by predators or scavengers. We've even noticed our cattle a couple of times over the years chewing on deer bones, even though we always regard cattle as strict herbivores. A few years back, a US Geological Survey study found that deer were eating a lot of eggs from the nests of ground birds—the researchers were shocked! Nature is a lot more fluid than we think it is. But clearly it's normal and natural for animals to eat other animals, and since we humans are part of nature, it's very normal for humans to be eating animals.

Now, that doesn't mean we have to eat animals. I feel I can personally make a choice to refrain from consuming meat for my own individual reasons. In my case, it's because of the particular connection I've always felt with animals. I think it would bother me somewhat to eat

meat. It would just make me feel uncomfortable. For me, factory farming is wrong not because it produces meat, but because it robs every animal of every shred of happiness. To put it another way, if I stole something, that would weigh on my conscience because it would be inherently wrong. Meat isn't inherently wrong. And if I ate some, my reaction would probably be limited to a feeling of regret.

I used to think that being a vegetarian exempted me from spending time trying to change how farm animals are treated. I felt that by abstaining from meat eating, I was doing my part. That seems silly to me now. The meat industry affects everybody in the sense that we are, all of us, living in a society in which food production is based on factory farming. Being a vegetarian does not relieve me from a responsibility for how our nation raises animals—especially at a time when total meat consumption is increasing both nationally and globally.

I have a lot of vegan friends and acquaintances, some of whom are connected with PETA or Farm Sanctuary, and many of them assume that eventually humanity will solve the factory-farming problem by getting people to quit eating animals. I disagree. At least, not in our lifetimes. If that were possible, I think it would be many generations from now. So in the interim, something else has to happen to address the intense suffering caused by factory farms. Alternatives need to be advocated for and supported.

Fortunately, there are glimmers of hope for the future. A return to more sensible farming methods is afoot. A collective will is emerging—a political will, and also a will of consumers, retailers, and restaurants. Various imperatives are coming together. One of these imperatives is better treatment of animals. We're awaking to the irony of seeking out shampoo that's not tested on animals while at the same time (and many times a day) buying meat that's produced in profoundly cruel systems.

There are also shifting economic imperatives, with the cost of fuel, agricultural chemicals, and grains all going up. And the farm subsidies, which have promoted factory farming for decades, are becoming increasingly untenable, especially in light of the current financial crisis. Things are starting to realign.

And the world doesn't, by the way, need to produce nearly as many animals as it's currently producing. Factory farming wasn't born or advanced out of a need to produce more food — to "feed the hungry" — but to produce it in a way that is profitable for agribusiness companies. Factory farming is all about money. That is the reason the factory farm system is failing and won't work over the long term: it's created a food industry whose primary concern isn't feeding people. Does anyone really doubt that the corporations that control the vast majority of animal agriculture in America are in it for the profit? In most industries, that's a perfectly good driving force. But when the commodities are animals, the factories are the earth itself, and the products are physically consumed, the stakes are not the same, and the thinking can't be the same.

For instance, developing animals physically incapable of reproduction makes no sense if you want to feed people, but it's logical if your primary concern is making money. Bill and I now have some turkeys on our ranch, and they're heritage birds — the same breeds that were being raised at the dawn of the twentieth century. We had to go back that far for our breeding stock because modern turkeys can barely walk, let alone mate naturally or raise their offspring. That's what you get in a system that is only incidentally interested in feeding people and totally uninterested in the animals themselves. Factory farming is the last system you'd create if you cared about sustainably feeding people over the long term.

The irony is that while factory farms don't benefit the public, they rely on us not only to support them, but to pay for their mistakes. They're

taking all their waste-disposal costs and passing them along to the environment and the communities they're operating in. Their prices are artificially low — what doesn't show up at the cash register is paid for over years and by everyone.

What must happen now is a move back toward pasture-based animal raising. This is not a pie-in-the-sky idea — there is historical precedent. Until the rise of factory farms in the mid-twentieth century, American animal farming was closely connected to grass and much less dependent on grains, chemicals, and machinery. Pasture-raised animals have better lives and are more environmentally sustainable. The grass system is also making more and more sense for hard economic reasons. Corn's rising price is going to change the way we eat. Cattle will be allowed to graze more, eating grasses as nature intended. And as the factory farm industry is forced to deal with the problem of concentrated manure instead of just passing the problem on to the public, that too will make grass-based farming more economically attractive. And that's the future: truly sustainable, humane farming.

She Knows Better

Thanks for sharing the transcript of Nicolette's thoughts with me. I work at PETA, and she is a meat producer, but I think of her as my colleague in the fight against factory farming, and she is my friend. I agree with everything that she says about the importance of treating animals well and about the artificially low prices of factory-farmed meat. I certainly agree that if someone is going to eat animals, they should eat only grass-fed, pasture-raised animals — especially cattle. But here's the elephant in the room: Why eat animals at all?

First, consider the environment and the food crisis: there is no ethical difference between eating meat and throwing vast quantities of food in

the trash, since the animals we eat can only turn a small fraction of the food that is fed to them into meat calories—it takes six to twenty-six calories fed to an animal to produce just one calorie of animal flesh. The vast majority of what we grow in the United States is fed to animals—that is land and food that we could use to feed humans or preserve wilderness—and the same thing is happening all over the world, with devastating consequences.

The UN special envoy on food called it a "crime against human-ity" to funnel 100 million tons of grain and corn to ethanol while almost a billion people are starving. So what kind of crime is animal agri-culture, which uses 756 million tons of grain and corn per year, much more than enough to adequately feed the 1.4 billion humans who are liv-ing in dire poverty? And that 756 million tons doesn't even include the fact that 98 percent of the 225-million-ton global soy crop is also fed to farmed animals. You're supporting vast inefficiency and pushing up the price of food for the poorest in the world, even if you're eating only meat from Niman Ranch. It was this inefficiency—not the environmental toll or even animal welfare—that inspired me to stop eating meat in the first place.

Some ranchers like to point out that there are marginal habitats where you can't grow foods but you can raise cattle, or that cattle can provide nutrients in times when crops fail. These arguments, though, are only seriously applied in the developing world. The foremost scientist on this issue, R. K. Pachauri, runs the Intergovernmental Panel on Cli-mate Change. He won the Nobel Peace Prize for his climate work, and he argues that vegetarianism is the diet that everyone in the developed world should consume, purely on environmental grounds.

Of course the animal rights argument is why I'm at PETA, and basic science also tells us that other animals are made of flesh, blood, and bone, just like we are. A pig farmer in Canada killed dozens of women, hanging

them on the meat hooks where the pig carcasses normally hung. When he was brought to trial, there was a huge visceral disgust and horror over the revelation that some of the women were fed to people who thought they were eating the farmer's pigs. The consumers couldn't tell the difference between ground pig flesh and human flesh. Of course they couldn't. The differences between human and pig (and chicken, cattle, etc.) anatomies are insignificant compared to the similarities—a corpse is a corpse, flesh is flesh.

Other animals have the same five senses that we do. And more and more, we're learning that they have behavioral, psychological, and emotional needs that evolution created in them just like it did in us. Other animals, like human beings, feel pleasure and pain, happiness and misery. The fact that animals are excited by many of the same emotions that we are is well established. To call all their complex emotions and behaviors "instinct" is stupid, as Nicolette clearly agrees. To ignore the obvious moral implications of these similarities is easy to do in today's world—it's convenient, politic, and common. It's also wrong. But it's not enough only to know what's right and wrong; action is the other, and more important, half of moral understanding.

Is Nicolette's love for her animals noble? It is when it leads her to see them as individuals and not want to harm them. But when it leads her to be complicit in branding, ripping babies away from mothers, and slitting the throats of animals, it's harder for me to understand it. Here's why: apply her argument for meat eating to the farming of dogs and cats—or even human beings. Most of us lose our sympathy. In fact, her arguments sound eerily similar (and are structurally identical) to the arguments of slaveholders who advocated treating slaves better without abolishing slavery. One could force someone into slavery and provide "a good life and an easy death," as Nicolette put it, speaking of farmed animals. Is that preferable to abusing them as slaves? Sure. But that is not what anyone wants.

Or try this thought experiment: Would you castrate animals without pain relief? Would you brand them? Would you slit their throats open? Please try watching these practices (the video "Meet Your Meat" is easily found on the Internet and a good place to start). Most people wouldn't do these things. Most of us don't even want to watch them. So where is the basic integrity in paying others to do these things for you? It's contract cruelty to animals, and a contract killing, and for what? A product no one needs — meat.

Eating meat may be "natural," and most humans may find it acceptable — humans certainly have been doing it for a very long time — but these are not moral arguments. In fact, the entirety of human society and moral progress represents an explicit transcendence of what's "natural." And the fact that most in the South supported slavery says nothing about its morality. The law of the jungle is not a moral standard, however much it may make meat eaters feel better about their meat eating.

After fleeing Nazi-occupied Poland, Nobel laureate Isaac Bashevis Singer compared species bias to the "most extreme racist theories." Singer argued that animal rights was the purest form of social-justice advocacy, because animals are the most vulnerable of all the downtrodden. He felt that mistreating animals was the epitome of the "might-makes-right" moral paradigm. We trade their most basic and important interests against fleeting human ones only because we can. Of course, the human animal is different from all other animals. Humans are unique, just not in ways that make animal pain irrelevant. Think about it: Do you eat chicken because you are familiar with the scientific literature on them and have decided that their suffering doesn't matter, or do you do it because it tastes good?

Usually, ethical decision making means choosing between unavoidable and serious conflicts of interest. In this case, the conflicting interests are these: a human being's desire for a palate pleasure, and an animal's

interest in not having her throat slit open. Nicolette will tell you that they give the animal a "good life and an easy death." But the lives they give animals aren't nearly as good as those most of us give our dogs and cats. (They may give animals a better life and death than Smithfield, but good?) And in any case, what kind of life ends at the age of twelve, the human-proportionate age of the oldest nonbreeding animals on farms like Bill and Nicolette's?

Nicolette and I agree about the importance of the influence our eating choices have on others. If you are a vegetarian, that's one unit of vegetarianism in your life. If you influence one other person, you've doubled your entire life's commitment as a vegetarian. And you can influence many more, of course. The public aspects of eating are critical whatever your diet of choice.

The decision to eat any meat at all (even if the meat is from producers that are less abusive) will cause others you know to eat factory-farmed meat where they might otherwise not have. What does it say that the leaders of the "ethical meat" charge, like my friends Eric Schlosser and Michael Pollan and even the Niman Ranch farmers, regularly pull money out of their pockets and send it off to the factory farms? To me, it says that the "ethical carnivore" is a failed idea; even the most prominent advocates don't do it full-time. I have met countless people who were moved by Eric's and Michael's arguments, but none of them now eat exclusively Niman-type meat. They are either vegetarians or they continue to eat at least some factory-farmed animals.

Saying that meat eating can be ethical sounds "nice" and "tolerant" only because most people like to be told that doing whatever they want to do is moral. It's very popular, of course, when a vegetarian like Nicolette gives meat eaters cover to forget the real moral challenge that meat presents. But today's social conservatives are yesterday's "extremists" on issues like women's rights, civil rights, children's rights, and so on. (Who

advocates half measures on the issue of slavery?) Why, when it comes to eating animals, is it suddenly problematic to point out what is scientifically obvious and irrefutable: other animals are more like us than they're unlike us? They are our "cousins," as Richard Dawkins puts it. Even saying "You're eating a corpse," which is irrefutable, is called hyperbolic. No, it's just true.

In fact, there is nothing harsh or intolerant about suggesting we shouldn't pay people — and pay them daily — to inflict third-degree burns on animals, rip out their testicles, or slit their throats. Let's describe the reality: that piece of meat came from an animal who, at best — and it's precious few who get away with only this — was burned, mutilated, and killed for the sake of a few minutes of human pleasure. Does the pleasure justify the means?

He Knows Better

I respect the views of people who decide — for whatever reasons — to refrain from eating meat. In fact, that was what I told Nicolette on our first date when she told me she was a vegetarian. I said, "Great. I respect that."

Most of my adult life has been spent trying to build an alternative to factory animal farming, most obviously through my work with Niman Ranch. I wholeheartedly agree that many modern industrialized meat-production methods, which only came into use in the second half of the twentieth century, violate the basic values long associated with animal husbandry and slaughter. In many traditional cultures, it was widely recognized that animals deserve respect and that their lives should be taken only reverently. Because of this recognition, ancient traditions in Judaism, Islam, Native American cultures, and others throughout the world

contained specific rituals and practices relating to how animals used for food should be treated and slaughtered. Unfortunately, the industrialized system has abandoned the notions that individual animals are entitled to good lives and should always be treated with respect. That's why I have vocally opposed much of what's happening in today's industrialized animal production.

With that being said, I'll explain why I feel good about raising animals for food using traditional, natural methods. As I told you a few months ago, I grew up in Minneapolis, the son of Russian Jewish immigrants who started Niman's Grocery, a corner store. It was the kind of place where service was the top priority; customers were known by name, and lots of orders were placed by phone and delivered right to people's doorsteps. As a kid, I did a lot of those deliveries. I also went with my father to the farmers' markets, stocked the shelves, bagged groceries, and did lots of other odd jobs. My mother, who also worked in the store, was a capable cook who made just about everything from scratch, using, of course, ingredients we were provisioning for our family's business. Food was always treated as something uniquely precious, not to be taken for granted or wasted. Neither was it regarded as mere fuel to run our bodies. The gathering, preparation, and consumption of food in our family involved time, care, and ritual.

In my twenties, I made my way to Bolinas and bought some property. My late wife and I tilled a large patch of the land for a vegetable garden; we planted fruit trees; and we got ourselves some goats, chickens, and pigs. For the first time in my life, most of my food was the product of my own labors. And it was incredibly satisfying.

It was at this time in my life, too, that I had to directly face the weightiness of eating meat. We literally lived alongside our animals, and I personally knew each of them. So taking their lives was very real and not an easy thing to do. I vividly remember lying awake the night after we'd slaughtered our first pig. I agonized over whether I'd done the right thing.

But in the weeks that followed, as we, our friends, and family ate the pork from that pig, I realized that the pig had died for an important purpose — to provide us with delicious, wholesome, and highly nutritious food. I decided that as long as I always endeavored to provide our animals good, natural lives, and deaths that were free from fear or pain, raising animals for food was morally acceptable to me.

Of course, most people never have to confront the unpleasant fact that animal foods (including dairy and eggs) involve killing animals. They remain disconnected from this reality, buying their meats, fish, and cheeses at restaurants and supermarkets, already cooked or presented to them in pieces, making it easy to give little or no thought to the animals these foods come from. This is a problem. It has enabled agribusiness to shift livestock and poultry farming into unhealthy, inhumane systems with little public scrutiny. Few people have seen the insides of industrial dairies, egg or pig operations, and most consumers truly have no idea what is going on at such places. I'm convinced that the vast majority of people would be appalled with what goes on there.

In earlier times, Americans were closely connected to the ways and places their food was produced. This connectedness and familiarity assured that food production was happening in a way that matched the values of our citizens. But farming's industrialization broke this link and launched us into the modern era of disconnectedness. Our current food-production system, especially how animals are raised in confinement operations, violates the basic ethics of most Americans, who find animal farming morally acceptable but believe that every animal should be provided a decent life and a humane death. This has always been part of the American value system. When President Eisenhower signed the Humane Methods of Slaughter Act in 1958, he remarked that based on the mail he'd received on the law, one would think Americans were only interested in humane slaughter.

At the same time, the vast majority of Americans and people of other

nations have always believed that meat eating was morally acceptable. This is both cultural and natural. It's cultural in that people who were raised in households where meat and dairy are consumed generally adopt the same patterns. Slavery is a poor analogy. Slavery—while widespread in certain epochs and in certain geographies—was never a universal, daily practice that sustained every household, like the consuming of meat, fish, or dairy has always been in human societies the world over.

I say meat eating is natural because vast numbers of animals in nature eat the flesh of other animals. This includes, of course, humans and our prehuman ancestors, who began eating meat over 1.5 million years ago. In most parts of the world and for most of animal and human history, meat eating has never been simply a matter of pleasure. It's been the basis for survival.

Meat's nourishment as well as meat eating's ubiquity in nature are powerful indications to me that it's appropriate. Some attempt to argue that it's wrong to look to natural systems to determine what is morally acceptable because behaviors like rape and infanticide have been found to exist in the wild. But this argument doesn't hold water because it points to aberrant behaviors. Such events do not occur as a matter of course in animal populations. Clearly, it would be foolish to look to aberrant behaviors to determine what is normal and acceptable. But the norms of natural ecosystems hold boundless wisdom about economy, order, and stability. And meat eating is (and always has been) the norm in nature.

But what about the argument that we humans should choose not to eat meat, regardless of natural norms, because meat is inherently wasteful of resources? This claim is also flawed. Those figures assume that livestock is raised in intensive confinement facilities and fed grains and soy from fertilized crop fields. Such data is inapplicable to grazing animals kept entirely on pasture, like grass-fed cattle, goats, sheep, and deer.

The leading scientist investigating energy usage in food production has long been David Pimentel of Cornell University. Pimentel is not an advocate of vegetarianism. He even notes that "all available evidence suggests that humans are omnivores." He frequently writes of livestock's important role in world food production. For example, in his seminal work Food, Energy, and Society, *he notes that livestock plays "an important role . . . in providing food for humans." He goes on to elaborate as follows: "First, the livestock effectively convert forage growing in the marginal habitat into food suitable for humans. Second, the herds serve as stored food resources. Third, the cattle can be traded for . . . grain during years of inadequate rainfall and poor crop yields."*

Moreover, asserting that animal farming is inherently bad for the environment fails to comprehend national and world food production from a holistic perspective. Plowing and planting land for crops is inherently environmentally damaging. In fact, many ecosystems have evolved with grazing animals as integral components over tens of thousands of years. Grazing animals are the most ecologically sound way to maintain the integrity of those prairies and grasslands.

As Wendell Berry has eloquently explained in his writings, the most ecologically sound farms raise plants and animals together. *They are modeled on natural ecosystems, with their continual and complex interplay of flora and fauna. Many (probably most) organic fruit and vegetable farmers depend on manure from livestock and poultry for fertilizer.*

The reality is that all food production involves altering the environment to a certain extent. Sustainable farming's goal is to minimize the disruption. Pasture-based agriculture, especially when part of a diversified farming operation, is the least disruptive way to produce food, minimizing water and air pollution, erosion, and impacts on wildlife. It also allows animals to thrive. Fostering such farming systems is my life's work, and I'm proud of it.

3.

Do We Know Better?

PETA's Bruce Friedrich (the voice that followed Nicolette's in the previous section), on the one hand, and the Nimans, on the other, represent the two dominant institutional responses to our present system of animal agriculture. Their two visions are also two strategies. Bruce argues for animal *rights*. Bill and Nicolette argue for animal *welfare*.

From a certain angle of vision, the two responses seem united: they both seek a lesser violence. (When animal rights advocates argue that *animals are not here for us to use*, they are calling for a minimization of the harm we inflict.) From this point of view, the more important difference between the positions—the one that is at the core of what motivates us to choose one or the other—is a wager about what ways of living will actually result in this lesser violence.

The advocates of animal rights that I've encountered in my research don't spend much time critiquing (let alone campaigning against) a scenario where generation after generation of farmed animals are raised by good shepherds like Frank, Paul, Bill, and Nicolette. This scenario—the idea of robustly humane animal agriculture—isn't so much seen as objectionable to most people who work in the name of animal rights as it is hopelessly romantic. They don't believe in it. From the vantage of animal rights, the animal welfare position is like proposing we take away basic legal rights for children, offer huge financial incentives for working children to death, place no social taboo on using goods made from child labor,

and somehow expect that toothless laws advocating "child welfare" will ensure they are treated well. The point of the analogy is not that children are morally on the same level as animals, but that both are vulnerable and almost infinitely exploitable if others don't intervene.

Of course, those who "believe in meat" and want meat eating to continue without factory farming think vegetarian advocates are the unrealistic ones. Sure, a small (or even large) group may want to go veg, but people in general want meat, always have, always will, and that's that. Vegetarians are at best kindly but unrealistic. At worst they are delusional sentimentalists.

No doubt these *are* different conclusions about the world in which we live and the foods that should be on our plates, but how much of a difference do these differences make? The idea of a just farm system rooted in the best traditions of animal welfare *and* the idea of a vegetarian farm system rooted in an animal rights ethic are both strategies for reducing (never eliminating) the violence inherent in being alive. They aren't just opposing values, as is often portrayed. They represent different ways of getting a job done that both agree needs doing. They reflect different intuitions about human nature, but they both appeal to compassion and prudence.

Both proposals require pretty significant leaps of faith, and both expect quite a bit of us as individuals—and as a society. Both require advocacy, not just making a decision and keeping it to yourself. Both strategies, if they are going to achieve their aims, suggest that we need to do more than just change our diets; we need to ask others to join us. And while the differences between these two positions matter, they are minor compared to their common ground, and inconsequential compared to their distance from positions that defend factory farming.

Long after I had made my personal decision to be vegetarian, it remained unclear to me to what extent I could genuinely respect a different decision. Are other strategies simply wrong?

4.

I Can't Go to the Word *Wrong*

BILL, NICOLETTE, AND I WALKED the rolling pasture to oceanside cliffs. Below us, waves broke on sculptural rock formations. One at a time, the grazing cattle came into view, black against a sea of green, heads down, face muscles pummeling tufts of grass. There could be no honest disputing that at least while grazing, those cows had it very good.

"And what about eating an animal you know as an individual?" I asked.

BILL: *It's not like eating a pet. At least I'm able to make a distinction. And some of it's maybe because we have enough numbers, and there's a tipping point where your animals are no longer individual pets.... But I wouldn't treat them any better or worse if I wasn't going to eat them.*

Really? Would he brand his dog?
"What about mutilations, like branding?"

BILL: *Part of it is that they are just big-ticket animals, and there is a system in place which may or may not be archaic today. In order to sell the animals, they have to be branded and inspected. And it prevents a*

lot of theft. It protects the investment. There are better ways of doing it being explored now — retina scanning, or putting chips in them. We do hot-iron branding and we've experimented with freeze branding, but both are painful to the animals. Until we find a better system, we consider the hot-iron branding a necessity.

NICOLETTE: *The one thing that we do that I'm uncomfortable with is the branding. We've been talking about this for years.... There is a real problem with cattle rustling.*

I asked Bernie Rollin, an internationally respected animal welfare expert at Colorado State University, what he thought of Bill's argument that branding was still necessary to prevent theft.

Let me tell you how cattle are rustled today: they pull in a truck and slaughter the animal on the spot—do you think branding makes any difference there? Branding is cultural. These brands have been in families for years, and ranchers don't want to give them up. They know it's painful, but they did it with their fathers and their grandfathers. I know one rancher, a good rancher, who told me that his kids don't come home for Thanksgiving and they don't come home for Christmas, but they come home for branding.

Niman Ranch is pushing the current paradigm on many fronts, and that's probably the best anyone can do if they want to create a model that can be replicated immediately. But that attention to immediacy also means intermediacy. Branding is an area of compromise—a concession not to necessity or practicality or demands for a certain taste, but to a habit of irrational, unnecessary violence, a tradition.

The beef industry is still by far the most ethically impressive segment of the meat industry, and so I wish the truth weren't so ugly here. The Animal Welfare Institute–approved welfare protocols that Niman Ranch follows—again, about the best there are—also allow disbudding (removal of horn buds with hot irons or caustic pastes) and castration. Less obviously a problem, but worse from a welfare point of view, is that Niman Ranch cattle all spend their last months on a feedlot. A Niman Ranch feedlot is not exactly like an industrial feedlot (because of the smaller scale, lack of drugs, better feed, better upkeep, and greater attention paid to each animal's welfare), but Bill and Nicolette are still putting cattle on a diet that fits poorly with a cow's digestive system, and doing so for months. Yes, Niman feeds a gentler blend of grains than the industry standard. But the animals' most basic "species specific" behavior is still being traded for a taste preference.

BILL: *What's important to me now is that I really feel like we can change the way people eat and the way these animals eat. It's going to take a joint effort of like minds. For me, as I evaluate my life and where I want to be at the end of it, if I can look back and say, "We created a model and everyone can copy us," even if they crush us in the marketplace, at least we effected that change.*

This was Bill's wager and he had staked his life on it. Was it Nicolette's?

"Why don't you eat meat?" I asked. "It's been bothering me all afternoon. You keep arguing that there's nothing inherently wrong with it, but it's obvious that it's wrong for you. I'm not asking a question about other people, but about you."

NICOLETTE: *I feel I can make a choice and I don't want it on my conscience. But that's because of my personal connection with animals. It would bother me. I think it just makes me feel uncomfortable.*

"Can you explain what makes you feel that way?"

NICOLETTE: *I think because I know it's not necessary. But I don't feel there's anything wrong with it. See, I can't go to the word wrong.*

BILL: *That moment of slaughter, for me, in my experience—and I would suspect for most sensitive animal husbandry farmers—that's when you understand destiny and dominion. Because you have brought that animal to its death. It's alive, and you know when that door goes up and it goes in there that it's over. It's the most troubling moment for me, that moment when they are lined up at the slaughterhouse. I don't know quite how to explain it. That's the marriage of life and death. That's when you realize, "God, do I really want to exercise dominion and transform this wonderful living creature into commodity, into food?"*

"And how do you resolve that?"

BILL: *Well, you just take a deep breath. It doesn't get easier with numbers. People think it gets easier.*

You take a deep breath? For a moment that sounds like a perfectly reasonable response. It sounds romantic. For a moment, ranching feels *more* honest: facing the hard issues of life and death, dominion and destiny.

Or is the deep breath really just a resigned sigh, a halfhearted promise to think about it later? Is the deep breath confrontation or

shallow avoidance? And what about the exhalation? It isn't enough to breathe the world's pollution in. Not responding is a response—we are equally responsible for what we don't do. In the case of animal slaughter, to throw your hands in the air is to wrap your fingers around a knife handle.

5.

Take a Deep Breath

VIRTUALLY ALL COWS COME TO the same end: the final trip to the kill floor. Cattle raised for beef are still adolescents when they meet their end. While early American ranchers kept cattle on the range for four or five years, today they are slaughtered at twelve to fourteen months. Though we could not be more intimate with the end product of this journey (it's in our homes and mouths, our children's mouths...), for most of us, the journey itself is unfelt and invisible.

Cattle seem to experience the trip as a series of distinct stresses: scientists have identified a different set of hormonal stress reactions to handling, transport, and slaughter itself. If the kill floor is working optimally, the initial "stress" of handling, as indicated by hormone levels, can actually be greater than that of either transport or slaughter.

Although acute pain is fairly easy to recognize, what counts as a good life for animals is not obvious until you know the species—even the herd, even the individual animal—in question. Slaughter might be ugliest to contemporary urbanites, but if you consider the cow's-eye view, it's not hard to imagine how after a

life in cow communities, interactions with strange, loud, pain-inflicting, upright creatures might be more frightening than a controlled moment of death.

When I wandered among Bill's herd, I developed some sense of why this is so. If I stayed a good distance from the grazing cattle, they seemed unaware I was even there. Not so: Cows have nearly 360-degree vision and keep a vigilant watch on their environs. They know the other animals around them, select leaders, and will defend their herd. Whenever I approached an animal just shy of the reach of an outstretched arm, it was as if I had crossed some invisible boundary and the cow quickly jerked away. As a rule, cattle have a heavy dose of a prey-species flight instinct, and many common handling procedures—roping, shouting, tail twisting, shocking with electric prods, and hitting—terrify the animals.

One way or another, they are herded onto trucks or trains. Once aboard, cattle face a journey of up to forty-eight hours, during which they are deprived of water and food. As a result, virtually all of them lose weight and many show signs of dehydration. They are often exposed to extremes of heat and cold. A number of animals will die from the conditions or arrive at the slaughterhouse too sick to be considered fit for human consumption.

I couldn't get near the inside of a large slaughter facility. Just about the only way for someone outside the industry to see industrial cattle slaughter is to go undercover, and that is not only a project that takes half a year or more, it can be life-threatening work. So the description of slaughter I will provide here comes from eyewitness accounts and the industry's own statistics. I'm going to try to let workers on the kill floor speak the realities in their own words as much as possible.

In his bestselling book *The Omnivore's Dilemma*, Michael Pollan traces the life of an industry-raised beef cow, #534, which he

personally purchased. Pollan provides a rich and thorough account of the raising of cattle but stops short of any serious probing into slaughter, discussing its ethics from a safely abstract distance, signaling a fundamental failure of his often clear-eyed and revelatory journey.

"Slaughter," Pollan reports, was "the one event in his [#534's] life I was not allowed to witness or even learn anything about, save its likely date. This didn't exactly surprise me: The meat industry understands that the more people know about what happens on the kill floor, the less meat they're likely to eat." Well said.

But, Pollan continues, "that's not because slaughter is necessarily inhumane, but because most of us would simply rather not be reminded of exactly what meat is or what it takes to bring it to our plates." This strikes me as somewhere between a half-truth and an evasion. As Pollan explains, "Eating industrial meat takes an almost heroic act of not knowing, or, now, forgetting." That heroism is needed precisely because one has to forget a lot more than the mere *fact* of animal deaths: one has to forget not only *that* animals are killed, but *how*.

Even among writers who deserve great praise for bringing factory farming into public view, there is often an insipid disavowal of the real horror we inflict. In his provocative and often brilliant review of *The Omnivore's Dilemma*, B. R. Myers explains this accepted intellectual fashion:

> The technique goes like this: One debates the other side in a rational manner until pushed into a corner. Then one simply drops the argument and slips away, pretending that one has not fallen short of reason but instead *transcended* it. The irreconcilability of one's belief with reason is then held up as a great

mystery, the humble readiness to live with which puts one above lesser minds and their cheap certainties.

There is one other rule to this game: never, absolutely never, emphasize that virtually all of the time one's choice is between cruelty and ecological destruction, and ceasing to eat animals.

It isn't hard to figure out why the beef industry won't let even an enthusiastic carnivore near its slaughter facilities. Even in abattoirs where most cattle die quickly, it's hard to imagine that any day passes in which several animals (tens, hundreds?) don't meet an end of the most horrifying kind. A meat industry that follows the ethics most of us hold (providing a good life and an easy death for animals, little waste) is not a fantasy, but it cannot deliver the immense amount of cheap meat per capita we currently enjoy.

At a typical slaughter facility, cattle are led through a chute into a knocking box—usually a large cylindrical hold through which the head pokes. The stun operator, or "knocker," presses a large pneumatic gun between the cow's eyes. A steel bolt shoots into the cow's skull and then retracts back into the gun, usually rendering the animal unconscious or causing death. Sometimes the bolt only dazes the animal, which either remains conscious or later wakes up as it is being "processed." The effectiveness of the knocking gun depends on its manufacture and maintenance, and the skill of its application—a small hose leak or firing the gun before pressure sufficiently builds up again can reduce the force with which the bolt is released and leave animals grotesquely punctured but painfully conscious.

The effectiveness of knocking is also reduced because some plant managers believe that animals can become "too dead" and

therefore, because their hearts are not pumping, bleed out too slowly or insufficiently. (It's "important" for plants to have a quick bleed-out time for basic efficiency and because blood left in the meat promotes bacterial growth and reduces shelf life.) As a result, some plants deliberately choose less-effective knocking methods. The side effect is that a higher percentage of animals require multiple knocks, remain conscious, or wake up in processing.

No jokes here, and no turning away. Let's say what we mean: animals are bled, skinned, and dismembered while conscious. It happens all the time, and the industry and the government know it. Several plants cited for bleeding or skinning or dismembering live animals have defended their actions as common in the industry and asked, perhaps rightly, why they were being singled out.

When Temple Grandin conducted an industrywide audit in 1996, her studies revealed that the vast majority of cattle slaughterhouses were unable to regularly render cattle unconscious with a single blow. The USDA, the federal agency charged with enforcing humane slaughter, responded to these numbers not by stepping up enforcement, but by changing its policy to cease tracking the number of humane slaughter violations and removing any mention of humane slaughter from its list of rotating tasks for inspectors. The situation has improved since then, which Grandin attributes largely to audits demanded by fast-food companies (which these companies demanded after being targeted by animal rights groups) but remains disturbing. Grandin's most recent estimates — which optimistically rely on data from announced audits — still found one in four cattle slaughterhouses unable to reliably render animals unconscious on the first blow. For smaller facilities, there are virtually no statistics available, and experts agree that these slaughterhouses can be significantly worse in their treatment of cattle. No one is spotless.

Cattle at the far end of the lines leading to the kill floor do not appear to understand what's coming, but if they survive the first knock, they sure as hell appear to know they are fighting for their lives. Recalls one worker, "Their heads are up in the air; they're looking around, trying to hide. They've already been hit before by this thing, and they're not going to let it get at them again."

The combination of line speeds that have increased as much as 800 percent in the past hundred years and poorly trained workers laboring under nightmarish conditions guarantees mistakes. (Slaughterhouse workers have the highest injury rate of any job— 27 percent annually—and receive low pay to kill as many as 2,050 cattle a shift.)

Temple Grandin has argued that ordinary people can become sadistic from the dehumanizing work of constant slaughter. This is a persistent problem, she reports, that management must guard against. Sometimes animals are not knocked *at all*. At one plant, a secret video was made by workers (not animal activists) and given to the *Washington Post*. The tape revealed conscious animals going down the processing line, and an incident where an electric prod was jammed into a steer's mouth. According to the *Post*, "More than twenty workers signed affidavits alleging that the violations shown on the tape are commonplace and that supervisors are aware of them." In one affidavit, a worker explained, "I've seen thousands and thousands of cows go through the slaughter process alive.... The cows can get seven minutes down the line and still be alive. I've been in the side puller where they're still alive. All the hide is stripped out down the neck there." And when workers who complain are listened to at all, they often get fired.

I'd come home and be in a bad mood.... Go right downstairs and go to sleep. Yell at the kids, stuff like that. One time I got really

upset— [my wife] knows about this. A three-year-old heifer was walking up through the kill alley. And she was having a calf right there, it was half in and half out. I knew she was going to die, so I pulled the calf out. Wow, did my boss get mad.... They call these calves "slunks." They use the blood for cancer research. And he wanted that calf. What they usually do is when the cow's guts fall onto the gut table, the workers go along and rip the uterus open and pull these calves out. It's nothing to have a cow hanging up in front of you and see the calf inside kicking, trying to get out.... My boss wanted that calf, but I sent it back down to the stockyards.... [I complained] to the foremen, the inspectors, the kill floor superintendent. Even the superintendent over at the beef division. We had a long talk one day in the cafeteria about this crap that was going on. I've gotten so mad, some days I'd go and pound on the wall because they won't do anything about it.... I've never seen a [USDA] vet near the knocking pen. Nobody wants to come back there. See, I'm an ex-Marine. The blood and guts don't bother me. It's the inhumane treatment. There's just so much of it.

In twelve seconds or less, the knocked cow—unconscious, semi-conscious, fully conscious, or dead—moves down the line to arrive at the "shackler," who attaches a chain around one of the hind legs and hoists the animal into the air.

From the shackler, the animal, now dangling from a leg, is mechanically moved to a "sticker," who cuts the carotid arteries and a jugular vein in the neck. The animal is again mechanically moved to a "bleed rail" and drained of blood for several minutes. A cow has in the neighborhood of five and a half gallons of blood, so this takes some time. Cutting the flow of blood to the animal's brain will kill it, but not instantly (which is why the animals are supposed to be unconscious). If the animal is partially conscious or

improperly cut, this can restrict the flow of blood, prolonging consciousness further. "They'd be blinking and stretching their necks from side to side, looking around, really frantic," explained one line worker.

The cow should now be carcass, which will move along the line to a "head-skinner," which is exactly what it sounds like—a stop where the skin is peeled off the head of the animal. The percentage of cattle still conscious at this stage is low but not zero. At some plants it is a regular problem—so much so that there are informal standards about how to deal with these animals. Explains a worker familiar with such practices, "A lot of times the skinner finds out an animal is still conscious when he slices the side of its head and it starts kicking wildly. If that happens, or if a cow is already kicking when it arrives at their station, the skinners shove a knife into the back of its head to cut the spinal cord."

This practice, it turns out, immobilizes the animal but does not render it insensible. I can't tell you how many animals this happens to, as no one is allowed to properly investigate. We only know that it is an inevitable by-product of the present slaughter system and that it will continue to happen.

After the head-skinner, the carcass (or cow) proceeds to the "leggers," who cut off the lower portions of the animal's legs. "As far as the ones that come back to life," says a line worker, "it looks like they're trying to climb the walls....And when they get to the leggers, well, the leggers don't want to wait to start working on the cow until somebody gets down there to reknock it. So they just cut off the bottom part of the leg with the clippers. When they do that, the cattle go wild, just kicking in every direction."

The animal then proceeds to be completely skinned, eviscerated, and cut in half, at which point it finally looks like the stereotyped image of beef—hanging in freezers with eerie stillness.

6.

Proposals

IN THE NOT-SO-DISTANT history of America's animal-protection organizations, those advocating vegetarianism, small in number but well organized, were definitively at odds with those advocating an *eat with care* stance. The ubiquity of factory farming and industrial slaughter has changed this, closing a once large gap between nonprofits like PETA that advocate veganism and those like HSUS that say nice things about veganism but primarily advocate welfare.

Of all the ranchers I met in my research, Frank Reese holds a special status. I say this for two reasons. The first is that he is the only farmer I met who doesn't do anything on his ranch that is plainly cruel. He doesn't castrate his animals like Paul or brand them like Bill. Where other farmers have said "We have to do this to survive" or "Consumers demand this," Frank has taken big risks (he'd lose his home if his farm failed completely) and asked his customers to eat differently (his birds need to be cooked longer or they don't taste right; they also are more flavorful and so can be used more sparingly in soups and a variety of other dishes, so he provides recipes and occasionally even prepares meals for customers to reeducate them in older ways of cooking). His work requires tremendous compassion and tremendous patience. And its value is not only moral, but, as a new generation of omnivores demands real welfare, economic.

Frank is one of the only farmers I know of who has succeeded in preserving the genetics of "heritage" poultry (he is the first and *only* rancher authorized by the USDA to call his birds "heritage"). His

preservation of traditional genetics is incredibly important because the single biggest factor preventing the emergence of tolerable turkey and chicken farms is the present reliance on factory farm hatcheries to supply baby birds to growers — almost the only hatcheries there are. Virtually none of these commercially available birds are capable of reproducing, and serious health problems have been bred into their genes in the process of engineering them (the chickens we eat, like turkeys, are dead-end animals — by design they can't live long enough to reproduce). Because the average farmer can't run his own hatchery, concentrated industry control of genetics locks farmers and their animals into the factory system. Aside from Frank, most all other small poultry farmers — even the few good farmers that pay for heritage genetics and raise their birds with great regard for their welfare — usually must have the birds they raise each year sent to them by mail from factory-style hatcheries. As one might imagine, sending chicks by mail poses serious welfare problems, but an even more serious welfare concern is the conditions under which the parent and grandparent birds are reared. Reliance on such hatcheries where the welfare of breeding birds may be as bad as in the worst factory farms, is the Achilles' heel of many otherwise excellent small producers. For these reasons, Frank's traditional genetics and skill in breeding give him the potential to create an alternative to poultry factory farms in a way almost no one else can.

But Frank, like many of the farmers who hold a living knowledge of traditional husbandry techniques, clearly won't be able to realize his potential without help. Integrity, skill, and genetics alone do not create a successful farm. When I first met him, the demand for his turkeys (he now has chickens, too) couldn't have been higher — he would sell out six months in advance of slaughter time. Though his most loyal customers tended to be blue-collar, his birds were prized by chefs and foodies from Dan Barber and Mario Batali to Martha

Stewart. Nevertheless, Frank was losing money and subsidizing his ranch with other work.

Frank has his own hatchery, but he still needs access to other services, especially a well-run slaughterhouse. The loss of not only local hatcheries, but also slaughterhouses, weigh stations, grain storage, and other services farmers require is an immense barrier to the growth of husbandry-based ranching. It's not that consumers won't buy the animals such farmers raise; it's that farmers can't produce them without reinventing a now destroyed rural infrastructure.

About halfway through writing this book, I called Frank as I had done periodically with various questions about poultry (as do many others inside the poultry world). Gone was his gentle, ever-patient, all-is-well voice. In its place was panic. The one slaughterhouse he had managed to find that would slaughter his birds according to standards he found tolerable (still not ideal) had, after more than a hundred years, been bought and closed down by an industry company. This was not merely an issue of convenience; there were quite literally no other plants left in the region that could accommodate his pre-Thanksgiving slaughter. Frank faced the prospect of enormous economic loss and, what scared him more, the possibility of having to kill all his birds outside a USDA-approved plant, which would mean the birds could not be sold and would literally rot.

The shuttering of the slaughter plant wasn't unusual. The destruction of the basic infrastructure that supported small poultry farmers is nearly total in America. At one level, this is the result of the normal process of corporations pursuing profit by making sure they have access to resources their competitors don't. There is, obviously, a lot of money at stake here: billions of dollars, which could either be spread among a handful of megacorporations or among hundreds of thousands of small farmers. But the question of whether the likes of Frank get crushed or begin to nibble at the 99 percent market share enjoyed

by the factory farm is more than financial. At stake is the future of an ethical heritage that generations before us labored to build. At stake is all that is done in the name of "the American farmer" and "American rural values"—and the invocation of these ideals is enormously influential. Billions of dollars in government funds marked for agriculture; state agricultural policies that shape the landscape, air, and water of our country; and foreign policies that affect global issues from starvation to climate change are, in our democracy, executed in the name of our farmers and the values that guide them. Except they're not exactly farmers anymore; they're corporations. And these corporations are not simply business magnates (who are quite capable of conscience). They are usually massive corporations with legal obligations to maximize profitability. For the sake of sales and public image, they promote the myth that they're Frank Reese, even as they labor to drive the real Frank Reese into extinction.

The alternative is that small farmers and their friends— sustainability and welfare advocates—will come to own this heritage. Few will actually farm, but in Wendell Berry's phrase, we will all farm by proxy. To whom will we give our proxy? In the former scenario, we give over immense moral and financial muscle to a small number of men who even themselves have limited control over the machine-like agribusiness bureaucracies they administer to immense personal gain. In the latter scenario, our proxy would be entrusted not only to actual farmers, but to thousands of experts whose lives have been centered around the civic rather than the corporate bottom line—with people like Dr. Aaron Gross, founder of Farm Forward, a sustainable-farming and farmed-animal advocacy organization that is charting new paths toward a food system that reflects our diverse values.

The factory farm has succeeded by divorcing people from their food, eliminating farmers, and ruling agriculture by corporate fiat. But what if farmers like Frank and longtime allies like the American

Livestock Breeds Conservancy got together with younger groups like Farm Forward that are plugged into networks of enthusiastically selective omnivores and activist vegetarians: students, scientists, and scholars; parents, artists, and religious leaders; lawyers, chefs, businesspeople, and farmers? What if instead of Frank spending his time hustling to secure a slaughter facility, such new alliances allowed him to put greater and greater energies into using the best of modern technology and traditional husbandry to reinvent a more humane and sustainable — and *democratic* — farm system?

I Am a Vegan Who Builds Slaughterhouses

I've now been vegan for more than half my life, and while many other concerns have kept me committed to veganism — sustainability and labor issues most of all, but also concerns with personal and public health — it's the animals that are at the center of my concern. Which is why people who know me well are surprised about the work I've been doing to develop plans for a slaughterhouse.

I've advocated for plant-based diets in a number of contexts and would still say that eating as few animal products as possible — ideally none — is a powerful way to be a part of the solution. But my understanding of the priorities of activism has changed, and so has my self-understanding. I once liked to think of being vegan as a cutting-edge, countercultural statement. It's now quite clear that the values that led me to a vegan diet come from the small farming in my family's background more than anywhere else.

If you know about factory farming and you've inherited anything like a traditional ethic about raising animals, it's hard not to have something

238

deep inside you recoil at what animal agriculture has become. And I'm not talking about some saintly farm ethic, either. I'm talking about a ranch ethic that tolerated castration, branding, and meant that you killed the runts and one fine day took hold of animals that perhaps knew you mostly as the bringer of food and cut their throats. There is a lot of violence in traditional techniques. But there was also compassion, something that tends to be less remembered, perhaps out of necessity. The formula for a good animal farm has been turned on its head. Instead of speaking of care, you'll often hear a knee-jerk response from farmers when the topic of animal welfare is raised: "No one gets in this business because they hate animals." It's a curious statement. It's a statement that says something by way of not saying it. The implication, of course, is that these men often wanted to be animal farmers because they liked *animals, enjoyed caring for and protecting them. I'm not saying that this is without its contradictions, but there is truth in it. It's also a statement that implies an apology without giving one. Why, after all, does it need to be said that they don't hate* animals?

Sadly, people in animal agriculture today are increasingly unlikely to be bearers of traditional rural values. Many of the people at city-based animal advocacy organizations, whether they know it or not, are from a strictly historical perspective far better representatives of rural values like respect for neighbors, straightforwardness, land stewardship, and, of course, respect for the creatures given into their hands. Since the world has changed so much, the same values don't lead to the same choices anymore.

I've had a lot of hope for more sustainable grass-based cattle ranches and seen a new vigor among the remaining small family hog farms, but when it came to the poultry industry, I had all but given up hope until I met Frank Reese and visited his incredible farm. Frank and the handful of farmers he's given some of his birds to are the only ones in a position to develop a proper

alternative to the poultry factory farm model from the genetics up—and that's what's needed.

When I spoke to Frank about the barriers he faced, his frustration with a half-dozen issues that couldn't be easily addressed without a significant cash influx came into focus. The other thing that was clear was that the demand for his product wasn't only significant, but positively immense—an entrepreneur's dream. Frank was regularly refusing orders for more birds than he had raised in his entire life because he didn't have the capacity to meet them. The organization I founded, Farm Forward, offered to help him create a business plan. A few months later, our director and I were in Frank's living room with the first possible investor.

We then set to the cat-herding work of bringing together the considerable influence of many of Frank's existing admirers— reporters, academics, foodies, politicians—and coordinating their energy in the ways that would deliver results most quickly. Plans for expansion were moving along. Frank had added several breeds of heritage chickens to his turkey flocks. The first of a series of new buildings that he needed was under construction, and he was in negotiations with a major retailer for a large contract. And that's when the slaughterhouse he used was bought and closed.

We had actually anticipated this. Still, Frank's growers—the farmers who raise many of the birds he hatches, and stood to lose most of a year's salary—were scared. Frank decided the only long-term solution was to build a slaughter facility that he owned, ideally a mobile slaughterhouse that could be right on the farm and eliminate the stress of transport. Of course he was right. So we started figuring out the mechanics and economics of doing this. It was new territory for me—intellectually, of course, but also emotionally. I thought the work would require regular speeches to myself correcting my resistance to kill animals. But if anything made me uncomfortable, it was my lack of discomfort. Why, I kept wondering, aren't I at least uneasy about this?

My grandfather on my mother's side wanted to stay in farming. He was forced out like so many others, but my mother had already grown up on a working farm. She was in a small town in the Midwest with a graduating high school class of forty. For a time, my grandfather raised pigs. He castrated and even used some confinement that was moving in the direction of today's hog factory farms. Still, they were animals to him, and if one got sick, he made sure that individual got extra care and attention. He didn't pull out a calculator and figure out whether it would be more profitable to let the animal languish. The thought would have been unchristian to him, cowardly, indecent.

That small victory of caring over the calculator is all you need to know to understand why I'm vegan today. And why I help build slaughterhouses. This is not paradoxical or ironic. The very same impulse that makes me personally committed to eschewing meats, eggs, and dairy has led me to devote my time to helping create a slaughterhouse that Frank would own and that could be a model for others. If you can't beat them, join them? No. It's a question of properly identifying who the them *is.*

7.

My Wager

AFTER HAVING SPENT NEARLY THREE years learning about animal agriculture, my resolve has become strong in two directions. I've become a committed vegetarian, whereas before I waffled among any number of diets. It's now hard to imagine that changing. I simply don't want anything to do with the factory farm, and refraining from meat is the only realistic way for me to do that.

In another direction, though, the vision of sustainable farms that give animals a good life (a life as good as we give our dogs or cats) and an easy death (as easy a death as we give our suffering and terminally ill companion animals) has moved me. Paul, Bill, Nicolette, and most of all Frank are not only good people, but extraordinary people. They should be among the people a president consults when selecting a secretary of agriculture. Their farms are what I want our elected officials to strive to create and our economy to support.

The meat industry has tried to paint people who take this two-fold stance as absolutist vegetarians hiding a radicalized agenda. But ranchers can be vegetarians, vegans can build slaughterhouses, and I can be a vegetarian who supports the best of animal agriculture.

I feel certain that Frank's ranch will be run honorably, but how sure can I be about the day-to-day running of other farms that follow his model? How sure do I need to be? Is the strategy of the selective omnivore "naive" in a way that vegetarianism is not?

How easy is it to avow a responsibility to the beings most within our power and at the same time raise them only to kill them? Marlene Halverson puts the strange situation of the animal farmer eloquently:

> The ethical relationship of farmers to farm animals is unique. The farmer must raise a living creature that is destined to an endpoint of slaughter for food, or culling and death after a lifetime of production, without becoming emotionally attached or, conversely, without becoming cynical about the animal's need for a decent life while the animal is alive. The farmer must *somehow* raise an animal as a commercial endeavor without regarding the animal as a mere commodity.

Is this a reasonable thing to ask of farmers? Given the pressures of our industrial era, is meat by necessity a disavowal, a frustration

if not an outright denial of compassion? Contemporary agriculture has given us cause for skepticism, but no one knows what tomorrow's farms will look like.

What we do know, though, is that if you eat meat today, your typical choice is between animals raised with either more (chicken, turkey, fish, and pork) or less (beef) cruelty. Why do so many of us feel we have to choose between such options? What would render such utilitarian calculations of the least horrible option beside the point? At what moment would the absurd choices readily available today give way to the simplicity of a firmly drawn line: *this is unacceptable?*

Just how destructive does a culinary preference have to be before we decide to eat something else? If contributing to the suffering of billions of animals that live miserable lives and (quite often) die in horrific ways isn't motivating, what would be? If being the number one contributor to the most serious threat facing the planet (global warming) isn't enough, what is? And if you are tempted to put off these questions of conscience, to say *not now*, then *when?*

We have let the factory farm replace farming for the same reasons our cultures have relegated minorities to being second-class members of society and kept women under the power of men. We treat animals as we do because we want to and can. (Does anyone really wish to deny this anymore?) The myth of consent is perhaps *the* story of meat, and much comes down to whether this story, when we are realistic, is plausible.

It isn't. Not anymore. It wouldn't satisfy anyone who didn't have an interest in eating animals. At the end of the day, factory farming isn't about feeding people; it's about money. Barring some rather radical legal and economic changes, it must be. And whether or not it's right to kill animals for food, we know that in today's dominant systems it's impossible to kill them without (at least) inflicting occasional torture. This is why even Frank—the most well-intentioned

farmer one could imagine—apologizes to his animals as they are sent off to slaughter. He's made a compromise rather than cut a fair deal.

A not particularly funny thing happened at Niman Ranch recently. Just before this book went to press, Bill was driven out of his namesake company. As he tells it, his own board forced him to leave, quite simply because they wanted to do things more profitably and less ethically than he would allow while remaining at the helm. It seems that even this company—literally the most impressive national meat provider in the United States—has sold out. I included Niman Ranch in this book because it was the best evidence that selective omnivores have a viable strategy. What am I—are we—to make of its fall?

For now, Niman Ranch remains the only nationally available brand that I can say represents a robust improvement in the lives of animals (pigs much more than cattle). But how good would you feel sending your money to these people? If animal agriculture has become a joke, perhaps this is the punch line: even Bill Niman has said he would no longer eat Niman Ranch beef.

I have placed my wager on a vegetarian diet *and* I have enough respect for people like Frank, who have bet on a more humane animal agriculture, to support their kind of farming. This is not in the end a complicated position. Nor is it a veiled argument for vegetarianism. It *is* an argument for vegetarianism, but it's also an argument for another, wiser animal agriculture and more honorable omnivory.

If we are not given the option to live without violence, we are given the choice to center our meals around harvest or slaughter, husbandry or war. We have chosen slaughter. We have chosen war. That's the truest version of our story of eating animals.

Can we tell a new story?

Storytelling

Where will it end?

1.

The Last Thanksgiving of My Childhood

THROUGHOUT MY CHILDHOOD, WE CELEBRATED Thanksgiving at my uncle and aunt's house. My uncle, my mother's younger brother, was the first person on that side of the family to be born on this side of the Atlantic. My aunt can trace her lineage back to the *Mayflower*. That unlikely pairing of histories was no small part of what made those Thanksgivings so special, and memorable, and, in the very best sense of the word, American.

We would arrive around two o'clock. The cousins would play football on the sloping sliver of a front yard until my little brother got hurt, at which point we would head up to the attic to play football on the various video game systems. Two floors beneath us, Maverick salivated at the stove's window, my father talked politics and cholesterol, the Detroit Lions played their hearts out on an unwatched TV, and my grandmother, surrounded by her family, thought in the language of her dead relatives.

Two dozen or so mismatched chairs circumscribed four tables of slightly different heights and widths, pushed together and covered in matching cloths. No one was fooled into thinking this setup was perfect, but it was. My aunt placed a small pile of popcorn kernels on each plate, which, in the course of the meal, we were supposed to transfer to the table as symbols of things we were thankful for. Dishes came out continuously; some went clockwise, some counter, some zigzagged down the length of the table: sweet potato casserole, homemade rolls, green beans with almonds, cranberry concoctions, yams, buttery mashed potatoes, my grandmother's wildly

incongruous kugel, trays of gherkins and olives and marinated mushrooms, and a cartoonishly large turkey that had been put in the oven when last year's was taken out. We talked and talked: about the Orioles and Redskins, changes in the neighborhood, our accomplishments, and the anguish of others (our own anguish was off-limits), and all the while, my grandmother would go from grandchild to grandchild, making sure no one was starving.

Thanksgiving is the holiday that encompasses all others. All of them, from Martin Luther King. Day to Arbor Day to Christmas to Valentine's Day, are in one way or another about being thankful. But Thanksgiving is freed from any particular thing we are thankful for. We aren't celebrating the Pilgrims, but what the Pilgrims celebrated. (The Pilgrims weren't even a feature of the holiday until the late nineteenth century.) Thanksgiving is an American holiday, but there's nothing specifically American about it—we aren't celebrating America, but American ideals. Its openness makes it available to anyone who feels like expressing thanks, and points beyond the crimes that made America possible, and the commercialization, kitsch, and jingoism that have been heaved onto the shoulders of the holiday.

Thanksgiving is the meal we aspire for other meals to resemble. Of course most of us can't (and wouldn't want to) cook all day every day, and of course such food would be fatal if consumed with regularity, and how many of us really want to be surrounded by our extended families every single night? (It can be challenge enough to have to eat with myself.) But it's nice to imagine all meals being so deliberate. Of the thousand-or-so meals we eat every year, Thanksgiving dinner is the one that we try most earnestly to get right. It holds the hope of being a *good* meal, whose ingredients, efforts, setting, and consuming are expressions of the best in us. More than any other meal, it is about good eating and good thinking.

And more than any other food, the Thanksgiving turkey embodies the paradoxes of eating animals: what we do to living turkeys is just about as bad as anything humans have ever done to any animal in the history of the world. Yet what we do with their dead bodies can feel so powerfully good and right. The Thanksgiving turkey is the flesh of competing instincts—of remembering and forgetting.

I'm writing these final words a few days before Thanksgiving. I live in New York now and only rarely—at least according to my grandmother—get back to DC. No one who was young is young anymore. Some of those who transferred kernels to the table are gone. And there are new family members. (*I* am now *we*.) As if the musical chairs I played at birthday parties were preparation for all of this ending and beginning.

This will be the first year we celebrate in my home, the first time I will prepare the food, and the first Thanksgiving meal at which my son will be old enough to eat the food the rest of us eat. If this entire book could be decanted into a single question—not something easy, loaded, or asked in bad faith, but a question that fully captured the problem of eating and not eating animals—it might be this: Should we serve turkey at Thanksgiving?

2.

What Do Turkeys Have to Do with Thanksgiving?

WHAT IS ADDED BY HAVING a turkey on the Thanksgiving table? Maybe it tastes good, but taste isn't the reason it's there—most people don't eat very much turkey throughout the year. (Thanksgiving Day

accounts for 18 percent of annual turkey consumption.) And despite the pleasure we take in eating vast amounts, Thanksgiving is not about being gluttonous—it is about the opposite.

Perhaps the turkey is there because it is fundamental to the ritual—it is how we celebrate Thanksgiving. Why? Because Pilgrims might have eaten it at their first Thanksgiving? It's more likely that they didn't. We know that they didn't have corn, apples, potatoes, or cranberries, and the only two written reports from the legendary Thanksgiving at Plymouth mention venison and wildfowl. Though it's conceivable that they ate wild turkey, we know that the turkey wasn't made part of the ritual until the nineteenth century. And historians have now discovered an even earlier Thanksgiving than the 1621 Plymouth celebration that English-American historians made famous. Half a century before Plymouth, early American settlers celebrated Thanksgiving with the Timucua Indians in what is now Florida—the best evidence suggests that the settlers were Catholic rather than Protestant, and spoke Spanish rather than English. They dined on bean soup.

But let's just make believe that the Pilgrims invented Thanksgiving and were eating turkey. Putting aside the obvious fact that the Pilgrims did many things that we wouldn't want to do now (and that we want to do many things they didn't), the turkeys *we* eat have about as much in common with the turkeys the Pilgrims might have eaten as does the ever-punch-lined tofurkey. At the center of *our* Thanksgiving tables is an animal that never breathed fresh air or saw the sky until it was packed away for slaughter. At the end of *our* forks is an animal that was incapable of reproducing sexually. In *our* bellies is an animal with antibiotics in its belly. The very genetics of our birds are radically different. If the Pilgrims could have seen into the future, what would they have thought of the turkey on our table? Without exaggeration, it's unlikely that they would have recognized it as a turkey.

And what would happen if there were no turkey? Would the tradition be broken, or injured, if instead of a bird we simply had the sweet potato casserole, homemade rolls, green beans with almonds, cranberry concoctions, yams, buttery mashed potatoes, pumpkin and pecan pies? Maybe we could add some Timucuan bean soup. It's not so hard to imagine it. See your loved ones around the table. Hear the sounds, smell the smells. There is no turkey. Is the holiday undermined? Is Thanksgiving no longer Thanksgiving?

Or would Thanksgiving be enhanced? Would the choice not to eat turkey be a more active way of celebrating how thankful we feel? Try to imagine the conversation that would take place. *This is why our family celebrates this way.* Would such a conversation feel disappointing or inspiring? Would fewer or more values be transmitted? Would the joy be lessened by the hunger to eat that particular animal? Imagine your family's Thanksgivings after you are gone, when the question is no longer "Why don't we eat this?" but the more obvious one: "Why did they ever?" Can the imagined gaze of future generations shame us, in Kafka's sense of the word, into remembering?

The secrecy that has enabled the factory farm is breaking down. The three years I spent writing this book, for example, saw the first documentation that livestock contribute more to global warming than anything else; saw the first major research institution (the Pew Commission) recommend the total phaseout of multiple dominant intensive-confinement practices; saw the first state (Colorado) illegalize common factory farm practices (gestation and veal crates) as a result of negotiations with industry (rather than campaigns against industry); saw the first supermarket chain of any kind (Whole Foods) commit to a systematic and extensive program of animal welfare labeling; and saw the first major national newspaper (the *New York Times*) editorialize against factory farming as a whole, arguing

251

that "animal husbandry has been turned into animal abuse," and "manure...has been turned into toxic waste."

When Celia Steele raised that first flock of confined chicks, she could not have foreseen the effects of her actions. When Charles Vantress crossed a red-feathered Cornish and a New Hampshire to produce the 1946 "Chicken of Tomorrow," the ancestor of today's factory broilers, he could not have comprehended what he was contributing to.

We can't plead ignorance, only indifference. Those alive today are the generations that came to know better. We have the burden and the opportunity of living in the moment when the critique of factory farming broke into the popular consciousness. We are the ones of whom it will be fairly asked, *What did you do when you learned the truth about eating animals?*

3.

The Truth About Eating Animals

SINCE 2000 — *AFTER* TEMPLE GRANDIN reported improvement in slaughterhouse conditions—workers have been documented using poles like baseball bats to hit baby turkeys, stomping on chickens to watch them "pop," beating lame pigs with metal pipes, and knowingly dismembering fully conscious cattle. One needn't rely on undercover videos by animal rights organizations to know of these atrocities—although they are plentiful and sufficient. I could have filled several books—an encyclopedia of cruelty—with worker testimonials.

Gail Eisnitz comes close to creating such an encyclopedia in her

book *Slaughterhouse*. Researched over a ten-year period, it is filled with interviews with workers who, combined, represent more than two million hours of slaughterhouse experience; no work of investigative journalism on the topic is as comprehensive.

> One time the knocking gun was broke all day, they were taking a knife and cutting the back of the cow's neck open while he's still standing up. They would just fall down and be ashaking. And they stab cows in the butt to make 'em move. Break their tails. They beat them so bad....And the cow be crying with its tongue stuck out.

> This is hard to talk about. You're under all this stress, all this pressure. And it really sounds mean, but I've taken [electric] prods and stuck them in their eyes. And held them there.

> Down in the blood pit they say that the smell of blood makes you aggressive. And it does. You get an attitude that if that hog kicks at me, I'm going to get even. You're already going to kill the hog, but that's not enough. It has to suffer....You go in hard, push hard, blow the windpipe, make it drown in its own blood. Split its nose. A live hog would be running around the pit. It would just be looking up at me and I'd be sticking, and I would just take my knife and—eerk—cut its eye out while it was just sitting there. And this hog would just scream. One time I took my knife—it's sharp enough—and I sliced off the end of a hog's nose, just like a piece of bologna. The hog went crazy for a few seconds. Then it just sat there looking kind of stupid. So I took a handful of salt brine and ground it into his nose. Now that hog really went nuts, pushing its nose all over the place. I still had a bunch of salt left on my hand—I was wearing a rubber glove—and I stuck the salt right up the hog's ass. The poor hog didn't know whether to shit or go blind....I wasn't

the only guy doing this kind of stuff. One guy I work with actually chases hogs into the scalding tank. And everybody—hog
drivers, shacklers, utility men—uses lead pipes on hogs. Everybody knows it, all of it.

These statements are disturbingly representative of what Eisnitz
discovered in interviews. The events described are not sanctioned
by industry, but they should not be regarded as uncommon.

Undercover investigations have consistently revealed that farmworkers, laboring under what Human Rights Watch describes as
"systematic human rights violations," have often let their frustrations loose on farmed animals or simply succumbed to the demands
of supervisors to keep slaughter lines moving at all costs and without second thoughts. Some workers clearly are sadistic in the literal
sense of that term. But I never met such a person. The several dozen
workers I met were good people, smart and honest people doing
their best in an impossible situation. The responsibility lies with the
mentality of the meat industry that treats both animals and "human
capital" like machines. One worker put it this way:

> The worst thing, worse than the physical danger, is the emotional
> toll. If you work in the stick pit for any period of time, you develop
> an attitude that lets you kill things but doesn't let you care. You
> may look a hog in the eye that's walking around down in the
> blood pit with you and think, God, that really isn't a bad-looking
> animal. You may want to pet it. Pigs down on the kill floor have
> come up and nuzzled me like a puppy. Two minutes later I had
> to kill them—beat them to death with a pipe....When I worked
> upstairs taking hogs' guts out, I could cop an attitude that I was
> working on a production line, helping to feed people. But down
> in the stick pit I wasn't feeding people. I was killing things.

Just how common do such savageries have to be for a decent person to be unable to overlook them? If you knew that one in one thousand food animals suffered actions like those described above, would you continue to eat animals? One in one hundred? One in ten? Toward the end of *The Omnivore's Dilemma*, Michael Pollan writes, "I have to say there is a part of me that envies the moral clarity of the vegetarian.... Yet part of me pities him, too. Dreams of innocence are just that; they usually depend on a denial of reality that can be its own form of hubris." He's right that emotional responses can lead us to an arrogant disconnect. But is the person who makes an effort to act on the dream of innocence really the one to be pitied? And who, in this case, is denying reality?

When Temple Grandin first began to quantify the scale of abuse in slaughterhouses, she reported witnessing "deliberate acts of cruelty occurring on a regular basis" at 32 percent of the plants she surveyed during announced visits in the United States. It's such a shocking statistic I had to read it three times. *Deliberate* acts, occurring on a *regular* basis, witnessed by an *auditor*—witnessed during *announced* audits that gave the slaughterhouse time to clean up the worst problems. What about cruelties that weren't witnessed? And what about accidents, which must have been far more common?

Grandin has emphasized that conditions have improved as more meat retailers demand slaughter audits from their suppliers, but how much? Reviewing the most recent audit of chicken slaughter conducted by the National Chicken Council, Grandin found that 26 percent of slaughterhouses had abuses so severe they *should* have failed. (The industry itself, disturbingly, found the audit results perfectly acceptable and gave all plants a pass even when live birds were thrown, tossed in the trash, and found scalded alive.) According to Grandin's most recent survey of beef plants, fully 25 percent

of the slaughterhouses had abuses so severe that they automatically failed her audit ("hanging a sensible animal on the rail" is given as a paradigmatic example of the kind of abuse that dictates an automatic failure). In recent surveys, Grandin witnessed a worker dismembering a fully conscious cow, cows waking up on the bleed rail, and workers "poking cows in the anus area with an electric prod." What went on when she was not looking? And what about the vast majority of plants that don't open their doors to audits in the first place?

Farmers have lost—have had taken from them—a direct, human relationship with their work. Increasingly, they don't own the animals, can't determine their methods, aren't allowed to apply their wisdom, and have no alternative to high-speed industrial slaughter. The factory model has estranged them not only from how they labor (hack, chop, saw, stick, lop, cut), but what they produce (disgusting, unhealthy food) and how the product is sold (anonymously and cheaply). Human beings cannot be human (much less humane) under the conditions of a factory farm or slaughterhouse. It's the most perfect workplace alienation in the world right now. Unless you consider what the animals experience.

4.

The American Table

WE SHOULDN'T KID OURSELVES ABOUT the number of ethical eating options available to most of us. There isn't enough nonfactory chicken produced in America to feed the population of Staten Island and not enough nonfactory pork to serve New York City, let alone the country. Ethical meat is a promissory note, not a reality. Any

ethical-meat advocate who is serious is going to be eating a lot of vegetarian fare.

A good number of people seem to be tempted to continue supporting factory farms while also buying meat outside that system when it is available. That's nice. But if it is as far as our moral imaginations can stretch, then it's hard to be optimistic about the future. Any plan that involves funneling money to the factory farm won't end factory farming. How effective would the Montgomery bus boycott have been if the protesters had used the bus when it became inconvenient not to? How effective would a strike be if workers announced they would go back to work as soon as it became difficult to strike? If anyone finds in this book encouragement to buy some meat from alternative sources while buying factory farm meat as well, they have found something that isn't here.

If we are at all serious about ending factory farming, then the absolute least we can do is stop sending checks to the absolute worst abusers. For some, the decision to eschew factory-farmed products will be easy. For others, the decision will be a hard one. To those for whom it sounds like a hard decision (I would have counted myself in this group), the ultimate question is whether it is worth the inconvenience. We *know*, at least, that this decision will help prevent deforestation, curb global warming, reduce pollution, save oil reserves, lessen the burden on rural America, decrease human rights abuses, improve public health, and help eliminate the most systematic animal abuse in world history. What we don't know, though, may be just as important. How would making such a decision change *us*?

Setting aside the direct material changes initiated by opting out of the factory farm system, the decision to eat with such deliberateness would itself be a force with enormous potential. What kind of world would we create if three times a day we activated our

compassion and reason as we sat down to eat, if we had the moral imagination and the pragmatic will to change our most fundamental act of consumption? Tolstoy famously argued that the existence of slaughterhouses and battlefields is linked. Okay, we don't fight wars because we eat meat, and some wars should be fought—which is not to mention that Hitler was a vegetarian. But compassion is a muscle that gets stronger with use, and the regular exercise of choosing kindness over cruelty would change us.

It might sound naive to suggest that whether you order a chicken patty or a veggie burger is a profoundly important decision. Then again, it certainly would have sounded fantastic if in the 1950s you were told that where you sat in a restaurant or on a bus could begin to uproot racism. It would have sounded equally fantastic if you were told in the early 1970s, before César Chávez's workers' rights campaigns, that refusing to eat grapes could begin to free farmworkers from slave-like conditions. It might sound fantastic, but when we bother to look, it's hard to deny that our day-to-day choices shape the world. When America's early settlers decided to throw a tea party in Boston, forces powerful enough to create a nation were released. Deciding what to eat (and what to toss overboard) is the founding act of production and consumption that shapes all others. Choosing leaf or flesh, factory farm or family farm, does not in itself change the world, but teaching ourselves, our children, our local communities, and our nation to choose conscience over ease can. One of the greatest opportunities to live our values—or betray them—lies in the food we put on our plates. And we will live or betray our values not only as individuals, but as nations.

We have grander legacies than the quest for cheap products. Martin Luther King Jr. wrote passionately about the time when "one must take a position that is neither safe, nor politic, nor popular." Sometimes we simply have to make a decision because "one's

conscience tells one that it is right." These famous words of King's, and the efforts of Chávez's United Farm Workers, are also our legacy. We might want to say that these social-justice movements have nothing to do with the situation of the factory farm. Human oppression is not animal abuse. King and Chávez were moved by a concern for suffering humanity, not suffering chickens or global warming. Fair enough. One can certainly quibble with, or even become enraged by, the comparison implicit in invoking them here, but it is worth noting that César Chávez and King's wife, Coretta Scott King, were vegans, as is King's son Dexter. We interpret the Chavez and King legacies—we interpret America's legacy—too narrowly if we assume in advance that they cannot speak against the oppression of the factory farm.

5.

The Global Table

NEXT TIME YOU SIT DOWN for a meal, imagine that there are nine other people sitting with you at the table, and that together you represent all the people on the planet. Organized by nations, two of your tablemates are Chinese, two Indian, and a fifth represents all the other countries in Northeast, South, and Central Asia. A sixth represents the nations of Southeast Asia and Oceana. A seventh represents sub-Saharan Africa, and an eighth represents the remainder of Africa and the Middle East. A ninth represents Europe. The remaining seat, representing the countries of South, Central, and North America, is for you.

If we allocate seats by native language, only Chinese speakers

would get their own representative. All English and Spanish speakers together would have to share a chair.

Organized by religion, three people are Christian, two are Muslim, and three practice Buddhism, traditional Chinese religions, or Hinduism. Another two belong to other religious traditions or identify as nonreligious. (My own Jewish community, which is smaller than the margin of error in the Chinese census, can't even squeeze half of a tuches onto a chair.)

If seated by nourishment, one person is hungry and two are obese. More than half eat a mostly vegetarian diet, but that number is shrinking. The stricter vegetarians and vegans have one seat at the table, but barely. And more than half of the time any one of you reaches for eggs, chicken, or pork, they will have come from a factory farm. If current trends continue for another twenty years, the beef and mutton you reach for also will.

The United States is not even close to getting its own seat when the table is organized by population, but it would have somewhere between two and three seats when people are seated by how much food they consume. No one loves to eat as much as we do, and when we change what we eat, the world changes.

I've restricted myself to mostly discussing how our food choices affect the ecology of our planet and the lives of its animals, but I could have just as easily made the entire book about public health, workers' rights, decaying rural communities, or global poverty—all of which are profoundly affected by factory farming. Factory farming, of course, does not cause all the world's problems, but it is remarkable just how many of them intersect there. And it is equally remarkable, and completely improbable, that the likes of you and me would have real influence over factory farming. But no one can seriously doubt the influence of US consumers on global farm practices.

I realize that I'm coming dangerously close to suggesting that

quaint notion that every person can make a difference. The reality is more complicated, of course. As a "solitary eater," your decisions will, in and of themselves, do nothing to alter the industry. That said, unless you obtain your food in secret and eat it in the closet, you don't eat alone. We eat as sons and daughters, as families, as communities, as generations, as nations, and increasingly as a globe. We can't stop our eating from radiating influence even if we want to.

As anyone who has been a vegetarian for a number of years might tell you, the influence that this simple dietary choice has on what others around you eat can be surprising. The body that represents restaurants in America, the National Restaurant Association, has advised every restaurant in the nation to have at least one vegetarian entrée. Why? It's simple: their own polling data indicates that more than a third of restaurant operators have observed an uptick in demand for vegetarian meals. A leading restaurant industry periodical, *Nation's Restaurant News*, advises restaurants to "add vegetarian or vegan dishes to the mix. Vegetarian dishes, aside from being less expensive...also mitigate the veto vote. Usually, if you have a vegan in your party, that will dictate where the party eats."

Millions upon millions of advertising dollars are spent simply to make sure that we see people drinking milk or eating beef in movies, and millions more are spent to make sure that when I have a soda in my hand, you can tell (probably from some distance) whether it is Coke or Pepsi. The National Restaurant Association doesn't make these recommendations, and multinational corporations don't spend millions on product placement, to make us feel good about the influence we have on others around us. They simply recognize the fact that eating is a social act.

When we lift our forks, we hang our hats somewhere. We set ourselves in one relationship or another to farmed animals, farmworkers, national economies, and global markets. Not making a

decision — eating "like everyone else" — is to make the easiest decision, a decision that is increasingly problematic. Without question, in most places and in most times, to decide one's diet by not deciding — to eat like everyone else — was probably a fine idea. Today, to eat like everyone else is to add another straw to the camel's back. Our straw may not be the backbreaker, but the act will be repeated — every day of our lives, and perhaps every day of the lives of our children and our children's children....

The seating arrangements and servings at the global table we all eat from change. The two Chinese at our table have four times the amount of meat on their plates as they did a few decades ago — and the pile keeps getting higher. Meanwhile, the two people at the table without clean drinking water are eyeballing China. Today, animal products still account for only 16 percent of the Chinese diet, but farmed animals account for more than 50 percent of China's water consumption — and at a time when Chinese water shortages are already cause for global concern. The desperate person at our table, who is struggling to find enough food to eat, might reasonably worry even more at how much of the world's march toward US-style meat eating will make the basic grains he or she relies on for life even less available. More meat means more demand for grains and more hands fighting over them. By 2050, the world's livestock will consume as much food as four billion people. Trends suggest that the one hungry person at our table could easily become two (270,000 more people become hungry each day). This will almost certainly happen as the obese also gain another seat. It's too easy to imagine a near future in which most of the seats at the global table are filled by either obese or malnourished people.

But it doesn't have to be this way. The best reason to think that there could be a better future is the fact that we know just how bad the future could be.

Rationally, factory farming is so obviously wrong, in so many ways. In all of my reading and conversations, I've yet to find a credible defense of it. But food is not rational. Food is culture, habit, and identity. For some, that irrationality leads to a kind of resignation. Food choices are likened to fashion choices or life-style preferences—they do not respond to judgments about how we should live. And I would agree that the messiness of food, the almost infinite meanings it proliferates, does make the question of eating—and eating animals especially—surprisingly fraught. Activists I spoke with were endlessly puzzled and frustrated by the disconnect between clear thinking and people's food choices. I sympathize, but I also wonder if it is precisely the irrationality of food that holds the most promise.

Food is never simply a calculation about which diet uses the least water or causes the least suffering. And it is in this, perhaps, that our greatest hope for actually motivating ourselves to change lies. In part, the factory farm requires us to suppress conscience in favor of craving. But at another level, the ability to reject the factory farm can be exactly what we most desire.

The debacle of the factory farm is not, I've come to feel, just a problem about ignorance—it's not, as activists often say, a problem that arose because "people don't know the facts." Clearly that is one cause. I've filled this book with an awful lot of facts because they are a necessary starting point. And I've presented what we know scientifically about the legacy we are creating with our daily food choices because that also matters a great deal. I'm not suggesting our reason should not guide us in many important ways, but simply that being human, being humane, is more than an exercise of reason. Responding to the factory farm calls for a capacity to care that dwells beyond information, and beyond the oppositions of desire and reason, fact and myth, and even human and animal.

The factory farm will come to an end because of its absurd economics someday. It is radically unsustainable. The earth will eventually shake off factory farming like a dog shakes off fleas; the only question is whether we will get shaken off along with it.

Thinking about eating animals, especially publicly, releases unexpected forces into the world. The questions are charged like few others. From one angle of vision, meat is just another thing we consume, and matters in the same way as the consumption of paper napkins or SUVs—if to a greater degree. Try changing napkins at Thanksgiving, though—even do it bombastically, with a lecture on the immorality of such and such a napkin maker—and you'll have a hard time getting anyone worked up. Raise the question of a vegetarian Thanksgiving, though, and you'll have no problem eliciting strong opinions—*at least* strong opinions. The question of eating animals hits chords that resonate deeply with our sense of self—our memories, desires, and values. Those resonances are potentially controversial, potentially threatening, potentially inspiring, but always filled with meaning. Food matters and animals matter and eating animals matters even more. The question of eating animals is ultimately driven by our intuitions about what it means to reach an ideal we have named, perhaps incorrectly, "being human."

6.

The First Thanksgiving of His Childhood

FOR WHAT, AT THANKSGIVING, AM I giving thanks? As a child, the first kernel I transferred to the table was symbolic of my thankfulness for my health and the health of my family. Strange choice for

a kid. Maybe it was a sentiment made in the shade cast by no family tree, or a response to my grandmother's mantra of "You should be healthy"—which couldn't help but sound like an accusation, as in, "You aren't healthy, but you should be." Whatever the cause, even as a young child, I thought of health as something unreliable. (It wasn't only because of the pay and prestige that so many children and grandchildren of survivors became doctors.) The next kernel represented my happiness. The next my loved ones—the family surrounding me, of course, but also my friends. And those would be my first three kernels today—health, happiness, and loved ones. But it's no longer my own health, happiness, and loved ones that I am giving thanks for. Perhaps it will be different when my son is old enough to participate in the ritual. For now, though, I give my thanks for, through, and on behalf of him.

How can Thanksgiving be a vehicle for expressing that most sincere thankfulness? What rituals and symbols would facilitate an appreciation for health, happiness, and loved ones?

We celebrate together, and that makes sense. And we don't just gather, we eat. This wasn't always so. The federal government first thought to promote Thanksgiving as a day of fasting, since that was how it had been frequently observed for decades. According to Benjamin Franklin, whom I think of as a kind of patron saint of the holiday, it was "a farmer of plain sense" who proposed that feasting "would be more becoming the gratitude." The voice of that farmer, who I suspect was a stand-in for Franklin himself, is now the conviction of a nation.

Producing and eating our own food is, historically, much of what made us Americans and not subjects of European powers. While other colonies required massive imports to survive, early American immigrants, thanks to help from Native Americans, were almost entirely self-sustaining. Food is not so much a symbol of freedom

265

as the first requirement of freedom. We eat foods that are native to America on Thanksgiving to acknowledge that fact. In many ways, Thanksgiving initiates a distinctly American ideal of ethical consumerism. The Thanksgiving meal is America's founding act of conscientious consumption.

But what about the food we feast upon? Does what we consume make sense?

All but a negligible number of the 45 million turkeys that find their way to our Thanksgiving tables were unhealthy, unhappy, and—this is a radical understatement—unloved. If people come to different conclusions about the turkey's place on the Thanksgiving table, at least we can all agree on those three things.

Today's turkeys are natural insectivores fed a grossly unnatural diet, which can include "meat, sawdust, leather tannery by-products," and other things whose mention, while widely documented, would probably push your belief too far. Given their vulnerability to disease, turkeys are perhaps the worst fit of any animal for the factory model. So they are given more antibiotics than any other farmed animals. Which encourages antibiotic resistance. Which makes these indispensable drugs less effective for humans. In a perfectly direct way, the turkeys on our tables are making it harder to cure human illness.

It shouldn't be the consumer's responsibility to figure out what's cruel and what's kind, what's environmentally destructive and what's sustainable. Cruel and destructive food products should be illegal. We don't need the option of buying children's toys made with lead paint, or aerosols with chlorofluorocarbons, or medicines with unlabeled side effects. And we don't need the option of buying factory-farmed animals.

However much we obfuscate or ignore it, we know that the factory farm is inhumane in the deepest sense of the word. And we know that there is something that matters in a deep way about the

lives we create for the living beings most within our power. Our response to the factory farm is ultimately a test of how we respond to the powerless, to the most distant, to the voiceless—it is a test of how we act when no one is forcing us to act one way or another. Consistency is not required, but engagement with the problem is.

Historians tell a story about Abraham Lincoln, that while returning to Washington from Springfield, he forced his entire party to stop to help some small birds he saw in distress. When chided by the others, he responded, quite plainly, "I could not have slept to-night if I had left those poor creatures on the ground and not restored them to their mother." He did not make (though he might have) a case for the moral value of the birds, their worth to themselves or the ecosystem or God. Instead he observed, quite simply, that once those suffering birds came into his view, a moral burden had been assumed. He could not be himself if he walked away. Lincoln was a hugely inconsistent personality, and of course he ate birds far more often than he aided them. But presented with the suffering of a fellow creature, he responded.

Whether I sit at the global table, with my family or with my conscience, the factory farm, for me, doesn't merely appear unreasonable. To accept the factory farm feels inhuman. To accept the factory farm—to feed the food it produces to my family, to support it with my money—would make me less myself, less my grandmother's grandson, less my son's father.

This is what my grandmother meant when she said, "If nothing matters, there's nothing to save."

Acknowledgments

Little, Brown has been the perfect home for this book and for me. I want to thank Michael Pietsch for his early and enduring faith in *Eating Animals*; Geoff Shandler for his wisdom, precision, and humor; Liese Mayer for months of profound and eclectic help; Michelle Aielli, Amanda Tobier, and Heather Fain for their seemingly endless creativity, energy, and openness.

Lori Glazer, Bridget Marmion, Debbie Engel, and Janet Silver were enormously encouraging of *Eating Animals* when it was still only an idea, and I don't know that I would have had the confidence to work on something so outside of my zone of comfort were it not for their early support.

If would be impossible to mention all of those who shared their knowledge and expertise with me, but I owe particular thanks to Diane and Marlene Halverson, Paul Shapiro, Noam Mohr, Miyun Park, Gowri Koneswaran, Bruce Freidrich, Michael Greger, Bernie Rollin, Daniel Pauly, Bill and Nicolette Niman, Frank Reese, the Fantasma family, Jonathan Balcombe, Gene Baur, Patrick Martins, Ralph Meraz, the League of Independent Workers of the San Joaquin Valley, and all of the farmworkers who have asked to remain anonymous.

Danielle Krauss, Matthew Mercier, Tori Okner, and Johanna Bond aided in the research (and collation of research) over the past three years, and were indispensable partners.

Joseph Finnerty's legal eye has provided me with necessary

Acknowledgments

confidence to share my explorations. Betsy Uhrig's eye for errors large and small has made this book finer and more exact—any mistakes are untirely mine own.

Tom Manning's chapter headings help give statistics an immediacy and poignancy that numbers, on their own, could not accomplish. His vision has been a tremendous help.

Ben Goldsmith, of Farm Forward, has aided in more ways than I can recount, and his work on farming advocacy is an inspiration.

As always, Nicole Aragi has been a careful friend, a careful reader, and the very best agent imaginable.

I was accompanied on my journey into factory farming by Aaron Gross. He was the Chewbacca to my Han, my Bullwinkle, my Jiminy Cricket. More than anything, he was an incredibly good conversation partner and scholar, and while this book is the record of a deeply personal quest, I couldn't have done it without him. There is not only a massive amount of sheer statistical information to consider when writing about animal food, but a complex cultural and intellectual history. There are a lot of smart people who have written on this topic before—from ancient philosophers to contemporary scientists. Aaron's assistance helped me engage more voices, broaden the book's horizons, and deepen its individual investigations. He was nothing less than my partner. It's often said that such-and-such wouldn't have been possible without so-and-so. But in the most literal sense, I wouldn't have, and couldn't have, written this book without Aaron. He is a great mind, a great advocate of more sensible and humane farming, and a great friend.

Notes

Storytelling

Page

1   *Americans choose...* Extrapolated on the basis of data provided in François Couplan and James Duke, *The Encyclopedia of Edible Plants of North America* (CT: Keats Publishing, 1998); "Edible Medicinal and Useful Plants for a Healthier World," Plants for a Future, http://www .pfaf.org/leaflets/edible_uses.php (accessed September 10, 2009).

12   *upwards of 99 percent of all meat...* These are my own calculations based on the most current available data. There are vastly more chickens raised for meat than any other kind of farmed animal and virtually all are factory farmed. Here is the percentage of each industry that is factory farmed:

Chickens raised for meat: 99.94% (2007 census inventory and EPA regulations)
Chickens raised for eggs: 96.57% (2007 census inventory and EPA regulations)
Turkeys: 97.43% (2007 census inventory and EPA regulations)
Pigs: 95.41% (2007 census inventory and EPA regulations)
Cows raised for beef: 78.2% (2008 NASS report)
Cows raised for dairy: 60.16% (2007 census inventory and EPA regulations)

All or Nothing or Something Else

Page

19   *modern industrial fishing...* See page 191.

22   *Sixty-three percent of American households...* American Pets Products Manufacturers Association (APPMA), 2007–2008, as quoted in

S. C. Johnson, "Photos: Americans Declare Love for Pets in National Contest," Thomson Reuters, April 15, 2009, http://www.reuters.com/article/pressRelease/idUS127052+15Apr-2009+PRN20090415 (accessed June 5, 2009).

22 *Keeping companion animals*...Keith Vivian Thomas, *Man and the Natural World: A History of the Modern Sensibility* (New York: Pantheon Books, 1983), 119.

$34 billion on their companion animals..."Pets in America," PetsinAmerica.org, 2005, http://www.petsinamerica.org/thefutureofpets.htm (accessed June 5, 2009). Note: The Pets in America project is "presented in conjunction with" the Pets in America exhibit at the McKissick Museum, University of South Carolina.

the spread of pet-keeping...Thomas, *Man and the Natural World*, 119.

25 *electrocute his children*..."My biggest nightmare would be if the kids ever came up to me and said, 'Dad, I'm a vegetarian.' Then I would sit them on the fence and electrocute them." Victoria Kennedy, "Gordon Ramsay's Shocking Recipe for Raising Kids," *Daily Mirror*, April 25, 2007, http://www.mirror.co.uk/celebs/news/2007/04/25/gordon-ramsay-s-shocking-recipe-for-raising-kids-115875-18958425/ (accessed June 9, 2009).

sometimes eat their dogs..."Inquiries revealed that dog meat is a prized food item here," as quoted in "Dog meat, a delicacy in Mizoram," *The Hindu*, December 20, 2004, http://www.hindu.com/2004/12/20/stories/2004122003042000.htm (accessed June 9, 2009).

26 *Fourth-century tombs*..."Wall paintings in a fourth-century Koguryo Kingdom tomb depict dogs being slaughtered along with pigs and sheep." Rolf Potts, "Man Bites Dog," Salon.com, October 28, 1999, http://www.salon.com/wlust/feature/1998/10/28feature.html (accessed June 30, 2009).

the Sino-Korean character...Ibid.

The Romans ate...Calvin W. Schwabe, *Unmentionable Cuisine* (Charlottesville: University of Virginia Press, 1979), 168.

Dakota Indians enjoyed...Hernán Cortés, *Letters from Mexico*, translated by Anthony Pagden (New Haven, CT: Yale University Press, 1986), 103, 398.

not so long ago Hawaiians ate...S. Fallon and M. G. Enig, "Guts and Grease: The Diet of Native Americans," Weston A. Price Foundation,

January 1, 2000, http://www.westonaprice.org/traditional_diets/native
_americans.html (accessed June 23, 2009).

26 *The Mexican hairless dog*... Schwabe, *Unmentionable Cuisine*, 168, 176.
Captain Cook ate dog... Captain James Cook, *Explorations of Captain
James Cook in the Pacific: As Told by Selections of His Own Journals, 1768–
1779*, edited by Grenfell Price (Mineola, NY: Dover Publications,
1971), 291.

dogs are still eaten... "Philippines Dogs: Factsheets," Global Action
Network, 2005, http://www.gan.ca/campaigns/philippines+dogs/fact
sheets.en.html (accessed July 7, 2009); "The Religious History of Eating Dog Meat," dogmeattrade.com, 2007, http://www.dogmeattrade
.com/facts.html (accessed July 7, 2009).

as medicine in China and Korea... Kevin Stafford, *The Welfare of Dogs*
(New York: Springer, 2007), 14.

to enhance libido in Nigeria... Senan Murray, "Dogs' dinners
prove popular in Nigeria," *BBC News*, March 6, 2007, http://news
.bbc.co.uk/1/hi/world/africa/6419041.stm (accessed June 23, 2009).

For centuries, the Chinese... Schwabe, *Unmentionable Cuisine*, 168.

and many European countries... Ibid., 173.

27 *Three to four million dogs and cats*... Humane Society of the United
States, "Pet Overpopulation Estimates," http://www.hsus.org/pets/
issues_affecting_our_pets/pet_overpopulation_and_ownership_sta
tistics/hsus_pet_overpopulation_estimates.html.

About twice as many dogs... "Animal Shelter Euthanasia," American Humane Association, 2009, http://www.americanhumane.org/
about-us/newsroom/fact-sheets/animal-shelter-euthanasia.html
(accessed June 23, 2009).

28 *Stewed Dog*... "Ethnic Recipes: Asian and Pacific Island Recipes: Filipino Recipes: Stewed Dog (Wedding Style)," Recipe Source, http://www
.recipesource.com/ethnic/asia/filipino/00/rec0001.html (accessed June
10, 2009).

29 *more than 31,000 different species*... The impressive Fishbase.org cat-
alogs 31,200 species known under 276,500 common names across the
globe. Fishbase, January 15, 2009, http://www.fishbase.org (accessed
June 10, 2009).

I am among... "Nearly all women respondents (99%) reported that
they frequently talked to their pets (vs. 95% of men) and an astonishing

93% of women think that their pets communicate with them (vs. 87% of men)." Business Wire, "Man's Best Friend Actually Woman's Best Friend; Survey Reveals That Females Have Stronger Affinity for Their Pets Than Their Partners," bnet, March 30, 2005, http://findar ticles.com/p/articles/mi_m0EIN/is_2005_March_30/ai_n13489499/ (accessed June 10, 2009).

30 *respond to sounds from as far away...* "Juvenile fish follow the crackle and fizz from a coral reef to help them find it. The 'frying bacon' sound of snapping shrimps for example can be picked up 20 kilometres away." Staff, "Fish Tune Into the Sounds of the Reef," *New Scientist*, April 16, 2005, http://www.newscientist.com/article/mg18624956.300-fish -tune-into-the-sounds-of-the-reef.html (accessed June 23, 2009).

The massive power... Richard Ellis, *The Empty Ocean* (Washington, DC: Island Press, 2004), 14. Ellis cites Robert Morgan, *World Sea Fisheries* (New York: Pitman, 1955), 106.

"If possible..." J. P. George, *Longline Fishing* (Rome: Food and Agriculture Organization of the United Nations, 1993), 79.

In the old days... Ellis, *The Empty Ocean*, 14, 222.

32 *$140 billion–plus a year industry...* "In addition to the $142 billion in sales, there are millions of dollars' worth of goods and services generated by the industry's economic ripple effect, including jobs in packaging, transportation, manufacturing and retail." American Meat Institute, "The United States Meat Industry at a Glance: Feeding Our Economy," meatAMI.com, 2009, http://www.meatami.com/ht/d/sp/i/47465/pid/47465/#feedingoureconomy (accessed May 29, 2009).

that occupies nearly a third of the land... Food and Agriculture Organization of the United Nations, Livestock, Environment and Development Initiative, "Livestock's Long Shadow: Environmental Issues and Options" Rome, 2006, xxi, ftp://ftp.fao.org/docrep/fao/010/a0701e/a0701e00.pdf (accessed August 11, 2009).

shapes ocean ecosystems... The health of an ocean is not easy to measure, but through a powerful new statistic called the Marine Trophic Index (MTI), scientists now have a way to get a rough snapshot of the state of ocean life. It's not a pretty picture. Imagine every living thing in the ocean is assigned a particular "trophic level" between 1 and 5, a marker of its place in the food chain. Number 1 is assigned to plants, since they form the base of marine food webs. The creatures that eat the

plants, like the tiny animals known as plankton, are assigned a trophic level of 2. The creatures that eat the plankton have a trophic level of 3 and so on. Top-level predators would be assigned to trophic level 5. If we could count all the creatures in the ocean and assign them all a number, we could calculate an average trophic level of life in the oceans—a kind of rough-and-ready snapshot of ocean life *as a whole*. That grand calculation is, in fact, exactly what MTI estimates. A higher MTI indicates longer, more diverse food chains and more vibrant oceans. If the oceans, for example, were filled with nothing but plants, the ocean would have an MTI of 1. If it were filled only with plants and plankton, the MTI would work out to be somewhere between 1 and 2. If the oceans have longer food webs with more diverse creatures, the MTI will become correspondingly higher. There is no right or wrong MTI, but consistent drops in MTI are clearly bad news: bad news for people who eat fish and bad news for the fish themselves. MTI has dropped steadily since the 1950s, when industrial-fishing techniques became the norm. Daniel Pauly and Jay McLean, *In a Perfect Ocean* (Washington, DC: Island Press, 2003), 45–53.

32 ***and may well determine the future...*** The livestock sector is the biggest single contributor to greenhouse gases. Food and Agriculture Organization, "Livestock's Long Shadow," xxi, 112, 267; Pew Charitable Trusts, Johns Hopkins Bloomberg School of Public Health, and Pew Commission on Industrial Animal Production, "Putting Meat on the Table: Industrial Farm Animal Production in America," 2008, http://www.ncifap.org/ (accessed August 11, 2009).

33 ***For every ten tuna...*** R. A. Myers and B. Worm, "Extinction, Survival, or Recovery of Large Predatory Fishes," *Philosophical Transactions of the Royal Society of London Series B—Biological Sciences*, January 29, 2005, 13–20, http://www.pubmedcentral.nih.gov/articlerender.fcgi?artinstid=163 (accessed June 24, 2009).

   Many scientists predict the total collapse... Boris Worm and others, "Impacts of Biodiversity Loss on Ocean Ecosystem Services," *Science*, November 3, 2006, http://www.sciencemag.org (accessed May 26, 2009).

   research scientists at the Fisheries Centre... D. Pauly and others, "Global Trends in World Fisheries: Impacts on Marine Ecosystems and Food Security," Royal Society, January 29, 2005, http://www.pubmedcentral.nih.gov/articlerender.fcgi?artid=1636108 (accessed June 23, 2009).

34 *roughly 450 billion land animals*... According to FAO statistics (accessible at http://faostat.fao.org/site/569/DesktopDefault.aspx?PageID =569#ancor), out of roughly sixty billion animals farmed each year, more than fifty billion are chickens raised for flesh and are almost certainly factory-farmed. This provides a rough estimate for the number of animals factory-farmed globally.

Ninety-nine percent of all... See note for page 12.

transmit information to the control rooms... Stephen Sloan, *Ocean Bankruptcy* (Guilford; CT: Lyons Press, 2003), 75.

35 *the 1.4 billion hooks*... R. L. Lewison and others, "Quantifying the effects of fisheries on threatened species: the impact of pelagic longlines on loggerhead and leatherback sea turtles," *Ecology Letters* 7, no. 3 (2004): 225.

on each of which... "This secondary line is hooked and baited with squid, fish, or in cases we have discovered, with fresh dolphin meat," as quoted in "What is a Longline?" Sea Shepherd Conservation Society, 2009, http://www.seashepherd.org/sharks/longlining.html (accessed June 10, 2009).

the 1,200 nets... Ellis, *The Empty Ocean*, 19.

the ability of a single vessel... J. A. Koslow and T. Koslow, *The Silent Deep: The Discovery, Ecology and Conservation of the Deep Sea* (Chicago: University of Chicago Press, 2007), 131, 198.

Technologies of war... Ibid., 199.

in the last decade of... Sloan, *Ocean Bankruptcy*, 75.

36 **SHAME**... The discussion of Benjamin, Derrida, and Kafka in this section is indebted to conversations with religion professor and critical theorist Aaron Gross.

Suddenly he began... Max Brod, *Franz Kafka* (New York: Schocken, 1947), 74.

38 *an unequal struggle*... Jacques Derrida, *The Animal That Therefore I Am*, edited by Marie-Louise Mallet and translated by David Wills (New York: Fordham University Press, 2008), 28, 29.

Sea horses come not only in... Ellis, *The Empty Ocean*, 78.

We desire to look... Ibid., 77–79.

39 *Sea horses, more than most animals*... I gathered these several facts about sea horses from "Sea Horse," Encyclopaedia Britannica Online, 2009, http://www.britannica.com/EBchecked/topic/664988/sea-horse

(accessed July 7, 2009); Environmental Justice Foundation Charitable Trust, *Squandering the Seas: How Shrimp Trawling Is Threatening Ecological Integrity and Food Security Around the World* (London: Environmental Justice Foundation, 2003), 18; Richard Dutton, "Bonaire's Famous Seahorse Is the Holy Grail of Any Scuba Diving Trip," http://bonaireunderwater.info/imgpages/bonaire_seahorse.html (accessed July 7, 2009).

40 ***twenty of the roughly thirty-five***...As listed in Environmental Justice Foundation, *Squandering the Seas*, 18.

sea horses are one..."Report for Biennial Period, 2004–2005," part I, vol. 2, International Commission for the Conservation of Atlantic Tunas, Madrid, 2005, http://www.iccat.int/en/pubs_biennial.htm (accessed June 12, 2009).

shrimp trawling devastates...Environmental Justice Foundation, *Squandering the Seas*, 19.

Words / Meaning

Page

43 ***Animal agriculture makes***...See page 58.

45 ***Anthropologist Tim Ingold***...Timothy Ingold, *What Is an Animal?* (Boston: Unwin Hyman, 1988), 1. A striking example of the different ways in which the animal world is conceptualized in other cultures is found in the remarkable ethnographic work of Eduardo Batalha Viveiros de Castro on the Araweté people of South America: "The difference between men and animals is not clear.... I cannot find a simple manner of characterizing the place of 'Nature' in Araweté cosmology[;]...there isno taxon for 'animal'; there are few generic terms, such as 'fish,' 'bird,' and a number of metonyms for other species according to their habitat, food habits, function for man (*do pi*, 'for eating,' *temina ni*, 'potential pets'), and relation to shamanism and food taboos. The distinctions with the domain of animals are essentially the same that apply for other categories of beings...[like] humans...and spirits." Eduardo Viveiros de Castro, *From the Enemy's Point of View: Humanity and Divinity in an Amazonian Society*, translated by Catherine V. Howard (Chicago: University of Chicago Press, 1992), 71.

46 **To ask "What is an animal?"**... Recent interdisciplinary research in the humanities has documented a dizzying variety of ways in which our interactions with animals reflect or shape how we understand ourselves. Studies of children's dog stories and public support for animal welfare are given as examples among others in *Animal Others and the Human Imagination*, edited by Aaron Gross and Anne Vallely (New York: Columbia University Press, forthcoming).

Anthropodenial... The word *anthropodenial* was coined by Frans de Waal. Frans de Waal, *Anthropodenial* (New York: Basic Books, 2001), 63, 69.

Anthropomorphism is a risk... E. Cenami Spada, "Amorphism, mechanomorphism, and anthropomorphism," in *Anthropomorphism, Anecdotes, and Animals*, edited by R. W. Mitchell and others (Albany, NY: SUNY Press, 1997), 37–49.

47 **sixty-seven square inches**... The United Egg Producers recommends that hens be given at least 67 square inches per hen. HSUS reports that this minimum is what is typically used. "United Egg Producers Animal Husbandry Guidelines for U.S. Egg Laying Flocks," United Egg Producers Certified (Alpharetta, GA: United Egg Producers, 2008), http://www.uepcertified.com/program/guidelines/ (accessed June 24, 2009); "Cage-Free Egg Production vs. Battery-Cage Egg Production," Humane Society of the United States, 2009, http://www.hsus.org/farm/camp/nbe/compare.html (accessed June 23, 2009).

Such cages are stacked... Roger Pulvers, "A Nation of Animal Lovers—As Pets or When They're on a Plate," *Japanese Times*, August 20, 2006, http://search.japantimes.co.jp/cgi-bin/fl20060820rp.html (accessed June 24, 2009).

48 **close to a single square foot**... The range is from .7 to a full square foot. This is true of American and European broilers; in India (and other places) they are often kept in cages. Ralph A. Ernst, "Chicken Meat Production in California," University of California Cooperative Extension, June 1995, http://animalscience.ucdavis.edu/avian/pfs20.htm (accessed July 7, 2009); D. L. Cunningham, "Broiler Production Systems in Georgia: Costs and Returns Analysis," thepoultrysite.com, July 2004, http://www.thepoultrysite.com/articles/234/broiler-production-systems-in-georgia (accessed July 7, 2009).

48 *egg output has more than doubled*...American Egg Board, "History of Egg Production," 2007, http://www.incredibleegg.org/egg_facts_his tory2.html (accessed August 10, 2009).

engineered to grow...Frank Gordy, "Broilers," in *American Poultry History, 1823–1973*, edited by Oscar August Hanke and others (Madison, WI: American Poultry Historical Society, 1974), 392; Mike Donohue, "How Breeding Companies Help Improve Broiler Industry Efficiency," thepoultrysite.com, February 2009, http://www.thepoultrysite.com/articles/1317/how-breeding-companies-help-improve-broiler-industry-efficiency (accessed August 10, 2009).

life expectancy of fifteen to twenty years...Frank Reese, Good Shepherd Poultry Ranch, personal correspondence, July 2009.

growth rate has increased roughly 400 percent..."from 25 g per day to 100 g per day." T. G. Knowles and others, "Leg Disorders in Broiler Chickens: Prevalence, Risk Factors and Prevention," PLoS ONE, 2008, http://www.plosone.org/article/info:doi/10.1371/journal.pone.0001545 (accessed June 12, 2009).

more than 250 million chicks...M. C. Appleby and others, *Poultry Behaviour and Welfare* (Wallingford, UK: CABI Publishing, 2004), 184.

Most male layers are destroyed...Ibid.

Some are tossed...Gene Baur, *Farm Sanctuary* (New York: Touchstone, 2008), 150.

49 *fully conscious through macerators*...G. C. Perry, ed., *Welfare of the Laying Hen*, vol. 27, Poultry Science Symposium Series (Wallingford, UK: CABI Publishing, 2004), 386.

The average shrimp-trawling...Environmental Justice Foundation Charitable Trust, *Squandering the Seas: How Shrimp Trawling Is Threatening Ecological Integrity and Food Security Around the World* (London: Environmental Justice Foundation, 2003), 12.

Shrimp account for only...Ibid.

trawled shrimp from Indonesia...Ibid.

145 species regularly killed..."Report for Biennial Period, 2004–2005," part I, vol. 2, International Commission for the Conservation of Atlantic Tunas, Madrid, 2005, 206, http://www.iccat.int/en/pubs_biennial.htm (accessed June 12, 2009).

manta ray, devil ray...International Commission for the Conservation

of Atlantic Tunas, "Bycatch Species," March 2007, http://www
.iccat.int/en/bycatchspp.htm (accessed August 10, 2009).

51 *Under its CFE*...Nevada CFE, "Chapter 574—Cruelty to Animals:
Prevention and Punishment," NRS 574.200, 2007, http://leg.state
.nv.us/NRS/NRS-574.html#NRS574Sec200 (accessed June 26, 2009).

Certain states exempt...D. J. Wolfson and M. Sullivan, "Foxes in the
Henhouse," in *Animal Rights: Current Debates and New Directions*, edited
by C. R. Sunstein and M. Nussbaum (Oxford: Oxford University Press,
2005), 213.

56 *estimates put the number of downed cows*...D. Hansen and V. Bridges,
"A survey description of down-cows and cows with progressive or
non-progressive neurological signs compatible with a TSE from veterinary client herd in 38 states," *Bovine Practitioner* 33, no. 2 (1999): 179–187.

58 *A University of Chicago study*..."It is demonstrated that the greenhouse gas emissions of various diets vary by as much as the difference
between owning an average sedan versus a sport-utility vehicle under
typical driving conditions." G. Eshel and P. A. Martin, "Diet, Energy,
and Global Warming," *Earth Interactions* 10, no. 9 (2006): 1–17.

More recent and authoritative studies...Food and Agriculture Organization of the United Nations, Livestock, Environment and Development Initiative, "Livestock's Long Shadow: Environmental Issues and
Options," Rome, 2006, xxi, 112, 267, ftp://ftp.fao.org/docrep/fao/010/
a0701e/a0701e00.pdf (accessed August 11, 2009).

and the Pew Commission...Pew Charitable Trusts, Johns Hopkins
Bloomberg School of Public Health, and Pew Commission on Industrial
Animal Production, "Putting Meat on the Table: Industrial Farm Ani-
mal Production in America," 2008, 27, http://www.ncifap.org/ (accessed
August 11, 2009).

18 percent of greenhouse gas...This number is actually known to be
low, as the UN did not include the greenhouse gases associated with
live transport. Food and Agriculture Organization, "Livestock's Long
Shadow," xxi, 112.

around 40 percent more...Scientists at the Intergovernmental Panel
on Climate Change report that transport constitutes 13.1 percent of
greenhouse gas emissions; 18 percent (see above) is 38 percent more
than 13.1 percent. H. H. Rogner, D. Zhou, R. Bradley. P. Crabbé,
O. Edenhofer, B. Hare (Australia), L. Kuijpers, and M. Yamaguchi,

introduction to *Climate Change 2007: Mitigation. Contribution of Working Group III to the Fourth Assessment Report of the Intergovernmental Panel on Climate Change*, edited by B. Metz, O. R. Davidson, P. R. Bosch, R. Dave, and L. A. Meyer (New York: Cambridge University Press).

58 ***Animal agriculture is responsible***...Food and Agriculture Organization, "Livestock's Long Shadow," xxi.

omnivores contribute seven times...AFP, "Going veggie can slash your carbon footprint: Study," August 26, 2008, http://afp.google.com/article/ALeqM5gb6B3_ItBZn0mNPPt8J5nxjgtllw.

"is one of the top two or three..." Food and Agriculture Organization, "Livestock's Long Shadow," 391.

59 ***In other words, if one cares***...Food and Agriculture Organization, "Livestock's Long Shadow"; FAO Fisheries and Aquaculture Department, "The State of World Fisheries and Aquaculture 2008," Food and Agriculture Organization of the United Nations, Rome, 2009, http://www.fao.org/fishery/sofia/en (accessed August 11, 2009).

Intergovernmental Panel on Climate Change...P. Smith, D. Martino, Z. Cai, D. Gwary, H. Janzen, P. Kumar, B. McCarl, S. Ogle, F. O'Mara, C. Rice, B. Scholes, and O. Sirotenko, "Agriculture," in *Climate Change 2007: Mitigation.*

Center for Science in the Public Interest...Michael Jacobsen et al., "Six Arguments for a Greener Diet," Center for Science in the Public Interest, 2006, http://www.cspinet.org/EatingGreen/ (accessed August 12, 2009).

Pew Commission...Pew Charitable Trusts et al., "Putting Meat on the Table."

Union of Concerned Scientists...Doug Gurian-Sherman, "CAFOs Uncovered: The Untold Costs of Confined Animal Feeding Operations," Union of Concerned Scientists, 2008, http://www.ucsusa.org/food_and_agriculture/science_and_impacts/impacts_industrial_agriculture/cafos-uncovered.html; Margaret Mellon, "Hogging It: Estimates of Antimicrobial Abuse in Livestock," Union of Concerned Scientists, January 2001, http://www.ucsusa.org/publications/#Food_and_Environment.

Worldwatch Institute... Sara J. Scherr and Sajal Sthapit, "Mitigating Climate Change Through Food and Land Use," Worldwatch Institute, 2009, https://www.worldwatch.org/node/6128.; Christopher Flavin

et al., "State of the World 2008," Worldwatch Institute, 2008, https://www.worldwatch.org/node/5561#toc.

61 *"access to the outdoors"*... "Meat and Poultry Labeling Terms," United States Department of Agriculture, Food Safety and Inspection Service, August 24, 2006, http://www.fsis.usda.gov/FactSheets/Meat_&_Poultry_Labeling_Terms/index.asp (accessed July 3, 2009).

The USDA doesn't even have a definition... *Federal Register* 73, no. 198 (October 10, 2008): 60228–60230, Federal Register Online via GPO Access (wais.access.gpo.gov), http://www.fsis.usda.gov/OPPDE/rdad/FRPubs/2008-0026.htm (accessed July 6, 2009).

laying hens are debeaked... For a lucid review of what particular USDA labels mean, see HSUS, "A Brief Guide to Egg Carton Labels and Their Relevance to Animal Welfare," March 2009, http://www.hsus.org/farm/resources/pubs/animal_welfare_claims_on_egg_cartons.html (accessed August 11, 2009).

According to the USDA... "For consumers, 'fresh' means whole poultry and cuts have never been below 26°F." United States Department of Agriculture, Food Safety and Inspection Service, "The Poultry Label Says Fresh," www.fsis.usda.gov/PDF/Poultry_Label_Says_Fresh.pdf (accessed June 25, 2009).

64 *Pigeons follow highways*... The study of pigeons was conducted at Oxford University and is discussed in Jonathan Balcombe's *Pleasurable Kingdom: Animals and the Nature of Feeling Good* (New York: Macmillan, 2007), 53.

Gilbert White... Lyall Watson, *The Whole Hog* (Washington, DC: Smithsonian Books, 2004), 177.

Scientists have documented... Pigs communicate using jaw chomping, teeth clacking, grunts, roars, squeals, snarls, and snorts. According to the highly regarded ethologist Marc Bekoff, pigs indicate their intention to play with one another by using body language, "such play markers as bouncy running and head twisting." Marc Bekoff, *The Emotional Lives of Animals* (Novato, CA: New World Library, 2008), 97; Humane Society of the United States, "About Pigs," http://www.hsus.org/farm/resources/animals/pigs/pigs.html?print=t (accessed June 23, 2009).

pigs will come when called... We also know that mother pigs will grunt to piglets when it's time to suckle and that the piglets themselves have a special call to summon their mothers when separated. Peter-Christian

Schön and others, "Common Features and Individual Differences in Nurse Grunting of Domestic Pigs (*Sus scrofa*): A Multi-Parametric Analysis," *Behaviour* 136, no. 1 (January 1999): 49–66, http://www.hsus.org/farm/resources/animals/pigs/pigs.html?print=t (accessed August 12, 2009).

64 **play with toys**... Temple Grandin has demonstrated not only that pigs enjoy toys, but that they have "definite toy preferences." Temple Grandin, "Environmental Enrichment for Confinement Pigs," Livestock Conservation Institute, 1988, http://www.grandin.com/references/LCIhand.html (accessed June 26, 2009). For more discussion of play in pigs and other animals, see Bekoff, *The Emotional Lives of Animals*, 97.

coming to the aid... Wild pigs also have been documented rushing to the aid of unrelated adult pigs crying in distress. Bekoff, *The Emotional Lives of Animals*, 28.

65 **They not only**... Lisa Duchene, "Are Pigs Smarter Than Dogs?" *Research Penn State*, May 8, 2006, http://www.rps.psu.edu/probing/pigs.html (accessed June 23, 2009).

undo the latches... Ibid.

only 70 peer-reviewed... K. N. Laland and others, "Learning in Fishes: From three-second memory to culture," *Fish and Fisheries* 4, no. 3 (2003): 199–202.

today it tops 640... This is a rough estimate based on a quick search of the ISI Web of Knowledge and review of more than 350 abstracts.

Fish build complex nests... "Many fish build nests for rearing young just as birds do; others have permanent burrows or preferred hiding spots. But how do you cope if you are constantly on the move, looking for food? Rock-moving wrasse build new homes every night by collecting bits of rubble off the seafloor. Once construction is complete the wrasse settles down to sleep and abandons the dwelling the next morning." Culum Brown, "Not Just a Pretty Face," *New Scientist*, no. 2451 (2004): 42.

form monogamous relationships... For example, "most goby species form monogamous breeding pairs." M. Wall and J. Herler, "Postsettlement movement patterns and homing in a coral-associated fish," *Behavioral Ecology*, 2009, http://beheco.oxfordjournals.org/cgi/content/full/arn118/DC1 (accessed June 25, 2009).

hunt cooperatively with other species... Laland and others, "Learning in Fishes," 199–202. Laland and others cite M. Milinski and others,

"Tit for Tat: Sticklebacks, *Gasterosteus aculeatus*, 'trusting' a cooperative partner," *Behavioural Ecology* 1 (1990): 7–11 ; M. Milinski and others, "Do sticklebacks cooperate repeatedly in reciprocal pairs?" *Behavioral Ecology and Sociobiology* 27 (1990): 17–21; L. A. Dugatkin, *Cooperation Among Animals* (New York: Oxford University Press, 1997).

65 **use tools**... "The use of an anvil to crush shellfish as described above is clearly a case of substrate use. It does not hold up, however, to the restrictive definition of tool use—that an animal must directly handle an agent to achieve a goal (Beck 1980). An example that more closely fits the strict definition is the use of leaves as tablets for carrying eggs to safety when disturbed, as has been documented in South American cichlids (Timms and Keenleyside 1975; Keenleyside and Prince 1976). The catfish *Hoplosternum thoracatum* also has its eggs glued to leaves and with this 'baby carriage' may bring them into its foam nest if the leaves get detached (Armbrust 1958)." R. Bshary and others, "Fish Cognition: A primate eye's view," *Animal Cognition* 5, no. 1 (2001): 1–13.

They recognize one another... P. K. McGregor, "Signaling in territorial systems—a context for individual identification, ranging and eavesdropping," *Philosophical Transactions of the Royal Society of London Series B—Biological Sciences* 340 (1993): 237–244; Bshary and others, "Fish cognition," 1–13; S. W. Griffiths, "Learned recognition of conspecifics by fishes," *Fish and Fisheries* 4 (2003): 256–268, as cited in Laland and others, "Learning in Fishes," 199–202.

make decisions individually... "Fish are just as intelligent as rats.... Dr Mike Webster of St Andrews University has discovered fish show a high level of intelligence when they are in danger.... Dr Webster carried out a series of experiments to show how minnows escape being eaten by predators by using techniques of shared learning. He discovered that a solitary fish separated from the shoal by a clear plastic divider, will make its own decisions when there is no threat. But when a predator was placed in the shared pool, the single fish took its cue on how to act by watching the other fish. The biologist said: 'These experiments provide clear evidence that minnows increasingly rely on social learning as the basis for their foraging decisions as the perceived threat of a predator increases.' " Sarah Knapton, "Scientist finds fish are as clever as mammals," telegraph.co.uk, August 29, 2008, http://www

.telegraph.co.uk/earth/main.jhtml?view=DETAILS&grid=&xml=/
earth/2008/08/29/scifish129.xml (accessed June 23, 2009).

65 ***monitor social prestige***...Laland and others, "Learning in Fishes,"
199–202. Laland and others cite McGregor, "Signaling in territorial systems," 237–244 ; Bshary and others, "Fish Cognition," 1–13;
Griffiths, "Learned recognition of conspecifics by fishes," 256–268.

"Machiavellian strategies..." Laland and others, "Learning in Fishes,"
199–202. Laland and others cite Bshary and others, "Fish Cognition,"
1–13; R. Bshary and M. Wurth, "Cleaner fish *Labroides dimidiatus*
manipulate client reef fish by providing tactile stimulation," *Proceedings of the Royal Society of London Series B — Biological Sciences* 268 (2001):
1495–1501.

significant long-term memories... "In 2001, I published an article in
Animal Cognition (vol. 4, p. 109) discussing long-term memory in the
Australian freshwater rainbow fish. The fish were trained to locate a
hole in a net as it approached down the length of a fish tank. After five
attempts, they could reliably find the hole in the net. About 11 months
later they were re-tested and their ability to escape was undiminished,
even though they had not seen the apparatus during the intervening
period. Not bad for a fish that only lives two to three years in the wild."
Brown, "Not Just a Pretty Face," 42.

are skilled in passing knowledge...Laland and others, "Learning in
Fishes," 199–202.

They even have...Ibid.

lateralization of avian brains...Lesley J. Rogers, *Minds of Their Own*
(Boulder, CO: Westview Press, 1997), 124–129; Balcombe, *Pleasurable
Kingdom*, 31, 33–34.

66 ***Scientists now agree***...Rogers, *Minds of Their Own*, 124–129.

Rogers argues that our present knowledge...Lesley J. Rogers, *The
Development of Brain and Behavior in the Chicken* (Oxford: CABI, 1996),
217. A recent review of the scientific literature supports her. The
distinguished ethologist Peter Marler recently reviewed the existing research on social cognition in nonhuman primates and birds;
his review confirmed Rogers's observations and led him to argue
that the scientific literature reveals more similarities than differences between the minds of birds and primates. Balcombe, *Pleasurable
Kingdom*, 52.

66 *She argues they have sophisticated...* Rogers, *Minds of Their Own*, 74.

Like fish, chickens can... In some studies, injured birds learned to identify select feed with painkillers (and preferred it). In other studies, chickens learned to avoid blue-colored feed that contained chemicals that would make them sick. Even after the chemical had been removed, mother hens still taught their chicks to avoid blue feed. Since neither pain relief nor sickness would beset the birds instantly, determining that the feed was the key variable required the birds to do some impressive analysis. Bekoff, *The Emotional Lives of Animals*, 46.

They also deceive one another... Often roosters will find food and shout out a food call to a hen they are courting. In most cases, the hen comes running. Some roosters, however, some of the time, issue a food call without food and the hen will still come running (if the hen is far enough away not to see). Rogers, *Minds of Their Own*, 38; Balcombe, *Pleasurable Kingdom*, 51.

can delay satisfaction... For example, when chickens got a small food reward from pecking on a lever but received a larger reward if they waited twenty-two seconds, they learned to wait 90 percent of the time. (The other 10 percent, it seems, were on the impatient side or maybe they just preferred the small, instant reward.) Balcombe, *Pleasurable Kingdom*, 223.

bird brains process information... Ibid., 52.

67 *KFC buys nearly a billion...* "KFC buys a reported 850 million chickens per year (a number the company will not confirm)." Quoted in Daniel Zwerdling, "A View to a Kill," *Gourmet*, June 2007, http://www.gourmet.com/magazine/2000s/2007/06/aviewtoakill (accessed June 26, 2009).

KFC insists... "KFC's executives aren't budging. They insist they're already 'committed to the well-being and humane treatment of chickens.'" Quoted ibid.

workers were documented tearing... "KFC responds to chicken supplier scandal," foodproductiondaily.com, July 23, 2004, http://www.foodproductiondaily.com/Supply-Chain/KFC-responds-to-chicken-supplier-scandal (accessed June 29, 2009); "Undercover Investigations," Kentucky Fried Cruelty, http://www.kentuckyfriedcruelty.com/u-pilgrimspride.asp (accessed July 5, 2009).

On KFC's website... "Animal Welfare Program," Kentucky Fried Chicken (KFC), http://www.kfc.com/about/animalwelfare.asp (accessed July 2, 2009).

68 *Adele Douglass, told the* **Chicago Tribune**...Andrew Martin, "PETA Ruffles Feathers: Graphic protests aimed at customers haven't pushed KFC to change suppliers' slaughterhouse rules," *Chicago Tribune,* August 6, 2005.

Ian Duncan, the Emeritus Chair in Animal Welfare...Heather Moore, "Unhealthy and Inhumane: KFC Doesn't Do Anyone Right," *American Chronicle,* July 19, 2006, http://www.americanchronicle.com/articles/view/11651 (accessed June 29, 2009).

KFC's Animal Welfare Council..."Advisory Council," Kentucky Fried Chicken, http://www.kfc.com/about/animalwelfare_council.asp (accessed July 2, 2009).

in one, employees also urinated...This was documented by PETA investigators. PETA reports, "On nine separate days, PETA's investigator saw workers urinating in the live-hang area, including on the conveyor belt that moves birds to slaughter." See: "Tyson Workers Torturing Birds, Urinating on Slaughter Line," PETA, http://getactive.peta.org/campaign/tortured_by_tyson (accessed July 27, 2009).

69 *KOSHER?*...The entire, complex saga of Agriprocessors has been extensively documented by the Orthodox blog FailedMessiah.com.

The president of the Rabbinical...Rabbi Perry Paphael Rank (President, the Rabbinical Assembly), Letter to Conservative Rabbis, December 8, 2008.

The Orthodox chair...Aaron Gross, "When Kosher Isn't Kosher," *Tikkun* 20, no. 2 (2005): 55.

in a joint statement...Ibid.

70 *ORGANIC*..."The Issues: Organic," Sustainable Table, http://www.sustainabletable.org/issues/organic/ (accessed August 6, 2009); "Fact Sheet: Organic Labeling and Marketing Information," USDA Agricultural Marketing Service, http://www.ams.usda.gov/AMSv1.0/getfile?dDocName=STELDEV3004446&acct=nopgeninfo (accessed August 6, 2009).

71 *she saw more improvement*..."I saw more changes in 1999 than I had seen previously in my whole 30-year career." Amy Garber and James Peters, "Latest Pet Project: Industry agencies try to create protocol for improving living, slaughtering conditions," *Nation's Restaurant News,* September 22, 2003, http://findarticles.com/p/articles/mi_m3190/is_38_37/ai_108279089/?tag=content;col1 (accessed August 12, 2009).

71 *"There's enough understanding…"* Steve Kopperud, January 12, 2009, from a phone interview with Harvard student Lewis Ballard, who wrote his thesis on HSUS and PETA farmed animal welfare campaigns.

73 *96 percent of Americans…* David W. Moore, "Public Lukewarm on Animal Rights: Supports strict laws governing treatment of farm animals, but opposes ban on product testing and medical research," Gallup News Service, May 21, 2003, http://www.gallup.com/poll/8461/public -lukewarm-animal-rights.aspx (accessed June 26, 2009).

76 percent say that animal welfare… Jayson L. Lusk et al., "Consumer Preferences for Farm Animal Welfare: Results of a Nationwide Telephone Survey," Oklahoma State University, Department of Agricultural Economics, August 17, 2007, ii, 23, 24, available at asp.okstate.edu/baileynorwood/AW2/InitialReporttoAFB.pdf (accessed July 7, 2009).

nearly two-thirds advocate… Moore, "Public Lukewarm on Animal Rights."

farmed animals represent more than 99 percent… Wolfson and Sullivan, "Foxes in the Henhouse," 206. This includes not only pets but hunted animals, watched birds, animals dissected for educational purposes, and animals in zoos, laboratories, racetracks, fighting rings, and circuses. The authors give data for how they come to 98 percent but indicate that their calculations do not include farmed fish. Given the large number of farmed fish, it is safe to bump the 98 percent to 99 percent.

Hiding / Seeking

Page

The identifying characteristics of a character, and the timing and location of and participants in some of the events, in this chapter have been changed.

79 *In the typical cage…* See page 47.

85 *seven sheds, each about 50 feet wide…* These numbers are representative of a typical turkey factory farm in California (or most anywhere). John C. Voris, "Poultry Fact Sheet No. 16c: California Turkey Production," Cooperative Extension, University of California, September 1997, http://animalscience.ucdavis.edu/Avian/pfsl6C.htm (accessed August 16, 2009).

Notes

94 *I AM A FACTORY FARMER*...This monologue is derived from the statements of more than one factory farmer interviewed for this book.

95 **4 percent right off the bat**...Mortality rates in chicken production are typically around 1 percent a week, which would yield a 5 percent mortality rate over the life of most broiler chickens. This is seven times the mortality rate seen in laying hens of the same age, and this large number of deaths is attributed largely to their rapid rate of growth. "The Welfare of Broiler Chickens in the EU," Compassion in World Farming Trust, 2005, http://www.ciwf.org.uk/includes/documents/cm_docs/2008/w/welfare_of_broilers_in_the_eu_2005.pdf (accessed August 16, 2009).

97 *Mr. McDonald*...This is slang for a particular breed of chicken "designed" with fast-food corporations in mind, specifically McDonald's. Eric Schlosser, *Fast Food Nation* (New York: Harper Perennial, 2005), 140.

98 *you begin communicating with your chicks*...Jeffrey Moussaieff Masson, *The Pig Who Sang to the Moon* (New York: Vintage, 2005), 65.
the second verse of Genesis..."I have longed to gather your children together as a hen," Matthew 23:27 (NIV).
you view the animals you hunt...James Serpell, *In the Company of Animals* (Cambridge: Cambridge University Press, 2008), 5.
You draw them...It has long been observed by scholars that ancient cave paintings are dominated by images of animals. For example, "Cave art is essentially animal art; whether expressed in paintings, engravings, or sculptures, in huge friezes or the most delicate tracings, it is always—or nearly always—inspired by the animal world." Annette Laming-Emperaire, *Lascaux: Paintings and Engravings* (Baltimore: Penguin Books, 1959), 208.

99 **Domestication is an evolutionary**...Michael Pollan, *The Omnivore's Dilemma* (New York: Penguin, 2007), 320.

100 *"That which willing nods..."* Jacob Milgrom, *Leviticus 1–16*, Anchor Bible series (New York: Doubleday, 1991).
"You have come to me, Lord Bear..." Jonathan Z. Smith, *Imagining Religion: From Babylon to Jonestown*, Chicago Studies in the History of Judaism (Chicago: University of Chicago Press, 1988), 59.
the red heifer sacrificed...Saul Lieberman, *Greek in Jewish Palestine: Hellenism in Jewish Palestine* (New York: Jewish Theological Seminary of America, 1994), 159–160.

102 *"beauty always takes place..."* Elaine Scarry, *On Beauty and Being Just* (Princeton, NJ: Princeton University Press, 2001), 18.

THE FIRST ANIMAL ETHICS... The observation that an older ethic in which the animals' and farmers' interests overlapped became obsolete with the rise of factory farming is a basic premise of the philosophical and advocacy work of animal welfare expert and professor of philosophy Dr. Bernard Rollin. I am indebted to him for these reflections.

103 *in the late 1820s and '30s...* D. D. Stull and M. J. Broadway, *Slaughterhouse Blues: The Meat and Poultry Industry in North America*, Case Studies on Contemporary Social Issues (Belmont, CA: Wadsworth Publishing, 2003), 34.

Kill men, sticker-bleeders... Ibid., 70–71.

the efficiencies of these lines... Jeremy Rifkin, *Beyond Beef: The Rise and Fall of the Cattle Culture* (New York: Plume, 1993), 120.

104 *The pressure to improve...* Stull and Broadway, *Slaughterhouse Blues*, 33; Rifkin, *Beyond Beef*, 87–88.

The average distance our meat... R. Pirog and others, "Food, Fuel, and Freeways: An Iowa perspective on how far food travels, fuel usage, and greenhouse gas emissions," Leopold Center for Sustainable Agriculture, Ames, Iowa, 2001, http://www.leopold.iastate.edu/pubs/staff/ppp/index.htm (accessed July 16, 2009).

By 1908, conveyer systems... Stull and Broadway, *Slaughterhouse Blues*, 34.

doubling and even tripling... Schlosser, *Fast Food Nation*, 173; Steve Bjerklie, "The Era of Big Bird Is Here: The Eight-Pound Chicken Is Changing Processing and the Industry," *Business Journal for Meat and Poultry Processors*, January 1, 2008, http://www.meatpoultry.com/Feature_Stories.asp?ArticleID=90548 (accessed July 15, 2009).

with predictable increases... *Blood, Sweat, and Fear: Workers' Rights in US Meat and Poultry Plants* (New York: Human Rights Watch, 2004), 33–38.

In 1923, in the Delmarva... Stull and Broadway, *Slaughterhouse Blues*, 38; Steve Striffler, *Chicken: The Dangerous Transformation of America's Favorite Food* (New Haven, CT: Yale University Press, 2007), 34.

105 *With the help of newly discovered feed...* The addition of vitamins A and D to chicken feed allowed birds to survive confinement that otherwise

would have prevented adequate growth and bone development. Jim Mason, *Animal Factories* (New York: Three Rivers Press, 1990), 2.

105 ***By 1926, Steele had 10,000 birds*** ... Stull and Broadway, *Slaughterhouse Blues*, 38.

and by 1935, 250,000 ... History of Sussex County, "Celia Steele & the Broiler Industry," sussexcountyde.gov, 2009, http://www.sussexcoun tyde.gov/about/history/events.cfm?action=broiler (accessed July 15, 2009).

The average flock size in America ... W. O. Wilson, "Housing," in *American Poultry History: 1823–1973*, edited by Oscar August Hanke and others (Madison, WI: American Poultry Historical Society, 1974), 218.

Just ten years after Steele's breakthrough ... Striffler, *Chicken*, 34.

Poultry production is the region's primary ... Lynette M. Ward, "Environmental Policies for a Sustainable Poultry Industry in Sussex County, Delaware," Ph.D. dissertation, Environmental and Energy Policy, University of Delaware, 2003, 4, 15, http://northeast.manure management.cornell.edu/docs/Ward_2003_Dissertation.pdf (accessed August 16, 2009).

Nitrates contaminate one-third ... P. A. Hamilton and others, "Water-quality assessment of the Delmarva Peninsula," Report Number 03–40, http://pubs.er.usgs.gov/usgspubs/ofr/ofr9340. For discussion see Peter S. Goodman, "An Unsavory Byproduct: Runoff and Pollution," *Washington Post*, August 1, 1999, http://www.washingtonpost.com/wp-srv/local/daily/aug99/chicken1.htm (accessed July 6, 2009).

Steele's birds never would have survived ... Mason, *Animal Factories*, 2.

produced with the help of government subsidies ... Pollan, *The Omnivore's Dilemma*, 52–54.

delivered by chain-driven feeders ... Mason, *Animal Factories*, 2.

Debeaking ... Ibid.

106 ***"the broad-breasted appearance..."*** George E. "Jim." Coleman, "One Man's Recollections over 50 Years," *Broiler Industry* (1976): 56.

The 1940s also saw the introduction ... Mason, *Animal Factories*, 2.

excessive amounts of eggs (layers) ... P. Smith and C. Daniel, *The Chicken Book* (Boston: Little, Brown, 1975), 270–272.

From 1935 to 1995, the average weight ... William Boyd, "Making Meat: Science, Technology, and American Poultry Production,"

Technology and Culture 42 (October 2001): 636–637, as quoted in Striffler, *Chicken*, 46.

107 **companies own three-fourths...** Paul Aho, "Feather Success," Watt Poultry USA, February 2002, http://www.wattnet.com/Archives/Docs/202wp30. pdf?CFID=28327&CFTOKEN=64015918 (accessed July 13, 2009).

108 ***"However one interprets..."*** Jacques Derrida, *The Animal That Therefore I Am*, edited by Marie-Louise Mallet, translated by David Wills (New York: Fordham University Press, 2008), 25–26.

109 **As described in industry journals...** This choice collection of quotations from industry journals was compiled in Jim Mason's groundbreaking book on factory farming, *Animal Factories*, 1. The quotations are from (in order): *Farmer and Stockbreeder*, January 30, 1962; J. Byrnes, "Raising Pigs by the Calendar at Maplewood Farm," *Hog Farm Management*, September 1976; "Farm Animals of the Future," *Agricultural Research*, U.S. Department of Agriculture, April 1989.

In the past fifty years... Scott Derks, ed., *The Value of a Dollar: 1860–1999*, millennium ed. (Lakeville, CT: Grey House Publishing, 1999), 280; Bureau of Labor Statistics, Average Price Data, US City Average, Milk, Fresh, Whole, Fortified, Per Gallon.

99.9 percent of chickens raised for meat... See note for page 12.

Influence / Speechlessness

Page

121 **On average...** Calculated on the basis of USDA statistics by Noam Mohr.

123 **the first of six to be killed...** Michael Greger, "Hong Kong 1997," BirdFluBook.com, http://birdflubook.com/a.php?id=15 (accessed July 6, 2009).

124 **1918 pandemic killed more people faster...** Even a low estimate of twenty million dead makes the 1918 pandemic the most deadly pandemic in history. Y. Ghendon, "Introduction to pandemic influenza through history," *European Journal of Epidemiology* 10 (1994): 451–453. Depending on what death estimates one accepts, World War II might have claimed more lives than the 1918 pandemic in absolute terms, but it raged for six years, whereas the 1918 pandemic was over in two.

Notes

124 ***Spanish flu killed as many***...J. M. Barry, "Viruses of mass destruc-tion," *Fortune* 150, no. 9 (2004): 74–76.

recent revisions of the death toll...NPAS Johnson and J. Mueller, "Updating the Accounts: Global mortality of the 1918–1920 'Span-ish' influenza pandemic," *Bulletin of the History of Medicine* 76 (2002): 105–115.

one-quarter of Americans...A. W. Crosby, *Epidemic and Peace, 1918* (Westford, CT: Greenwood Press, 1976), 205.

125 ***highest in the twenty-five-to-twenty-nine-year-old group***... J. S. Nguyen-Van-Tam and A. W. Hampson, "The epidemiology and clini-cal impact of pandemic influenza," *Vaccine* 21 (2003): 1762–1768, 1765, http://birdfluexposed.com/resources/tam1772.pdf (accessed July 6, 2009).

average life expectancy for Americans... L. Garrett, "The Next Pan-demic? Probable cause," *Foreign Affairs* 84, no. 4 (2005).

twenty thousand Americans died in a week...Crosby, *Epidemic and Peace, 1918*, 60.

Steam shovels were used...Pete Davies, *The Devil's Flu* (New York: Henry Holt, 2000), 86.

"We know another pandemic is inevitable..." World Health Orga-nization, "World is ill-prepared for 'inevitable' flu pandemic," *Bul-letin of the World Health Organization*, 2004, http://who.int/bulletin/volumes/82/4/who%20news.pdf (accessed July 6, 2009).

"not only inevitable..." M. S. Smolinksi and others, *Microbial Threats to Health: The Threat of Pandemic Influenza* (Washington, DC: National Academies Press, 2005), 138.

a threat is imminent...Predicting how a pandemic will affect human populations is particularly difficult because it involves expertise spread across many scientific disciplines (pathology, epidemiology, sociology, and veterinary sciences, among others) and involves predicting com-plex interactions between pathogens, new technological tools (like geographic information systems, remote sensing data, and molecular epidemiology), and policy decisions by health authorities worldwide (that is, the whims of world leaders). "Report of the WHO/FAO/OIE joint consultation on emerging zoonotic diseases: in collaboration with the Health Council of the Netherlands," May 3–5, 2004, Geneva, Swit-zerland, 7.

126   *The world may be on the brink...* "Ten things you need to know about pandemic influenza," World Health Organization, 2005, http://www.who.int/csr/disease/influenza/pandemic10things/en/ (accessed July 16, 2009).

"a relatively conservative estimate..." Ibid.

*The results, published in 2005...*J. K. Taubenberger and others, "Characterization of the 1918 influenza virus polymerase genes," *Nature* 437, no. 889 (2005); R. B. Belshe, "The origins of pandemic influenza—lessons from the 1918 virus," *New England Journal of Medicine* 353, no. 21 (2005): 2209–2211.

the 1918 virus might have mutated... "Taubenberger and Reid's subsequent work has revealed a provocative fact: the 1918 flu pandemic was not set off by the same circumstances as the ones of 1957 and 1968. Those viruses had surface proteins that jumped directly from birds, coupled with human-adapted core genes. By contrast, in the 1918 virus, the surface genes are mammalian in character. Though probably originally derived from a bird, the first had spent years adapting to life in mammals, either pigs or humans." Madeline Drexler, *Secret Agents* (New York: Penguin, 2003). 189.

uniquely susceptible to both... Ibid., 173.

127   *He called it the "barnyard theory"...* Ibid., 170–171.

cause twenty thousand "excess deaths"... Ibid., 170.

a duck in central Europe... Ibid., 171.

the primordial source of all flu... Ibid.

128   *H1 through the recently discovered H16...* Joseph LaDou, *Current Occupational and Environmental Medicine* (New York: McGraw-Hill Professional, 2006), 263–264; R. A. M. Fouchier, "Characterization of a novel influenza A virus hemagglutinin subtype (H16) obtained from black-headed gulls," *Journal of Virology* 79, no. 5 (2005): 2814–2822; Drexler, *Secret Agents*, 171.

Domestic birds can also... Drexler, *Secret Agents*, 171.

Humans, for example... Ibid., 172.

The H stands for hemagglutinin... David S. Goodsell, "Hemagglutinin," RCSB Protein Data Bank, April 2006, http://www.rcsb.org/pdb/static.do?p=education_discussion/molecule_of_the_month/pdb76_1.html (accessed July 16, 2009).

129 *twenty sheds, each 45 feet wide...* Terrence o'Keefe and Gray Thorton, "Housing Expansion Plans," Walt Poultry Industry USA, June 2006, 30.

up to 60 feet by 504 feet... Ibid.

eight-tenths of a square foot... "About the Industry: Animal Welfare: Physical Well-Being of Chickens," National Chicken Council, 2007, http://www.nationalchickencouncil.com/aboutIndustry/detail .cfm?id=11 (accessed July 6, 2009).

130 *The muscles and fat tissues...* S. Boersma, "Managing Rapid Growth Rate in Broilers," *World Poultry* 17, no. 8 (2001): 20, http://www.world poultry.net/article-database/managing-rapid-growth-rate-in-broilers-id1337.html (accessed July 8, 2009).

leading to deformities... A regional report from the World's Poultry Science Association concludes that "one of the main factors responsible [for leg problems in conventional broilers in conventional production systems] is their high growth rate." G. S. Santotra and others, "Monitoring Leg Problems in Broilers: A survey of commercial broiler production in Denmark," *World's Poultry Science Journal* 57 (2001).

between 1 and 4 percent... "Flip-over Disease: Introduction," *The Merk Veterinary Manual* (Whitehouse Station, NJ: Merck, 2008), http:// www.merckvetmanual.com/mvm/index.jsp?cfile=htm/bc/202500.htm (accessed June 28, 2009).

ascites, kills even more... M. H. Maxwell and G. W. Robertson, "World broiler ascites survey 1996," *Poultry Int.* (April 1997), as cited in "Ascites," Government of Alberta, July 15, 2008, http://www1 .agric.gov.ab.ca/$department/deptdocs.nsf/all/pou3546?open document (accessed June 28, 2009).

Three out of four will have some degree... Santotra and others, "Monitoring Leg Problems in Broilers."

One out of four... T. G. Knowles and others, "Leg Disorders in Broiler Chickens: Prevalence, Risk Factors and Prevention," PLoS ONE, (2008), http://www.plosone.org/article/info:doi/10.1371/journal.pone .0001545; S. C. Kestin and others, "Prevalence of leg weakness in broiler chickens and its relationship with genotype," *Veterinary Record* 131 (1992): 190–194.

130 ***they are in pain...*** Citing studies published in the *Veterinary Record*, a recent HSUS white paper concludes, "Research strongly suggests that birds [that have trouble walking] are in pain." HSUS, "An HSUS Report: The Welfare of Animals in the Chicken Industry," 2, http://www.hsus.org/web-files/PDF/farm/welfare_broiler.pdf.

leave the lights on nearly twenty-four hours... I. Duncan, "Welfare Problems of Poultry," in *The Well-Being of Farm Animals: Challenges and Solutions*, edited by G. J. Benson and B. E. Rollin. (Ames, IA: Blackwell Publishing, 2004), 310; Christine Woodside, *Living on an Acre: A Practical Guide to the Self-Reliant Life* (Guilford, CT: Lyons Press, 2003), 234.

forty-second day... I. Duncan, "Welfare problems of meat-type chickens," Farmed Animal Well-Being Conference, University of California–Davis, June 28–29, 2001, http://www.upc-online.org/fall2001/well-being_conference_review.html (accessed on August 12, 2009).

131 ***(or increasingly the thirty-ninth)...*** "39-day blog following the life of a factory farmed chicken," Compassion in World Farming, http://www.chickenout.tv/39-day-blog.html; G. T. Tabler, I. L. Berry, and A. M. Mendenhall, "Mortality Patterns Associated with Commercial Broiler Production," *Avian Advice* (University of Arkansas) 6, no. 1 Spring (2004): 1–3.

Beyond deformities, eye damage... Jim Mason, *Animal Factories* (New York: Three Rivers Press, 1990), 29.

virtually all...chickens... "Nationwide Young Chicken Microbiological Baseline Data Collection Program," Food Safety and Inspection Service, November 1999–October 2000, http://www.fsis.usda.gov/Science/Baseline_Data/index.asp (accessed July 17, 2009); Nichols Fox, "Safe Food? Not Yet," *New York Times*, January 30, 1997, http://www.nytimes.com/1997/01/30/opinion/safe-food-not-yet.html?pagewanted=print (accessed August 16, 2009); K. L. Kotula and Y. Pandya, "Bacterial Contamination of Broiler Chickens Before Scalding," *Journal of Food Protection* 58, no. 12 (1995): 1326–1329, http://www.ingentaconnect.com./content/iafp/jfp/1995/00000058/00000012/art00007%3Bjsessionid=1ms4km94qohkn.alexandra (accessed August 16, 2009).

between 39 and 75 percent... C. Zhao and others, "Prevalence of *Campylobacter* spp., *Escherichia coli*, and *Salmonella* Serovars in Retail Chicken,

Turkey, Pork, and Beef from the Greater Washington, D.C., Area," *Applied and Environmental Microbiology* 67, no. 12 (December 2001): 5431–5436, http://aem.asm.org/cgi/content/abstract/67/12/5431?maxtoshow= &HITS=10&hits=10&RESULT FORMAT=&fulltext=coli&searchid =1&FIRSTINDEX=2400&resourcetype=HWFIG (accessed August 16, 2009); R. B. Kegode and others, "Occurrence of *Campylobacter* species, *Salmonella* species, and generic *Escherichia coli* in meat products from retail outlets in the Fargo metropolitan area," *Journal of Food Safety* 28, no. 1 (2008): 111–125, http://www.ars.usda.gov/research/publications/ publications.htm?SEQ_NO_115=196570 (accessed August 16, 2009).

131 *Around 8 percent of birds*...S. Russell and others, "Zero tolerance for salmonella raises questions," WattPoultry.com, 2009, http://www .wattpoultry.com/PoultryUSA/Article.aspx?id=30786 (accessed August 16, 2009).

at least one in four birds...Kotula and Pandya, "Bacterial Contamination of Broiler Chickens Before Scalding," 1326–1329.

which still occurs on some farms..."Dirty Birds: Even Premium Chickens Harbor Dangerous Bacteria," *Consumer Reports*, January 2007, www.usapeec.org/p_documents/newsandinfo_050612111938.pdf (accessed July 8, 2009).

Seventy to 90 percent are infected...Marian Burros, "Health Concerns Mounting over Bacteria in Chickens," *New York Times*, October 20, 1997, http://www.nytimes.com/1997/10/20/us/health-concerns-mounting-over-bacteria-in-chickens.html?scp=1&sq=%22Health%20 Concerns%20Mounting%20Over%20Bacteria%20in%20 Chickens%22&st=cse (accessed July 17, 2009). See also: Alan R. Sams, *Poultry Meat Processing* (Florence, KY: CRC Press, 2001), 143, http:// books.google.com/books?id=UCjhDRSP13wC&pg=PP1&dq=Poultry +Meat+Processing&ei=ag9hSprSFYrgkwSv8Om9Dg (accessed July 17, 2009); Kotula and Pandya, "Bacterial Contamination of Broiler Chickens Before Scalding," 1326–1329; Zhao and others, "Prevalence of *Campylobacter* spp., *Escherichia coli*, and *Salmonella* Serovars in Retail Chicken, Turkey, Pork, and Beef from the Greater Washington, D.C., Area," 5431–5436; J. C. Buzby and others, "Bacterial Foodborne Disease: Medical Costs and Productivity Losses," *Agricultural Economics Report*, no. AER741 (August 1996): 3, http://www.ers.usda.gov/Publications/ AER741/ (accessed August 16, 2009).

Notes

131   ***Chlorine baths are commonly used…*** G. C. Mead, *Food Safety Control in the Poultry Industry* (Florence, KY: CRC Press, 2005), 322; Sams, *Poultry Meat Processing*, 143, 150.

     the birds will be injected… "Buying This Chicken? You could pay up to $1.70 for broth," ConsumerReports.org, June 2008, http://www .consumerreports.org/cro/food/news/2008/06/poultry-companies-adding-broth-to-products/overview/enhanced-poultry-ov.htm?resultP ageIndex=1&resultIndex=8&searchTerm=chicken (accessed August 16, 2009).

     "ballooned with 10 to 30 percent…" Ibid.

     You will have to continuously find… *Blood, Sweat, and Fear: Workers' Rights in US Meat and Poultry Plants* (New York: Human Rights Watch, 2004), 108, footnote 298.

     Illegal aliens are often preferred… Ibid., 78–101.

132   ***typical working conditions…*** Ibid., 2.

     Approximately 30 percent… T. G. Knowles. "Handling and Transport of Spent Hens," *World's Poultry Science Journal* 50 (1994): 60–61.

133   ***This most likely paralyzes…*** There is some debate about whether the birds are insensible or conscious after being immobilized. At the very least, a large percentage are immobilized but conscious. For a careful and cautious review of the peer review literature, see: S. Shields and M. Raj, "An HSUS Report: The Welfare of Birds at Slaughter," October 3, 2008, http://www.hsus.org/farm/resources/research/welfare/welfare_of_birds_at_slaughter.html#038 (accessed August 16, 2009).

     about one-tenth the level necessary… Gail A. Eisnitz, *Slaughterhouse: The Shocking Story of Greed, Neglect, and Inhumane Treatment Inside the U.S. Meat Industry* (Amherst, NY: Prometheus Books, 2006), 166. Also see: E. W. Craig and D. L. Fletchere, "Processing and Products: A Comparison of High Current and Low Voltage Electrical Stunning Systems on Broiler Breast Rigor Development and Meat Quality," *Poultry Science* 76, no. 8 (1997): 1178–1179, http://poultsci.highwire.org/cgi/content/abstract/76/8/1178 (accessed August 16, 2009).

     When asked if these numbers… Daniel Zwerdling, "A View to a Kill," *Gourmet*, June 2007, 96, http://www.gourmet.com/magazine/2005/2007/06/aviewtoakill (accessed June 26, 2009).

133 *Government estimates obtained*...The Freedom of Information Act request indicates that three million chickens were scalded alive in 1993, when only seven billion birds were slaughtered. Adjusting for the fact that today nine billion birds are slaughtered, we can assume that at least 3.85 million birds are scalded alive today. Freedom of Information Act #94-363, Poultry Slaughtered, Condemned, and Cadavers, 6/30/94, cited in "Poultry Slaughter: The Need for Legislation," United Poultry Concerns, www.upc-online.org/slaughter/slaughter3web.pdf (accessed August 12, 2009).

the birds leave filled with pathogens...K. A. Liljebjelke and others, "Scald tank water and foam as sources of salmonella contamination for poultry carcasses during early processing," Poultry Science Association Meeting, 2009, http://www.ars.usda.gov/research/publications/public ations.htm?SEQ_NO_115=238456 (accessed July 11, 2009). For further discussion, see Eisnitz, *Slaughterhouse*, 166.

134 *Once a dangerous contaminant*...Caroline Smith DeWaal, "Playing Chicken: The Human Cost of Inadequate Regulation of the Poultry Industry," Center for Science in the Public Interest (CSPI), 1996, http://www.cspinet.org/reports/polt.html (accessed July 11, 2009).

As a result, inspectors condemn half...Ibid.

The inspector has approximately...Moira Herbst, "Beefs About Poultry Inspections: The USDA wants to change how it inspects poultry, focusing on microbial testing. Critics say the move could pose serious public health risks," *Business Week*, February 6, 2008, http://www.busi nessweek.com/bwdaily/dnflash/content/feb2008/db2008025_760284 .html (accessed July 11, 2009); Report to Congressional Requesters, "Food Safety—Risk-Based Inspections and Microbial Monitoring Needed for Meat and Poultry," Meat and Poultry Inspection, May 1994, http://fedbbs.access.gpo.gov/library/gao_rpts/rc94110.txt (accessed July 11, 2009).

"Every week," he reports...Scott Bronstein, "A Journal-Constitution Special Report—Chicken: How Safe? First of Two Parts," *Atlanta Journal-Constitution*, May 26, 1991.

thousands of birds are communally...R. Behar and M. Kramer, "Something Smells Foul," *Time*, October 17, 1994, http://www.time.com/time/ magazine/article/0,9171,981629-3,00.html (accessed July 6, 2009).

135 ***"water in these tanks…"*** Smith De Waal, "Playing Chicken." Also see: Eisnitz, *Slaughterhouse*, 168.

99 percent of US poultry producers… Russell and others, "Zero tolerance for salmonella raises questions."

placing the chicken carcasses… Behar and Kramer, "Something Smells Foul."

But that would also eliminate… Ibid.

8 percent limit… Ibid.

Consumers sued over the practice… "USDA Rule on Retained Water in Meat and Poultry," Food Safety and Inspection Service, April 2001, http://www.fsis.usda.gov/oa/background/waterretention.htm. See also: Behar and Kramer, "Something Smells Foul."

"arbitrary and capricious"… "Retained Water in Raw Meat and Poultry Products; Poultry Chilling Requirements," *Federal Register* 66 no. 6 (January 9, 2001), http://www.fsis.usda.gov/OPPDE/rdad/FRPubs/97-054F.html (accessed July 21, 2009).

the USDA's interpretation… Ibid.

the new law… L. L. Young and D. P. Smith, "Moisture retention by water- and air-chilled chicken broilers during processing and cutup operations," *Poultry Science* 83, no. 1 (2004): 119–122, http://ps.fass.org/cgi/content/abstract/83/l/119 (accessed July 21, 2009); "Water in Meat and Poultry," Food Safety and Inspection Service, August 6, 2007, http://www.fsis.usda.gov/Factsheets/Water_in_Meats/index.asp (accessed July 21, 2009); "Title 9—Animals and Animal Products," U.S. Government Printing Office, January 1, 2003, http://frweb gate.access.gpo.gov/cgi-bin/get-cfr.cgi?TITLE=9&PART=424&SECTION=21&TYPE=TEXT&YEAR=2003 (accessed July 21, 2009).

136 ***gift massive poultry producers…*** Behar and Kramer, "Something Smells Foul."

Today six billion chickens… These estimates are based on the number of chickens slaughtered for meat annually according to the most recent FAO statistics, available at http://faostat.fao.org/site/569/DesktopDefault.aspx?PageID=569#ancor.

137 ***Americans eat 150 times…*** W. Boyd and M. Watts, "Agro-Industrial Just-in-Time: The Chicken Industry and Postwar American Capitalism," in *Globalising Food: Agrarian Questions and Global Restructuring*, edited by D. Goodman and M. Watts (London: Routledge, 1997), 192–193.

137 *The statisticians who generate*...Agricultural Statistics Board, "Poultry slaughter: 2008 annual summary," Table: Poultry Slaughtered: Number, Live Weight, and Average Live Weight by Type, United States, 2008 and 2007 Total (continued), 2, U.S. Department of Agriculture, National Agricultural Statistics Service, February 2009, http://usda.mannlib.cornell.edu/usda/current/PoulSlauSu/PoulSlauSu-02-25-2009.pdf (accessed July 9, 2009).

Much like the virus it names... Douglas Harper, Online Etymological Dictionary, November 2001, http://www.etymonline.com/index.php?search=influenzA&searchmode=none (accessed September 9, 2009); *Oxford English Dictionary* entry for "influenza."

138 *what about the 500 million pigs*...According to the FAO, an estimated half of the world's 1.2 billion pigs (statistics available at http://faostat.fao.org/site/569/DesktopDefault.aspx?PageID=569#ancor) are intensively confined. FAO, "Livestock Policy Brief 01: Responding to the 'Livestock Revolution,'" ftp://ftp.fao.org/docrep/fao/010/a0260e/a0260e00.pdf (accessed July 28, 2009).

zoonotic...A zoonotic disease is defined as "any disease and/or infection which is naturally 'transmissible from vertebrate animals to man,'" according to Pan American Health Organisation, *Zoonoses and Communicable Diseases Common to Man and Animals*, as quoted in "Zoonoses and Veterinary Public Health (VPH)," World Health Organization, http://www.who.int/zoonoses/en/ (accessed July 8, 2009).

where we do know the origin...Buzby and others, "Bacterial Foodborne Disease," 3.

139 *poultry is by far the largest cause*...Gardiner Harris, "Poultry Is No. 1 Source of Outbreaks, Report Says," *New York Times*, June 11, 2009, http://www.nytimes.com/2009/06/12/health/research/12cdc.html (accessed July 21, 2009).

83 percent of all chicken meat..."Dirty Birds: Even Premium Chickens Harbor Dangerous Bacteria," 21.

the 76 million cases..."Preliminary Foodnet Data on the Incidence of Foodborne Illnesses—Selected Sites, United States, 2001," Centers for Disease Control, *MMWR* 51, no. 15 (April 19, 2002): 325–329, http://www.cdc.gov/mmwr/preview/mmwrhtml/mm5115a3.htm (accessed August 16, 2009).

140 *In the United States, about 3 million pounds...* The industry figure comes from the Animal Health Institute, described by the *New York Times* as "a trade group in Washington that represents 31 makers of veterinary drugs." Denise Grady, "Scientists See Higher Use of Antibiotics on Farms," *New York Times*, January 8, 2001, http://www.nytimes.com/2001/01/08/us/scientists-see-higher-use-of-antibiotics-on-farms.html (accessed July 6, 2009).

industry underreported its antibiotic use... "Hogging It! Estimates of Antimicrobial Abuse in Livestock," Union of Concerned Scientists, April 7, 2004, http://www.ucsusa.org/food_and_agriculture/science_and_impacts/impacts_industrial_agriculture/hogging-it-estimates-of.html (accessed July 21, 2009).

fully 13.5 million pounds... Ibid.

the percentage of bacteria resistant... Marian Burros, "Poultry Industry Quietly Cuts Back on Antibiotic Use," *New York Times*, February 10, 2002, http://www.nytimes.com/2002/02/10/national/10CHIC.html (accessed July 6, 2009).

eightfold increase in antimicrobial resistance... K. Smith and others, "Quinolone-Resistant *Campylobacter jejuni* Infections in Minnesota, 1992–1998," *New England Journal of Medicine* 340, no. 20 (1999): 1525, http://content.nejm.org/content/vol340/issue20/index.dtl (accessed July 10, 2009).

As far back as the late 1960s... Humane Society of the United States, "An HSUS Report: Human Health Implications of Non-Therapeutic Antibiotic Use in Animal Agriculture," *Farm Animal Welfare* http://www.hsus.org/web-files/PDF/farm/HSUS-Human-Health-Report-on-Antibiotics-in-Animal-Agriculture.pdf (accessed September 14, 2009).

American Medical Association... "Low-Level Use of Antibiotics in Livestock and Poultry," FMI Backgrounder, Food Marketing Institute, http://www.fmi.org/docs/media/bg/antibiotics.pdf (accessed August 5, 2009).

141 *Centers for Disease Control...* "An HSUS Report: Human Health Implications of Non-Therapeutic Antibiotic Use in Animal Agriculture." Also see this article for an early interpretation of CDC data: "Infections in the United States," *New England Journal of*

Medicine 338 (1998): 1333–1338, http://www.cdc.gov/enterics/publications/135-k_glynnMDR_salmoNEJM1998.pdf.

141 **Institute of Medicine...** A. D. Anderson and others, "Public Health Consequences of Use of Antimicrobial Agents in Food Animals in the United States," *Microbial Drug Resistance* 9, no. 4 (2003), http://www.cdc.gov/enterics/publications/2_a_anderson_2003.pdf.

World Health Organization... Ibid.

remarkable 2004 conference... *Report of the WHO, FAO, OIE Joint Consultation on Emerging Zoonotic Diseases: In collaboration with the Health Council of the Neatherlands,* World Health Organization, Food and Agriculture Organization of the United Nations, World Organization for Animal Health, Geneva, Switzerland, May 3–5, 2004, whqlibdoc.who.int/hq/2004/WHO_CDS_CPE_ZFK_2004.9.pdf (accessed August 16, 2009).

The scientists distinguished... Ibid.

142 **This demand for animal products...** Ibid.

"the rapid selection and amplification..." "Global Risks of Infectious Animal Diseases," Issue Paper, Council for Agricultural Science and Technology (CAST), no. 28, 2005, 6, http://www.cast-science.org/publicationDetails.asp?idProduct=69 (accessed July 9, 2009).

Breeding genetically uniform... Michael Greger, *Bird Flu* (Herndon, VA: Lantern Books, 2006), 183–213.

The "cost of increased efficiency"... "Global Risks of Infectious Animal Diseases," 6.

trace six of the eight... V. Trifonov and others, "The origin of the recent swine influenza A(H1N1) virus infecting humans," *Eurosurveillance* 14, no. 17 (2009), http://www.eurosurveillance.org/images/dynamic/EE/V14N17/art19193.pdf (accessed July 16, 2009). Also see: Debora MacKenzie, "Swine Flu: The Predictable Pandemic?" *New Scientist*, 2706 (April 29, 2009), http://www.newscientist.com/article/mg20227063.800-swine-flu-the-predictable-pandemic.html?full=true (accessed July 10, 2009).

143 **heart disease, number one...** "Leading Causes of Death," Centers for Disease Control and Prevention, http://www.cdc.gov/nchs/FASTATS/lcod.htm (accessed August 16, 2009).

143 *In 1917...* "ADA: Who We Are, What We Do," American Dietetic Association, 2009, http://www.eatright.org/cps/rde/xchg/ada/hs.xsl/home_404_ENU_HTML.htm (accessed July 6, 2009).

144 *Well-planned vegetarian diets...* "Vegetarian Diets," *American Dietetic Association* 109, no. 7 (July 2009): 1266–1282, http://eatright.org/cps/rde/xchg/ada/hs.xsl/advocacy_933_ENU_HTML.htm (accessed August 16, 2009).

Vegetarian diets tend to be lower... Ibid.

vegetarians and vegans (including athletes)... Ibid.

excess animal protein intake is linked... "The Protein Myth," Physicians Committee for Responsible Medicine, http://www.pcrm.org/health/veginfo/vsk/protein_myth.html (accessed July 16, 2009). And from a sports nutrition expert: "Excess protein should be avoided because it can be detrimental to normal physiologic functioning and, therefore, health....Likewise excess breakdown and thus excretion of protein have been shown to increase urinary calcium loss. Females who are already prone to bone disease (that is, osteoporosis) due to low bone density could be compromising their bone health by consuming a diet too high in protein. Certain high-protein diets may also put one at increased risk for coronary artery disease....Finally, excess protein intake is generally associated with possible kidney malfunction." J. R. Berning and S. N. Steen, *Nutrition for Sport and Exercise*, 2nd ed. (Sudbury, MA: Jones & Bartlett, 2005), 55.

Vegetarian diets are often... "Vegetarian Diets," 1266–1282.

145 *heart disease [which alone accounts...* "LCWK9. Deaths, percent of total deaths, and death rates for the 15 leading causes of death: United States and each state, 2006," Centers for Disease Control and Prevention, http://www.cdc.gov/nchs/data/dvs/LCWK9_2006.pdf (accessed August 16, 2009).

cancers account for nearly... Ibid.

"drive increased sales..." "About Us," Dairy Management Inc., 2009, http://www.dairycheckoff.com/DairyCheckoff/AboutUs/About-Us (accessed July 16, 2009); "About Us," National Dairy Council, 2009, http://www.nationaldairycouncil.org/nationaldairycouncil/aboutus (accessed July 16, 2009).

NDC promotes dairy consumption... For example, the National Dairy Council (NDC) has marketed dairy extensively to African

Americans, 70 percent of whom are lactose intolerant. "Support Grows for PCRM's Challenge to Dietary Guidelines Bias," *PCRM Magazine*, 1999,http://www.pcrm.org/magazine/GM99Summer/GM99Summer9.html (accessed July 16, 2009).

146 *the largest and most important supplier*... P. Imperato and G. Mitchell, *Acceptable Risks* (New York: Viking, 1985), 65; John Robbins, *Diet for a New America* (Tiburon, CA: HJ Kramer Publishing, 1998), 237–238.

Founded the same year that the ADA opened... For the start of ADA, see: "American Dietetic Association," National Health Information Center, February 7, 2007, http://www.healthfinder.gov/orgs/hr1846.htm (accessed July 16, 2009). For the USDA tasks, see: Marion Nestle, *Food Politics: How the Food Industry Influences Nutrition, and Health* (Berkeley: University of California Press, 2007), 33, 34.

Nestle has worked extensively... "The Surgeon General's Report on Nutrition and Health 1988," edited by Marion Nestle, Office of the Surgeon General and United States Department of Health and Human Services Nutrition Policy Board (United States Public Health Service, 1988), http://profiles.nlm.nih.gov/NN/B/C/Q/G/ (accessed July 8, 2009).

food companies, like cigarette companies... Nestle, *Food Politics*, 361.
They will "lobby Congress..." Ibid., xiii.

147 *in parts of the world where milk*... Marion Nestle, *What to Eat* (New York: North Point Press, 2007), 73.

The highest rates of osteoporosis... Ibid., 74.

USDA currently has an informal policy... "Pressures from food companies have led government officials and nutrition professionals to produce dietary guidelines that disguise 'eat less' messages with euphemisms. Their true meaning can be detected only through careful reading, interpretation, and analysis." Nestle, *Food Politics*, 67.

half a billion of our tax dollars... Erik Marcus, *Meat Market: Animals, Ethics, and Money* (Cupertino, CA: Brio Press, 2005), 100.

a modest $161 million... Ibid.

148 *India's and China's poultry industries*... Economic Research Service, USDA, "Recent Trends in Poultry Supply and Demand," in *India's Poultry Sector: Development and Prospects/WRS-04-03*, http://www.ers.usda.gov/publications/WRS0403/WRS0403c.pdf (accessed August 12, 2009).

148 *twenty-seven to twenty-eight birds annually*...Calculation based on USDA, U.S. Census Bureau, and FAO statistics. Thanks to Noam Mohr for help with this.

Slices of Paradise/Pieces of Shit

Page

149 *Nearly one-third*...See page 32.

155 *"The way the plants are physically laid out..."* Gail A. Eisnitz, *Slaughter-house: The Shocking Story of Greed, Neglect, and Inhumane Treatment Inside the U.S. Meat Industry* (Amherst, NY: Prometheus Books, 2006), 189.

"We aren't in a position to see..." Ibid., 196.

"about 80 percent..." By the standards the industry endorses through the American Meat Institute, 80 percent is considered a poor rate of success in rendering animals unconscious on the first try. Mario offered this number off the cuff, though, and did not explain how he was figuring it. It is quite possible that if his success rate were measured using, for example, the standard procedures developed by Temple Grandin, it would be much higher.

156 *Pigs exist in the wild*...L. R. Walker, *Ecosystems of Disturbed Ground* (New York: Elsevier Science, 1999), 442.

taxonomists count sixteen... "Family Suidae; hogs and pigs," University of Michigan Museum of Zoology, 2008, http://animaldiversity.ummz.umich.edu/site/accounts/information/Suidae.html (accessed July 17, 2009).

157 *about 90 percent of large hog farms*...U.S. Department of Agriculture, "Swine 2006, Part I: Reference of swine health and management practices in the United States," October 2007, http://www.aphis.usda.gov/vs/ceah/ncahs/nahms/swine/swine2006/Swine2006_PartI.pdf (accessed August 17, 2009).

pork industry to breed pigs...Madonna Benjamin, "Pig Trucking and Handling: Stress and Fatigued Pig," *Advances in Pork Production*, 2005, http://www.afac.ab.ca/careinfo/transport/articles/05benjamin.pdf (accessed July 26, 2009); E. A. Pajor and others, "The Effect of Selection for Lean Growth on Swine Behavior and Welfare," Purdue University

Swine Day, 2000, www.ansc.purdue.edu/swine/swineday/sday00/1.pdf (accessed July 12, 2009); Temple Grandin, "Solving livestock handling problems," *Veterinary Medicine*, October 1994, 989–998, http://www.grandin.com/references/solv.lvstk.probs.html (accessed July 26, 2009).

158 *affected 10 percent of slaughtered pigs...* Steve W. Martinez and Kelly Zering, "Pork Quality and the Role of Market Organization/AER-835," Economic Research Service/USDA, November 2004, http://www.ers.usda.gov/Publications/aer835/aer835c.pdf (accessed August 17, 2009).

driving a tractor too close... Nathanael Johnson, "The Making of the Modern Pig," *Harper's Magazine*, May 2006, http://www.harpers.org/archive/2006/05/0081030 (accessed July 26, 2009).

more than 15 percent of slaughtered pigs... Martinez and Zering, "Pork Quality and the Role of Market Organization/AER-835." The American Meat Science Association estimate that 15 percent of pork is affected by PSE was challenged by a later study that suggested much of this 15 percent was actually flesh that was only pale, only soft, or only watery. Estimates suggest that only 3 percent of pork has all three negative characteristics. American Meat Science Association, *Proceedings of the 59th Reciprocal Meat Conference*, June 18–21, 2006, 35 http://www.meatscience.org/Pubs/rmcarchv/2006/presentations/2006_Proceedings.pdf (accessed August 17, 2009).

reduced the number of pigs that died in transport... Temple Grandin, "The Welfare of Pigs During Transport and Slaughter," Department of Animal Science, Colorado State University, http://www.grandin.com/references/pig.welfare.during.transport.slaughter.html (accessed June 16, 2009).

160 *In fact, it's not uncommon...* While pigs do have heart attacks in transit, far more common is what the industry calls "fatigued pig syndrome," which is the industry term for pigs "that become nonambulatory without obvious injury, trauma, or disease, and refuse to walk." Benjamin, "Pig Trucking and Handling: Stress and Fatigued Pig."

162 *Today there are a tenth as many...* Fern Shen, "Maryland Hog Farm Causing Quite a Stink," *Washington Post*, May 23, 1999; Ronald L. Plain, "Trends in U.S. Swine Industry," U.S. Meat Export Federation Conference, September 24, 1997.

in the past ten years alone... "Statistical Highlights of US Agriculture 1995–1996," *USDA-NASS* 9, http://www.nass.usda.gov/Publications/

Statistical_Highlights/index.asp (accessed July 28, 2009); "Statistical Highlights of US Agriculture 2002–2003," *USDA-NASS* 35, http://www.nass.usda.gov/Publications/Statistical_Highlights/2003/contentl.htm (accessed July 28, 2009).

162   *Four companies now produce 60 percent*... Leland Swenson, president, the National Farmers Union, testimony before the House Judiciary Committee, September 12, 2000.

     In 1930, more than 20 percent... C. Dimitri and others, "The 20th Century Transformation of U.S. Agriculture and Farm Policy," USDA Economic Research Service, June 2005, http://www.ers.usda.gov/publications/eib3/eib3.htm (accessed July 15, 2009).

     agricultural production doubled between 1820 and 1920... Matthew Scully, *Dominion: The Power of Man, the Suffering of Animals, and the Call to Mercy* (New York: St. Martin's Griffin, 2003), 29.

     In 1950, one farmworker... "About Us," USDA, Cooperative State Research, Education, and Extension Service, June 9, 2009, http://www.csrees.usda.gov/qlinks/extension.html (accessed July 15, 2009).

     American farmers are four times... P. Gunderson and others, "The Epidemiology of Suicide Among Farm Residents or Workers in Five North-Central States, 1980," *American Journal of Preventive Medicine* 9 (May 1993): 26–32.

164   *The pork sold in practically every supermarket*... See note to page 12.

     Chipotle is, as of the writing of this book... Diane Halverson, "Chipotle Mexican Grill Takes Humane Standards to the Mass Marketplace," *Animal Welfare Institute Quarterly*, Spring 2003, http://www.awionline.org/ht/d/ContentDetails/id/11861/pid/2514 (accessed August 17, 2009).

165   *The factory hog farm is still expanding*... Danielle Nierenberg, "Happier Meals: Rethinking the Global Meat Industry," Worldwatch Paper #171, Worldwatch Institute, August 2005, 38, http://www.worldwatch.org/node/819 (accessed July 27, 2009); Danielle Nierenberg, "Factory Farming in the Developing World: In some critical respects this is not progress at all," Worldwatch Institute, May 2003, http://www.worldwatch.org/epublish/1/v16n3.

168   *His story might have ended*... Johnson, "The Making of the Modern Pig."

     about twenty-five to thirty dollars... Personal correspondence with head of Niman Ranch's pork division, Paul Willis, July 27, 2009.

168 *"our old sympathetic attempts..."* Wendell Berry, "The Idea of a Local Economy," *Orion*, Winter 2001, http://www.organicconsumers.org/btc/berry.cfm (accessed August 17, 2009).

which happens to 90 percent... Ninety percent of male piglets are castrated. "The Use of Drugs in Food Animals: Benefits and Risks," National Academy of Sciences, 1999.

170 *cut off pigs' tails...* An estimated 80 percent of industrial pigs have their tails cut off. Ibid.

or teeth... Dr. Allen Harper, "Piglet Processing and Swine Welfare," Virginia Tech Tidewater AREC, May 2009, http://pubs.ext.vt.edu/news/livestock/2009/05/aps-20090513.html (accessed July 17, 2009); Timothy Blackwell, "Production Practices and Well-Being: Swine," in *The Well-Being of Farm Animals*, edited by G. J. Benson and B. E. Rollin (Ames, IA: Blackwell publishing, 2004), 251.

excessive biting and cannibalism... Industry bodies themselves acknowledge the common problems with aggression. For example, the National Pork Producers Council and the National Pork Board have reported: "As pigs come in close contact with each other, they may at times attempt to bite or chew on their pen mates, especially on their tails. Once blood has been drawn from a tail, further biting may result, sometimes leading to cannibalism of the victimized pig." *Swine Care Handbook*, published by the National Pork Producers Council in cooperation with the National Pork Board, 1996, http://sanangelo.tamu.edu/ded/swine/swinecar.htm (accessed July 15, 2009). See also: *Swine Care Handbook*, published by the National Pork Producers Council in cooperation with the National Pork Board, 2003, 9–10; "Savaging of Piglets (Cannibalism)," ThePigSite.com, http://www.thepigsite.com/pighealth/article/260/savaging-of-piglets-canni balism (accessed July 27, 2009); J. McGlone and W. G. Pond, *Pig Production* (Florence, KY: Delmar Cengage Learning, 2002), 301–304; J. J. McGlone and others, "Cannibalism in Growing Pigs: Effects of Tail Docking and Housing System on Behavior, Performance and Immune Function," Texas Technical University, http://www.depts.ttu.edu/liru_afs/PDF/CANNIBALISMINGROWINGPIGS.pdf (accessed July 27, 2009); K. W. F. Jericho and T. L. Church, "Cannibalism in Pigs," *Canadian Veterinary Journal* 13, no. 7 (July 1972).

170   *80 percent of pregnant pigs in America*...U.S. Department of Agriculture, "Swine 2006, Part I: Reference of swine health and management practices in the United States."

1.2 million owned by Smithfield...RSPCA, "Improvements in Farm Animal Welfare: The USA," 2007, http://www.wspa-usa.org/download/44_improvements_in_farm_animal_welfare.pdf (accessed July 27, 2009).

172   *It's no trivial task to identify*...See FarmForward.com for details on how to find non-factory-farmed animal products.

Our methodologies...Wendell Berry, *The Art of the Commonplace*, edited by Norman Wirzba (Berkeley, CA: Counterpoint, 2003), 250.

173   *cost Americans $26 billion*..."CAFOs Uncovered: The Untold Costs of Confined Animal Feeding Operations," Union of Concerned Scientists, 2008, http://www.ucsusa.org/food_and_agriculture/science_and_impacts/impacts_industrial_agriculture/cafos-uncovered.html (accessed July 27, 2009).

174   *Today a typical pig factory farm will produce*...USDA, Economic Research Service, "Manure Use for Fertilizer and Energy: Report to Congress," June 2009, http://www.ers.usda.gov/Publications/AP/AP037/ (accessed August 17, 2009).

"can generate more raw waste..." "Concentrated Animal Feeding Operations: EPA Needs More Information and a Clearly Defined Strategy to Protect Air and Water Quality from Pollutants of Concern," U.S. Government Accountability Office, 2008, http://www.gao.gov/new.items/d08944.pdf (accessed July 27, 2009).

farmed animals in the United States produce...Pew Commission on Industrial Farm Animal Production, "Environment," http://www.ncifap.org/issues/environment/ (accessed August 17, 2009).

87,000 pounds of shit **per second**...The USDA cites a report by the Minority Staff of the U.S. Senate Committee on Agriculture, Nutrition & Forestry requested by Senator Tom Harkin (D-IA), which estimates livestock in the United States produce 1.37 billion tons of solid animal waste each year. Dividing this by the number of seconds in a year equals 86,884 pounds of waste per second. Ibid.

160 times greater than raw municipal sewage...This was calculated by John P. Chastain, a University of Minnesota Extension agricultural engineer, based on data from the Illinois Environmental Protection

Agency, in 1991. University of Minnesota Extension, Biosystems and Agricultural Engineering, *Engineering Notes*, Winter 1995, http://www .bbe.umn.edu/extens/ennotes/enwin95/manure.html (accessed June 16, 2009).

174 *no federal agency even collects...* "Concentrated Animal Feeding Operations: EPA Needs More Information and a Clearly Defined Strategy to Protect Air and Water Quality from Pollutants of Concern."

175 *31 million...* Smithfield, 2008 Annual Report, 15, http://investors .smithfieldfoods.com/common/download/download.cfm?compan yid=SFD&fileid=215496&filekey=CE5E396C-CF17-47B0-BAC6-BBEFDDC51975&filename=2008AR.pdf (accessed July 28, 2009).

According to conservative EPA figures... "Animal Waste Disposal Issues," U.S. Environmental Protection Agency, May 22, 2009, http:// www.epa.gov/oig/reports/1997/hogchpl.htm (accessed July 27, 2009).

in Smithfield's case, the number... According to a study by David Pimentel, which cites the USDA's 2004 figures, each hog produces 1,230 kg (2,712 pounds) of waste per year. So Smithfield's 31 million hogs produced roughly 84 billion pounds of waste in 2008. With the US population estimated at 299 million, that amounts to 281 pounds of shit produced for every American. D. Pimentel and others, "Reducing Energy Inputs in the US Food System," *Human Ecology* 36, no. 4 (2008): 459–471.

That means that Smithfield—a single legal entity... Calculated based on 2008 US census and "Animal Waste Disposal Issues."

"the waste nurses more than 100..." Jeff Tietz, "Boss Hog," *Rolling Stone*, July 8, 2008, http://www.rollingstone.com/news/story/21727641/ boss_hog/ (accessed July 27, 2009).

children raised on... Francis Thicke, "CAFOs crate toxic waste byproducts," Ottumwa.com, March 23, 2009, http://www.ottumwa.com/ archivesearch/local_story_082235355.html (accessed July 27, 2009).

This includes but is not limited to... Tietz, "Boss Hog."

176 *The impression the pig industry...* Jennifer Lee, "Neighbors of Vast Hog Farms Say Foul Air Endangers Their Health," *New York Times*, May 11, 2003; Tietz, "Boss Hog."

177 *At one point, three factory farms...* Tietz, "Boss Hog."

120,000 square feet... Ibid. The comparison with a casino floor is my own—the Luxor and Venetian boast 120,000-square-foot casinos.

177 *a single slaughterhouse*... Ibid.

Just as you would die of asphyxiation... Thicke, "CAFOs crate toxic waste byproducts."

A worker in Michigan... Tietz, "Boss Hog."

178 *In the rare cases*... "Overview," North Carolina in the Global Economy, August 23, 2007, http://www.soc.duke.edu/NC_GlobalEconomy/ hog/overview.shtml (accessed July 27, 2009); Rob Schofield, "A Corporation Running Amok," NC Policy Watch, April 26, 2008, http://www .ncpolicywatch.com/cms/2008/04/26/a-corporation-running-amok/ (accessed July 27, 2009).

Smithfield spilled more than 20 million... "Animal Waste Disposal Issues."

The spill remains the largest... Ibid.

The spill released enough liquid... http://www.evostc.state.ak.us/facts/ qanda.com; "Animal Waste Disposal Issues."

Smithfield was penalized... "The RapSheet on Animal Factories," Sierra Club, August 2002, 14, http://www.midwestadvocates .org/archive/dvorakbeef/rapsheet.pdf (accessed July 27, 2009); Ellen Nakashima, "Court Fines Smithfield $12.6 Million," *Washington Post*, August 9, 1997, http://pqasb.pqarchiver.com/washingtonpost/ access/13400463.html?dids=13400463:13400463&FMT=ABS&FMT S=ABS:FT&date=Aug+9%2C+1997&author=Ellen+Nakashima&pub =The+Washington+Post&edition=&startpage=A.01&desc=Court +Fines+Smithfield+%2412.6+Million%3B+Va.+Firm+Is+Assessed+Lar gest+Such+Pollution+Penalty+in+U.S.+History.

179 *At the time, $12.6 million*... "The RapSheet on Animal Factories."

a pathetically small amount... Calculation based on 2009 sales of $12.5 billion. "Smithfield Foods Reports Fourth Quarter and Full Year Results," *PR Newswire*, June 16, 2009, http://investors.smith fieldfoods.com/releasedetail.cfm?ReleaseID=389871 (accessed July 14, 2009).

Smithfield's former CEO Joseph Luter... Compensation Resources, Inc., 2009, http://www.compensationresources.com/press-room/ceo-s -fat-checks-belie-troubled-times.php (accessed July 28, 2009).

Smithfield is so large... Tietz, "Boss Hog."

chicken, hog, and cattle excrement... In addition to river pollution, factory farms have contaminated groundwater in seventeen states.

Sierra Club, "Clean Water and Factory Farms," http://www.sierraclub.org/factoryfarms/ (August 19, 2009).

179 *two hundred fish kills*... Merritt Frey et al., "Spills and Kills: Manure Pollution and America's Livestock Feedlots," Clean Water Network, Izaak Walton League of America and Natural Resources Defense Council, August 2000, 1, as cited in Sierra Club, "Clean Water: That Stinks," http://www.sierraclub.org/cleanwater/that_stinks (August 19, 2009).

if set head to tail fin... This assumes each fish is approximately six inches long.

180 *sore throats, headaches*... "An HSUS Report: The Impact of Industrial Animal Agriculture on Rural Communities," http://www.hsus.org/web-files/PDF/farm/hsus-the-impact-of-industrialized-animal-agriculture-on-rural-communities.pdf (accessed August 19, 2009).

"Studies have shown that..." "Confined Animal Facilities in California," California State Senate, November 2004, http://sor.govoffice3.com/vertical/Sites/%7B3BDD1595-792B-4D20-8D44-626EF05648C7%7D/uploads/%7BD51D1D55-1B1F-4268-80CC-C636EE939A06%7D.PDF (accessed July 28, 2009).

There are even some good reasons.... Nicholas Kristof, "Our Pigs, Our Food, Our Health," *New York Times*, March 11, 2009, http://www.nytimes.com/2009/03/12/opinion/12kristof.html?_r=3&adxnnl=1&adxnnlx=1250701592-DDwvJ/Oilp86iJ6xqYVYLQ (accessed August 18, 2009).

The American Public Health Association... "Policy Statement Database: Precautionary Moratorium on New Concentrated Animal Feed Operations," American Public Health Association, November 18, 2003, www.apha.org/advocacy/policy/policysearch/default.htm?id=1243 (accessed July 26, 2009).

the Pew Commission recently... Pew Charitable Trusts, Johns Hopkins Bloomberg School of Public Health, and Pew Commission on Industrial Animal Production, "Putting Meat on the Table: Industrial Farm Animal Production in America," 2008, 84, http://www.ncifap.org/_images/PCIFAP Final Release PCIFAP.pdf (accessed June 18, 2008).

181 *Smithfield has now spread*... Romania: D. Carvajal and S. Castle, "A U.S. Hog Giant Transforms Eastern Europe," *New York Times*,

May 5, 2009, http://www.nytimes.com/2009/05/06/business/global/06smithfield.html (accessed July 27, 2009).

181 ***Joseph Luter III's stock...*** "Joseph W. Luter III," Forbes.com, http://www.forbes.com/lists/2006/12/UQDU.html (accessed July 27, 2009).

His last name is pronounced... Personal phone message. He never called back and could never be reached after leaving me a message.

Undercover investigations... I am not aware of a single factory farm or industrial slaughterhouse in the nation that has agreed to disclose without restriction information obtained from ongoing, unannounced, and independent welfare audits.

182 ***workers sawed off pigs' legs...*** This was documented by PETA investigators. See: "Belcross Farms Investigation," GoVeg.com, http://www.goveg.com/belcross.asp (accessed July 27, 2009).

employees were videotaped... This was documented by PETA investigators. See: "Seaboard Farms Investigation," GoVeg.com, http://www.goveg.com/seaboard.asp (accessed July 27, 2009).

managers condoned these abuses... "Attorney General Asked to Prosecute Rosebud Hog Factory Operators," Humane Farming Association (HFA), http://hfa.org/campaigns/rosebud.html (accessed July 17, 2009).

An investigation at one... This was documented by PETA investigators. See: "Tyson Workers Torturing Birds, Urinating on Slaughter Line," PETA, http://getactive.peta.org/campaign/tortured_by_tyson (accessed July 27, 2009).

fully conscious chickens... This was documented by PETA investigators. See: "Thousands of Chickens Tortured by KFC Supplier," Kentucky Fried Cruelty, PETA, http://www.kentuckyfriedcruelty.com/u-pilgrimspride.asp (accessed July 27, 2009).

Pilgrim's Pride... Pilgrim's Pride has since gone bankrupt. This is no victory. All it means is reduced competition and greater concentration of power as the other giant firms buy up Pilgrim's Pride's assets. Michael J. de la Merced, "Major Poultry Producer Files for Bankruptcy Protection," *New York Times*, December 1, 2008, http://www.nytimes.com/2008/12/02/business/02pilgrim.html (accessed July 13, 2009).

they were the two largest chicken processors... "Top Broiler Producing Companies: Mid-2008," National Chicken Council, http://www

.nationalchickencouncil.com/statistics/stat_detail.cfm?id=31 (accessed July 17, 2009).

183 *the modern factory sow*...F. Hollowell and D. Lee, "Management Tips for Reducing Pre-weaning Mortality," *North Carolina Cooperative Extension Service Swine News* 25, no. 1 (February 2002), http://www.ncsu.edu/project/swine_extension/swine_news/2002/sn_v2501.htm (accessed July 28, 2009).

When she is approaching...Blackwell, "Production Practices and Well-Being: Swine," 249; SwineReproNet Staff, "Swine Reproduction Papers; Inducing Farrowing," SwineReproNet, Online Resource for the Pork Industry, University of Illinois Extenstion, available at http://www.livestocktrail.uiuc.edu/swinereporonet/paperDisplay.cfm?ContentID=6264 (accessed July 17, 2009).

After her piglets are weaned...Marlene Halverson, "The Price We Pay for Corporate Hogs," Institute for Agriculture and Trade Policy, July 2000, http://www.iatp.org/hogreport/indextoc.html (accessed July 27, 2009).

Four out of five times...U.S. Department of Agriculture, "Swine 2006, Part I: Reference of swine health and management practices in the United States."

Her bone density will decrease...G. R. Spencer, "Animal model of human disease: Pregnancy and lactational osteoporosis; Animal model: Porcine lactational osteoporosis," *American Journal of Pathology* 95 (1979): 277–280; J. N. Marchent and D. M. Broom, "Effects of dry sow housing conditions on muscle weight and bone strength," *Animal Science* 62 (1996): 105–113, as cited in Blackwell, "Production Practices and Well-Being: Swine," 242.

A worker at the farm...."Cruel Conditions at a Nebraska Pig Farm," GoVeg.com, http://www.goveg.com/nebraskapigfarm.asp (accessed July 28, 2009).

suffering caused by boredom... Blackwell, "Production Practices and Well-Being: Swine," 242.

would build a nest...Ibid., 247.

will be feed restricted..."Sow Housing," Texas Tech University Pork Industry Institute, http://www.depts.ttu.edu/porkindustryinstitute/SowHousing_files/sow_housing.htm (accessed July 15, 2009); Jim Mason, *Animal Factories* (New York: Three Rivers Press, 1990), 10.

Notes

184 *The pregnant animals*...D. C. Coats and M. W. Fox, *Old McDonald's Factory Farm: The Myth of the Traditional Farm and the Shocking Truth About Animal Suffering in Today's Agribusiness* (London: Continuum International Publishing Group, 1989), 37.

lame and diseased animals...Blackwell, "Production Practices and Well-Being: Swine," 242.

almost invariably be confined in a crate...Around 90 percent of farrowing sows are confined in crates. U.S. Department of Agriculture, "Swine 2006, Part I: Reference of swine health and management practices in the United States."

185 *it's necessary to "beat the shit*..." Eisnitz, *Slaughterhouse*, 219.

"One guy smashed a sow's nose..." Ibid.

Not surprisingly, when farmers select...I am indebted to welfare experts Diane and Marlene Halverson for this analysis of why sows on factory systems are so much more likely to crush their young than those in family farms.

pigs in crates showed... "The Welfare of Intensively Kept Pigs," *Report of the Scientific Veterinary Committee*, September 30, 1997, Section 5.2.11, Section 5.2.2, Section 5.2.7, http://ec.europa.eu/food/fs/sc/oldcomm4/out17_en.pdf (accessed July 17, 2009).

poor genetics, lack of movement...Cindy Wood, "Don't Ignore Feet and Leg Soundness in Pigs," *Virginia Cooperative Extension*, June 2001, http://www.ext.vt.edu/news/periodicals/livestock/aps-01_06/aps-0375.html.

186 *7 percent of breeding sows*...Ken Stalder, "Getting a Handle on Sow Herd Dropout Rates," *National Hog Farmer*, January 15, 2001, http://nationalhogfarmer.com/mag/farming_getting_handle_sow/.

in some operations the mortality rate...Keith Wilson, "Sow Mortality Frustrates Experts," *National Hog Farmer*, June 15, 2001, http://nationalhogfarmer.com/mag/farming_sow_mortality_frustrates/ (accessed July 27, 2009); Halverson, "The Price We Pay for Corporate Hogs."

Many pigs go insane...A. J. Zanella and O. Duran, "Pig Welfare During Loading and Transport: A North American Perspective," I Conferencia Vitrual Internacional Sobre Qualidade de Carne Suina, November 16, 2000.

186   *or drink urine*...Blackwell, "Production Practices and Well-Being: Swine," 253.

Others exhibit mourning...Halverson, "The Price We Pay for Corporate Hogs."

Common congenital diseases..."Congenital defects," PigProgress .net, 2009, http://www.pigprogress.net/health-diseases/c/congenital -defects-17.html (accessed July 17, 2009); B. Rischkowsky and others, "The State of the World's Animal Genetic Resources for Food and Agriculture," FAO, Rome, 2007, 402, http://www.fao.org/docrep/010/ a1250e/a1250e00.htm (accessed July 27, 2009); "Quick Disease Guide," ThePigSite.com, http://www.thepigsite.com/diseaseinfo (accessed July 27, 2009).

Inguinal hernias are common... Blackwell, "Production Practices and Well-Being: Swine," 251.

Within the first forty-eight hours... See notes for pages 168–170.

"needle teeth"... "Piglets are born with eight fully erupted 'needle teeth,' the deciduous canines and third incisors, which the animals use to deliver sideward bites to the faces of litter mates when fighting at the udder." D. M. Weary and D. Fraser, "Partial tooth-clippings of suckling pigs: Effects on neonatal competition and facial injuries," *Applied Animal Behavior Science* 65 (1999): 22.

so they are more lethargic...James Serpell, *In the Company of Animals* (Cambridge: Cambridge University Press, 2008), 9.

factory-farmed piglets often will be... Blackwell, "Production Practices and Well-Being: Swine," 251.

187   *consumers in America*...J. L. Xue and G. D. Dial, "Raising intact male pigs for meat: Detecting and preventing boar taint," American Association of Swine Practitioners, 1997, http://www.aasp.org/shap/ issues/v5n4/v5n4p151.html (accessed July 17, 2009).

By the time farmers begin weaning...Hollowell and Lee, "Management Tips for Reducing Pre-weaning Mortality."

The sooner the piglets start feeding..."Pork Glossary," U.S. Environmental Protection Agency, September 11, 2007, http://www.epa.gov/ oecaagct/ag101/porkglossary.html (accessed July 27, 2009).

"Solid food" in this case...K. J. Touchette and others, "Effect of spray-dried plasma and lipopolysaccharide exposure on weaned piglets:

I. Effects on the immune axis of weaned pigs," *Journal of Animal Science* 80 (2002): 494–501.

187   ***Left alone, piglets tend to wean***...P. Jensen, "Observations on the Maternal Behavior of Free-Ranging Domestic Pigs," *Applied Animal Behavior Science* 16 (1968): 131–142.

but on factory farms...Blackwell, "Production Practices and Well-Being: Swine," 250–251.

At these young ages...L. Y. Yue and S. Y. Qiao, "Effects of low-protein diets supplemented with crystalline amino acids on performance and intestinal development in piglets over the first 2 weeks after weaning," *Livestock Science* 115 (2008): 144–152; J. P. Lallès and others, "Gut function and dysfunction in young pigs: Physiology," *Animal Research* 53 (2004): 301–316.

The pens are deliberately overcrowded..."Overcrowding Pigs Pays—if It's Managed Properly," *National Hog Farmer*, November 15, 1993, as cited in Michael Greger, "Swine Flu and Factory Farms: Fast Track to Disaster," *Encyclopaedia Britannica's* Advocacy for Animals, May 4, 2009, http://advocacy.britannica.com/blog/advocacy/2009/05/swine-flu-and-factory-farms-fast-track-to-disaster/ (accessed August 5, 2009).

"We've thumped as many..." Eisnitz, *Slaughterhouse*, 220.

188   ***Fully 30 to 70 percent of the pigs***...L. K. Clark, "Swine respiratory disease," IPVS Special Report, B Pharmacia & Upjohn Animal Health, November–December 1998, *Swine Practitioner*, Section B, P6, P7, as cited in Halverson, "The Price We Pay for Corporate Hogs."

entire hog populations of entire states...R. J. Webby and others, "Evolution of swine H3N2 influenza viruses in the United States," *Journal of Virology* 74 (2000): 8243–8251.

189   ***But far from reducing demand***...R. L. Naylor and others, "Effects of aquaculture on world fish supplies," *Issues in Ecology*, no. 8 (Winter 2001): 1018.

Wild salmon catches worldwide...Ibid.

"key stressors in the aquaculture environment"...S. M. Stead and L. Laird, *Handbook of Salmon Farming* (New York: Springer, 2002), 374–375.

190   ***These problems are typical***...Philip Lymbery, "In Too Deep—Why Fish Farming Needs Urgent Welfare Reform," 2002, 1, http://www

.ciwf.org.uk/includes/documents/cm_docs/2008/i/in_too_deep_
summary_2001.pdf (accessed August 12, 2009).

190 **_The handbook calls them_** ... Stead and Laird, _Handbook of Salmon Farm-
ing_, 375.

known as the "death crown" ... "Fish Farms: Underwater Factories,"
Fishing Hurts, peta.org, http://www.fishinghurts.com/fishFarms1.asp
(accessed July 27, 2009).

swarming clouds of sea lice ... University of Alberta study, as cited in
"Farm sea lice plague wild salmon," _BBC News_, March 29, 2005, http://
news.bbc.co.uk/go/pr/fr/-/2/hi/science/nature/4391711.stm (accessed
July 27, 2009).

a 10 to 30 percent death rate ... Lymbery, "In Too Deep," 1.

starved for seven to ten days ... This is a recommended method for
killing salmon. See: Stead and Laird, _Handbook of Salmon Farming_, 188.

they may be stunned ... Slicing the gills of conscious fish is not only
painful but also a difficult procedure to perform on fully conscious animals. Because of this, some operations render fish unconscious (or at
least immobile) before slicing their gills. Two methods are prevalent
for salmon: beating the animals on the head and carbon dioxide anesthesia. Beating the salmon unconscious is called "percussive stunning."
Hitting fish on the head in the right place to stun them involves a high
degree "of skill and dexterity to carry out cleanly on a struggling fish,"
according to the _Handbook of Salmon Farming_. Misplaced blows only
cause the fish pain and don't render the animal unconscious. And the
imprecision of this method virtually guarantees that a certain number
of animals will become conscious while their gills are cut. The other
most common method of stunning involves using carbon dioxide as
anesthesia. The fish are transferred ashore into tanks saturated with
carbon dioxide and will become unconscious within minutes. Welfare
problems in carbon dioxide stunning include the stress of transferring
the fish into the chamber and the possibility that not all fish will be rendered fully unconscious. Stead and Laird, _Handbook of Salmon Farming_,
374–375.

191 **_Longlines today_** ... "Longline Bycatch," AIDA, 2007, http://www
.aida-americas.org/aida.php?page=turtles.bycatch_longline (accessed
July 28, 2009).

An estimated 27 million ... Ibid.

191 ***4.5 million sea animals***…"Pillaging the Pacific," Sea Turtle Restoration Project, 2004, http://www.seaturtles.org/downloads/Pillaging .5.final.pdf (accessed August 19, 2009).

The most common type…"Squandering the Seas: How shrimp trawling is threatening ecological integrity and food security around the world," Environmental Justice Foundation, London, 2003, 8.

The trawl is pulled…Ibid.

trawlers sweep up fish…Ibid., 14.

typically about a hundred different fish…Ibid., 11.

The average trawling operation…Ibid., 12.

The least efficient operations…Ibid.

We are literally reducing the diversity…See note for page 32 beginning with "shapes ocean ecosystems…"

192 ***As we gobble up the most desired fish***…Daniel Pauly et al., "Fishing Down Marine Food Webs," *Science* 279 (1998): 860.

193 ***fish die slowly and painfully***…P. J. Ashley, "Fish welfare: Current issues in aquaculture," *Applied Animal Behaviour Science* 200, no. 104 (2007): 199–235, 210.

2.5-foot-long salmon…Lymbery, "In Too Deep."

explosions of parasite populations…Kenneth R. Weiss, "Fish Farms Become Feedlots of the Sea," *Los Angeles Times*, December 9, 2002, http://www.latimes.com/la-me-salmon9dec09,0,7675555,full.story (accessed July 27, 2009).

You never have to wonder…Some may ask how we can be sure fish and other sea animals even experience pain. We have every reason to assume that at least fish do. Comparative anatomy tells us that fish have plenty of the anatomical and neurological gear that seems to play an important role in conscious perception. Most relevantly, fish have abundant nociceptors, the sensory receptors that appear to transmit pain signals to the brain (we can even count them). We also know that fish produce natural opioids, like enkephalins and endorphins, which the human nervous system uses to control pain.

Fish also exhibit "pain behavior." This has seemed obvious to me since the first time I was taken fishing as a child by my grandfather, and the people I know who fish recreationally don't deny fish pain as much as forget about it. As David Foster Wallace put it while reflecting on lobster pain in his magnificent essay "Consider the Lobster,"

Notes

"The whole animal-cruelty-and-eating issue is not just complex, it's also uncomfortable. It is, at any rate, uncomfortable for me, and for just about everyone I know who enjoys a variety of foods and yet does not want to see herself as cruel or unfeeling. As far as I can tell, my own main way of dealing with this conflict has been to avoid thinking about the whole unpleasant thing." Later, he describes the unpleasant thing that he has avoided thinking about: "However stuperous the lobster is from the trip home, for instance, it tends to come alarmingly to life when placed in boiling water. If you're tilting it from a container into the steaming kettle, the lobster will sometimes try to cling to the container's sides or even to hook its claws over the kettle's rim like a person trying to keep from going over the edge of a roof. And worse is when the lobster's fully immersed. Even if you cover the kettle and turn away, you can usually hear the cover rattling and clanking as the lobster tries to push it off." This seems—to Wallace, to me, and I have to imagine to most—not only to be physical pain but psychic, too. The lobster is not just thrashing about in agony—it begins fighting for its life before it touches the hot water. It is trying to escape. And it is hard not to identify some of this frantic behavior with some version of fear and panic. Lobsters, unlike fish, are not vertebrates, and so scientific investigations of how they might experience pain—or, more precisely, a type of pain essentially close to that found in humans—are more complicated than investigations into fish. (As it turns out, though, scientific knowledge reveals plenty of reasons to trust the intuitions most of us would have about lobster suffering when sympathizing with a lobster trying to fight his way out of a pot of boiling water. Wallace admirably reviews this science. As they are vertebrates that share the anatomical gear involved in experiencing pain and demonstrate pain behavior, the case for pain in fish is much stronger and leaves little room for skepticism. Kristopher Paul Chandroo, Stephanie Yue, and Richard David Moccia, "An evaluation of current perspectives on consciousness and pain in fishes," *Fish and Fisheries* 5 (2004): 281–295; Lynne U. Sneddon, Victoria A. Braithwaite, and Michael J. Gentle, "Do Fishes Have Nociceptors? Evidence for the Evolution of a Vertebrate Sensory System," *Proceedings: Biological Sciences.* 270, no. 1520 (June 7, 2003): 1115–1121, http://links.jstor.org/sici?sici=0962-8452%2820030607%29270%3A15 20%3C1115%3ADFHNEF%3E2.0.CO%3B2-O (accessed August 19,

2009); David Foster Wallace, "Consider the Lobster," in *Consider the Lobster* (New York: Little, Brown, 2005), 248.

I Do

Page

201 *Less than 1%*... See page 12.

203 *"There is no reason..."* Patricia Leigh Brown, "Bolinas Journal; Welcome to Bolinas: Please Keep on Moving," *New York Times*, July 9, 2000, http://query.nytimes.com/gst/fullpage.html?res=980DE0DA143 8F93AA35754C0A9669C8B63 (accessed July 28, 2009).

211 *it takes six to twenty-six calories*... Bruce Friedrich's calculation based on US government and academic sources.

The UN special envoy on food... Grant Ferrett, "Biofuels' crime against humanity," *BBC News*, October 27, 2007, http://news.bbc.co.uk/2/hi/americas/7065061.stm (accessed July 28, 2009).

uses 756 million tons... "Global cereal supply and demand brief," FAO, April 2008, http://www.fao.org/docrep/010/ai465e/ai465e04.htm (accessed July 28, 2009).

to adequately feed... "New Data Show 1.4 Billion Live on Less Than US$1.25 a Day," World Bank, August 26, 2008, http://web.worldbank.org/WBSITE/EXTERNAL/TOPICS/EXTPOVERTY/0, content MDK:21883042~menuPK:2643747~pagePK:64020865~piPK:149114~theSitePK:336992,00.html (accessed July 28, 2009); Peter Singer, *The Life You Can Save: Acting Now to End World Poverty* (New York: Random House, 2009), 122.

And that 756 million tons... Singer, *The Life You Can Save*, 122.

He won the Nobel Peace Prize... Dr. R. K. Pachauri, Blog, June 15, 2009, www.rkpachauri.org (accessed July 28, 2009).

212 *pleasure and pain, happiness and misery*... Bruce Friedrich is quoting from Charles Darwin in *The Descent of Man:* "There is no fundamental difference between man and the higher animals in their mental faculties.... The lower animals, like man manifestly feel pleasure and pain, happiness and misery." As cited in Bernard Rollin, *The Unheeded*

Cry: Animal Consciousness, Animal Pain, and Science (New York: Oxford University Press, 1989), 33.

212 **The fact that animals are excited...** Temple Grandin and Catherine Johnson, *Animals Make Us Human* (Boston: Houghton Mifflin Harcourt, 2009); Temple Grandin and Catherine Johnson, *Animals in Translation* (Fort Washington, PA: Harvest Books, 2006); Marc Bekoff, *The Emotional Lives of Animals* (Novato, CA: New World Library, 2008).

213 **He felt that mistreating animals...** Isaac Bashevis Singer, *Enemies, a Love Story* (New York: Farrar, Straus and Giroux, 1988), 145.

214 **the leaders of the "ethical meat" charge...** Bruce Friedrich's personal correspondence with Michael Pollan (July 2009). Eric Schlosser eats a factory-farmed burger in the important movie *Food, Inc.*

219 **"all available evidence..."** D. Pimentel and M. Pimentel, *Food, Energy and Society*, 3rd ed. (Florence, KY: CRC Press, 2008), 57.
"First, the livestock effectively convert..." Ibid.
Plowing and planting land... It destroys the root structures of naturally occurring vegetative cover, leading to wind and water erosion, the single largest cause of soil nutrient loss in the United States. Crop production is particularly damaging where topsoil is thin and where topography is hilly. On the other hand, such lands are well suited for livestock grazing, which, when properly managed, actually can improve topsoil and vegetative cover.

223 **Let me tell you how cattle...** Personal correspondence.

226 **today they are slaughtered...** B. Niman and J. Fletcher, *Niman Ranch Cookbook* (New York: Ten Speed Press, 2008), 37.
Cattle seem to experience... G. Mitchell and others, "Stress in cattle assessed after handling, after transport and after slaughter," *Veterinary Record* 123, no. 8 (1988): 201–205, http://veterinaryrecord.bvapublications.com/cgi/content/abstract/123/8/201 (accessed July 28, 2009).
If the kill floor... Ibid.; "The Welfare of Cattle in Beef Production," *Farm Sanctuary*, 2006, http://www.farmsanctuary.org/mediacenter/beef_report.html (accessed July 28, 2009).

227 **They know the other animals...** Cows remember as many as seventy individuals, work out hierarchies for both males and females (female hierarchies are more stable), choose particular cows as friends, and treat other cows as enemies. Cattle "elect" leaders that they choose on the

basis of both "social attractiveness" and actual knowledge of the land and its resources. Some herds follow their leader virtually all the time, and others are more independent (or disorganized) and follow their leader about half the time. "Stop, Look, Listen: Recognising the Sentience of Farm Animals," Compassion in World Farming Trust, 2006, http://www.ciwf.org.uk/includes/documents/cm_docs/2008/s/stop_look_listen_2006.pdf (accessed July 28, 2009); M. F. Bouissou and others, "The Social Behaviour of Cattle," in *Social Behaviour in Farm Animals*, edited by L. J. Keeling and H. W. Gonyou (Oxford: CABI Publishing, 2001); A. F. Fraser and D. M. Broom, *Farm Animal Behaviour and Welfare* (Oxford: CABI Publishing, 1997); D. Wood-Gush, *Elements of Ethology; A Textbook of Agricultural and Veterinary Students* (New York: Springer, 1983); P. K. Rout and others, "Studies on behavioural patterns in Jamunapari goats," *Small Ruminant Research* 43, no. 2 (2002): 185–188; P. T. Greenwood and L. R. Rittenhouse, "Feeding area selection: The leader-follower phenomena," *Proc. West. Sect. Am. Soc. Anim. Sci.* 48 (1997): 267–269; B. Dumont and others, "Consistency of animal order in spontaneous group movements allows the measurement of leadership in a group of grazing heifers," *Applied Animal Behaviour Science* 95, no. 1–2 (2005): 55–66 (page 64 specifically); V. Reinhardt, "Movement orders and leadership in a semi-wild cattle herd," *Behaviour* 83 (1983): 251–264.

227 *As a rule, cattle have a heavy dose...* "The Welfare of Cattle in Beef Production."

virtually all of them lose weight... T. G. Knowles and others, "Effects on cattle of transportation by road for up to 31 hours," *Veterinary Record* 145 (1999): 575–582.

228 *"Slaughter," Pollan reports...* Michael Pollan, *The Omnivore's Dilemma* (New York: Penguin, 2007), 304.

"that's not because slaughter..." Ibid., 304–305.

"Eating industrial meat..." Ibid., 84.

"The technique goes like this..." B. R. Myers, "Hard to Swallow," *Atlantic Monthly;* September 2007, www.theatlantic.com/doc/200709/omnivore (accessed September 10, 2009).

230 *The side effect is that...* Gail A. Eisnitz, *Slaughterhouse: The Shocking Story of Greed, Neglect, and Inhumane Treatment Inside the U.S. Meat Industry* (Amherst, NY: Prometheus Books, 2006), 122.

230 **Several plants cited...** Joby Warrick, "They Die Piece by Piece," *Washington Post*, April 10, 2001; Sholom Mordechai Rubashkin, "Rubashkin's response to the 'attack on Shechita,'" shmais.com, December 7, 2004, http://www.shmais.com/jnewsdetail.cfm?ID=148 (accessed November 28, 2007).

the vast majority of... Temple Grandin, "Survey of Stunning and Handling in Federally Inspected Beef, Veal, Pork, and Sheep Slaughter Plants," Agricultural Research Service, U.S. Department of Agriculture, Project Number 3602-32000-002-08G, http://www.grandin.com/survey/usdarpt.html (accessed August 18, 2009).

The USDA, the federal agency... Warrick, "They Die Piece by Piece."

has improved since then... Temple Grandin, "2002 Update" for "Survey of Stunning and Handling in Federally Inspected Beef, Veal, Pork, and Sheep Slaughter Plants."

still found one in four... Kurt Vogel and Temple Grandin, "2008 Restaurant Animal Welfare and Humane Slaughter Audits in Federally Inspected Beef and Pork Slaughter Plants in the U.S. and Canada," Department of Animal Science, Colorado State University, http://www.grandin.com/survey/2008.restaurant.audits.html (accessed August 18, 2009).

231 **"Their heads are up..."** Slaughterhouse worker Chris O'Day, as cited in Eisnitz, *Slaughterhouse*, 128.

increased as much as 800 percent... Warrick, "They Die Piece by Piece."

Slaughterhouse workers... Ibid.

ordinary people can become sadistic... Temple Grandin, "Commentary: Behavior of Slaughter Plant and Auction Employees Toward the Animals," *Anthrozoös* 1, no. 4 (1988): 205–213, http://www.grandin.com/references/behavior.employees.html (accessed July 14, 2009).

"More than twenty workers..." Warrick, "They Die Piece by Piece."

"I've seen thousands..." Ibid.

I'd come home... Slaughterhouse worker Ken Burdette, as cited in Eisnitz, *Slaughterhouse*, 131.

232 **In twelve seconds or less...** Warrick, "They Die Piece by Piece."

A cow has in the neighborhood... Monica Reynolds, "Plasma and Blood Volume in the Cow Using the T-1824 Hematocrit Method," *American Journal of Physiology* 173 (1953): 421–427.

233 **"They'd be blinking..."** Slaughterhouse worker Timothy Walker, as cited in Eisnitz, *Slaughterhouse*, 28–29.

233 *"A lot of times the skinner..."* Slaughterhouse worker Timothy Walker, as cited in Eisnitz, *Slaughterhouse*, 29.

"As for as the ones..." Slaughterhouse worker Chris O'Day, as cited in Eisnitz, *Slaughterhouse*, 128.

234 **sending chicks by mail...** Humane Society of the United States, "An HSUS Report: Welfare Issues with Transport of Day-Old Chicks," Dec 3, 2008, http://www.hsus.org/farm/resources/research/practices/chick_transport.html (accessed Sept 9, 2009).

an even more serious welfare concern... Humane Society of the United States, "An HSUS Report: The Welfare of Animals in the Chicken Industry," December 2, 2008, http://www.hsus.org/farm/resources/research/welfare/broiler_industry.html (accessed August 18, 2009).

237 **we will all farm by proxy...** Wendell Berry, *Citizenship Papers* (Berkeley, CA: Counterpoint, 2004), 167.

American Livestock Breeds Conservancy... ALBC describes itself as "a nonprofit membership organization working to protect over 150 breeds of livestock and poultry from extinction." American Livestock Breeds Conservancy, 2009, http://www.albc-usa.org/ (accessed July 28, 2009).

242 **The ethical relationship...** M. Halverson, "Viewpoints of agricultural producers who have made ethical choices to practice a 'high welfare' approach to raising farm animals," EurSafe 2006, the 6th Congress of the European Society for Agricultural and Food Ethics, Oslo, June 22–24, 2006.

Storytelling

Page
250 **the only two written reports...** "The History of Thanksgiving: The First Thanksgiving," history.com, http://www.history.com/content/thanksgiving/the-first-thanksgiving (accessed July 28, 2009); "The History of Thanksgiving: The Pilgrims' Menu," history.com, http://www.history.com/content/thanksgiving/the-first-thanksgiving/the-pilgrims-menu (accessed July 28, 2009).

250 *the turkey wasn't made part*...Rick Schenkman, "Top 10 Myths About Thanksgiving," History News Network, November 21, 2001, http://hnn.us/articles/406.html (accessed July 28, 2009).

Thanksgiving with the Timucua Indians...Michael V. Gannon, *The Cross in the Sand* (Gainesville: University Press of Florida, 1965), 26–27.

They dined on bean soup...Craig Wilson, "Florida Teacher Chips Away at Plymouth Rock Thanksgiving Myth," *USAToday*, November 21, 2007, http://www.usatoday.com/life/lifestyle/2007-11-20-first-thanksgiving_N.htm (accessed July 28, 2009).

251 *first documentation*...Food and Agriculture Organization of the United Nations, Livestock, Environment and Development Initiative, "Livestock's Long Shadow: Environmental Issues and Options," Rome 2006, xxi, 112, 26, ftp://ftp.fao.org/docrep/fao/010/a0701e/a0701e00.pdf (accessed August 11, 2009).

saw the first major research institution...Pew Charitable Trusts, Johns Hopkins Bloomberg School of Public Health, and Pew Commission on Industrial Animal Production, "Putting Meat on the Table: Industrial Farm Animal Production in America," 57–59, 2008, http://www.ncifap.org.

saw the first state (Colorado)...Humane Society of the United States, "Landmark Farm Animal Welfare Bill Approved in Colorado," http://www.hsus.org/farm/news/ournews/colo_gestation_crate_veal_crate_bill_051408.html (August 19, 2009).

saw the first supermarket chain...John Mackey, Letter to Stakeholders, Whole Foods Market, http://www.wholefoodsmarket.com/company/pdfs/ar08_letter.pdf (accessed August 19, 2009).

first major national newspaper..."The Worst Way to Farm," *New York Times*, May 31, 2008.

252 *after Temple Grandin reported*...Temple Grandin, "2002 Update" for "Survey of Stunning and Handling in Federally Inspected Beef, Veal, Pork, and Sheep Slaughter Plants," Agricultural Research Service, U.S. Department of Agriculture, Project Number 3602-32000-002-08G, http://www.grandin.com/survey/usdarpt.html (accessed August 18, 2009).

253 *One time the knocking gun*... Slaughterhouse worker Steve Parrish, as cited in Gail A. Eisnitz, *Slaughterhouse: The Shocking Story of Greed,*

Neglect, and Inhumane Treatment Inside the U.S. Meat Industry (Amherst, NY: Prometheus Books, 2006), 145.

253   **This is hard to talk about**... Slaughterhouse worker Ed Van Winkle, as cited in Eisnitz, *Slaughterhouse*, 81.

      Down in the blood pit... Slaughterhouse worker Donny Tice, as cited in Eisnitz, *Slaughterhouse*, 92–94.

254   **"systematic human rights violations"**... *Blood, Sweat, and Fear: Workers' Rights in US Meat and Poultry Plants* (New York: Human Rights Watch, 2004), 2.

      The worst thing... Slaughterhouse worker Ed Van Winkle, as cited in Eisnitz, *Slaughterhouse*, 87.

255   **"I have to say..."** Michael Pollan, *The Omnivore's Dilemma* (New York: Penguin, 2007), 362.

      she reported witnessing... Temple Grandin, "Commentary: Behavior of Slaughter Plant and Auction Employees Toward the Animals," *Anthrozoös* 1, no. 4 (1988): 205, http://www.grandin.com/references/behavior.employees.html (accessed July 28, 2009).

      26 percent of slaughterhouses had abuses... Temple Grandin, "2005 Poultry Welfare Audits: National Chicken Council Animal Welfare Audit for Poultry Has a Scoring System That Is Too Lax and Allows Slaughter Plants with Abusive Practices to Pass," Department of Animal Science, Colorado State University, http://www.grandin.com/survey/2005.poultry.audits.html (accessed July 28, 2009).

      live birds were thrown... Ibid.

      25 percent of the slaughterhouses... Kurt Vogel and Temple Grandin, "2008 Restaurant Animal Welfare and Humane Slaughter Audits in Federally Inspected Beef and Pork Slaughter Plants in the U.S. and Canada," Department of Animal Science, Colorado State University, http://www.grandin.com/survey/2008.restaurant.audits.html (accessed July 28, 2009).

256   **dismembering a fully conscious cow**... Grandin writes that the plant received "an automatic failure rating for cutting a leg off a sensible animal." Temple Grandin, "2007 Restaurant Animal Welfare and Humane Slaughter Audits in Federally Inspected Beef and Pork Slaughter Plants in the U.S. and Canada," Department of Animal Science, Colorado State University, http://www.grandin.com/survey/2007.restaurant.audits.html (accessed July 28, 2009).

Notes

256   *cows waking up...* Temple Grandin, "2006 Restaurant Animal Welfare Audits of Federally Inspected Beef, Pork, and Veal Slaughter Plants in the U.S.," Department of Animal Science, Colorado State University, http://www.grandin.com/survey/2006.restaurant.audits.html (accessed July 28, 2009); Vogel and Grandin, "2008 Restaurant Animal Welfare and Humane Slaughter Audits in Federally Inspected Beef and Pork Slaughter Plants in the U.S. and Canada."

  "poking cows in the anus area..." Grandin, "2007 Restaurant Animal Welfare and Humane Slaughter Audits in Federally Inspected Beef and Pork Slaughter Plants in the U.S. and Canada."

  There isn't enough nonfactory chicken... Of America's roughly eight billion broilers, roughly .06 percent are likely raised outside of factory farms. Assuming Americans eat around twenty-seven chickens apiece annually, this means that the nonfactory chicken meat supply could feed less than 200,000 persons. Similarly, of the nation's roughly 118 million pigs, roughly 4.59 percent are likely raised outside of factory farms. Assuming Americans eat roughly .9 hogs a year, the nonfactory pork supply could feed almost six million people. (For numbers of factory-farmed animals, see note for page 12.) Numbers of animals slaughtered annually come from the USDA, and the average number of chickens and pigs consumed by each American was calculated on the basis of USDA statistics by Noam Mohr.

258   *Hitler was a vegetarian...* The legend of Hitler's vegetarianism is quite persistent and widespread, but I have no idea if it's true. It is especially doubtful given various references to his eating sausages. For example, H. Eberle and M. Uhl, *The Hitler Book* (Jackson, TN: PublicAffairs, 2006), 136.

  "one must take a position..." This Martin Luther King Jr. quote is widely cited on the Internet; for example, see Quotiki.com, http://www.quotiki.com/quotes/3450 (accessed August 19, 2009).

260   *Organized by religion...* "Major Religions of the World Ranked by Number of Adherents," Adherents.com, August 9, 2007, http://www.adherents.com/Religions_By_Adherents.html (accessed July 29, 2009); "Population by religion, sex and urban/rural residence: Each census, 1984–2004," un.org, http://unstats.un.org/unsd/demographic/products/dyb/dybcensus/V2_table6.pdf (accessed July 28, 2009).

Notes

260 *one person is hungry*... The obese quietly became a larger percentage of the world than the undernourished in 2006. "Overweight 'Top World's Hungry,'" *BBC News*, August 15, 2006, http://news.bbc .co.uk/2/hi/health/4793455.stm (accessed July 28, 2009).

More than half eat a mostly vegetarian diet... E. Millstone and T. Lang, *The Penguin Atlas of Food* (New York: Penguin, 2003), 34.

vegetarians and vegans... There is no reliable data on the precise number of vegetarians worldwide. There isn't even a consensus on what it means to be vegetarian (in India, for example, eggs are considered non-vegetarian). That said, an estimated 42 percent of India's 1.2 billion citizens, roughly 500 million people, are believed to be vegetarian. "Project on Livestock Industrialization, Trade and Social-Health-Environment Impacts in Developing Countries," FAO, July 24, 2003, http://www.fao .org/WAIRDOCS/LEAD/X6170E/x6170e00.htm#Contents:section 2.3 (accessed July 29, 2009). If around 3 percent of the rest of the world is vegetarian, that grants vegetarians a seat at the table. This seems a reasonable assumption. In the United States, for example, between 2.3 and 6.7 percent of the population is vegetarian, depending on how you define it. Charles Stahler, "How Many Adults Are Vegetarian?" *Vegetarian Journal* 4 (2006), http://www.vrg.org/journal/vj2006issue4/ vj2006issue4poll.htm (accessed July 29, 2009).

more than half of the time... FAO, "Livestock Policy Brief 01: Responding to the 'Livestock Revolution,'" ftp://ftp.fao.org/docrep/ fao/010/a0260e/a0260e00.pdf (accessed July 28, 2009).

If current trents continue... Ibid.

261 *more than a third of restaurant operators*... Evan George, "Welcome to $oy City," *Los Angeles Downtown News*, November 22, 2006, http://www.downtownnews.com/articles/2006/11/27/news/news03.txt (accessed July 28, 2009).

"add vegetarian or vegan dishes..." Mark Brandau, "Indy Talk: Eric Blauberg, the Restaurant Fixer," October 22, 2008, *Nation's Restaurant News*, Independent Thinking, http://nrnindependentthink ing.blogspot.com/2008/10/indy-talk-erik-blauberg-restaurant.html (accessed July 28, 2009). Also see: "Having Words with Erik Blauberg: Chief Executive, EKB Restaurant Consulting," bnet.com, November 24, 2008, http://findarticles.com/p/articles/mi_m3190/is_46_42/ ai_n31044068/ (accessed July 28, 2009).

Notes

262 *four times the amount of meat*... Mia McDonald, "Skillful Means: The Challenges of China's Encounter with Factory Farming," Brighter-Green, http://www.brightergreen.org/files/brightergreen_china_print.pdf (accessed July 28, 2009).

animal products still account... Junguo Liu of the Swiss Federal Institute of Aquatic Science and Technology, as cited in Sid Perkins, "A thirst for meat: Changes in diet, rising population may strain China's water supply," *Science News*, January 19, 2008.

By 2050, the world's livestock... Colin Tudge, *So Shall We Reap* (New York: Penguin, 2003), as cited in Ramona Cristina Ilea, "Intensive Livestock Farming: Global Trends, Increased Environmental Concerns, and Ethical Solutions, *Journal of Agricultural Environmental Ethics* 22 (2009): 153–167.

one hungry person... "More people than ever are victims of hunger," FAO, http://www.fao.org/fileadmin/user_upload/newsroom/docs/Press%20release%20june-en.pdf (accessed July 28, 2009).

as the obese also gain another seat... Obesity worldwide is increasing rapidly. D. A. York and others, "Prevention Conference VII: Obesity, a Worldwide Epidemic Related to Heart Disease and Stroke: Group 1: Worldwide Demographics of Obesity," *Circulation: Journal of the American Heart Association* 110 (2004): 463–470, http://www.circ.ahajournals.org/cgi/reprint/110/18/e463 (accessed July 28, 2009).

265 *According to Benjamin Franklin*... Benjamin Franklin, *The Compleated Autobiography*, edited by Mark Skousen (Washington, DC: Regnery Publishing, 2006), 332.

thanks to help from Native Americans... James E. McWilliams, *A Revolution in Eating: How the Quest for Food Shaped America* (New York: Columbia University Press, 2005), 7, 8. "For all the challenges that the colonists faced, they rarely starved. English visitors were astonished at the region's material abundance."

266 *"meat, sawdust, leather..."* "A COK Report: Animal Suffering in the Turkey Industry," Compassion over Killing, http://www.cok.net/lit/turkey/disease.php (accessed July 28, 2009). This article cites A. R. Y. El Boushy and A. F. B. van der Poel, *Poultry Feed from Waste—Processing and Use* (New York: Chapman and Hall, 1994).

267 *"I could not have slept..."* James Baldwin, *Abraham Lincoln: A True Life* (New York: American Book Company, 1904), 130–131.

Index

abortion as analogy, 13

Abu Ghraib torture scandal, 40

activists, animal. *See* factory farming
(opposition to)

ADA (American Dietetic Association),
143–46

agribusiness, 135, 172, 209, 217, 237.
See also factory farming

Agricultural Research (industry journal),
109

Agriprocessors (Postville, Iowa), 69

AIDS (acquired immunodeficiency
syndrome), 124, 180

America. *See* United States

American Livestock Breeds Conservancy, 237–38

American Meat Science Association, 158

American Medical Association, 140

American Public Health Association,
180

Amundsen, Roald, 26

Anderson, Pamela, 72

animal(s)

activism on behalf of, *see* factory
farming (opposition to)

definition of, 45–46; environmentalist
definition, 58

domestication of, 99–100; and care,
102–3 (*see also* pet-keeping)

experimentation on, 93

farmed, personalities of, 101–2

intelligence of, 23, 25, 64–66, 76, 101,
195

myth of animal consent, 99–101, 243

rescue of, 82, 88–89, 90 (*see also*
euthanization)

animal agriculture

and the environment: as benefit to,
219–20; as burden on, 174

factory farm domination of, 109

and global warming, 43, 58

pasture-based, 220

research into, 12–13, 33

rural values lost from, 239

vs. starving people, 211

animal ethics. *See* "ethical carnivore"

animal experience, 13–14, 46–47.
See also suffering

Animal Farm (Orwell), 25

animal rights, 70–72, 211–15, 220–22

denial of, 93

See also animal welfare

animal science departments, 107, 206

animal welfare, 94, 220–22, 224, 239

American view of, 73

euthanization and, 27, 56, 72, 76,
90, 92

industry view of, 129; labeling
program, 251; legislation
disregarded, 51; welfare audits by
KFC, 67–68

"organic" and, 70

production costs vs., 95

welfare standards for pigs, 170–72

See also PETA (People for the Ethical
Treatment of Animals)

Animal Welfare Guidelines, 129

Animal Welfare Institute, 224

anthropocentrism, 46

anthropodenial, 46, 47

anthropomorphism, 46–47

antibiotic use. *See* factory farming

Applied Animal Behaviour Science
(industry journal), 193

Index

Index

Index

Lam Hoi-ka, 123–24
light. *See* food and light
Lincoln, Abraham, 267
line workers, 103–4, 133–34
    injuries to/health of, 104, 132, 231–32
    stress on, 254
    turnover of, 131–32
livestock
    American Livestock Breeds
        Conservancy, 237–38
    and the environment, 59 (*see also*
        environment, the)
    food consumed by, 211, 262
    percentage of planet dedicated to, 149
    worldwide role of, 219
    See also cattle; factory farming; pigs;
        poultry industry; slaughterhouses
Lobb, Richard L., 133, 134
Luter, Joseph III, 179, 181

Man and the Natural World (Thomas), 22
Martins, Patrick, 151–52
"Meet Your Meat" video, 213
Montgomery bus boycott, 257
MRSA (methicillin-resistant
    Staphylococcus aureaus bacteria),
    180
Murphy, Wendell, 178
Murphy Family Farms, 167, 178
Myers, B. R., 228
myth of animal consent, 99–101, 243

National Academy of Sciences Institute
    of Medicine, 125, 141
National Chicken Council, 129, 133,
    134, 255
National Hog Farmer (industry journal),
    185
National Institutes of Health, 148
National Joint Council of Food Inspec-
    tion Locals, 155
National Pork Producers Council, 158
National Restaurant Association, 261
National School Lunch Program, 147
Nation's Restaurant News (industry
    journal), 261
Native American culture, 216, 265

"natural"
    food described as, 61, 131
    meat-eating as, debated, 213, 218
NDC (National Dairy Council),
    145–46
Nestle, Marion, 146–47
New England Journal of Medicine, 140
New York Times, 180, 203, 251–52
Nigeria, 26
Niman, Amy, 204
Niman, Bill, and Niman Ranch, 165,
    167–71, 197, 203–25, 227, 234, 242
    founder forced out, 244
Niman, Nicolette Hahn, 203–15,
    220–25, 242
Nobel Peace Prize, 211
North Carolina, hog factory farms in,
    142, 167, 177, 181
    regulation powers revoked, 178
nutritional information, 143–48

OIE (World Organization for Animal
    Health), 141, 142
Omnivore's Dilemma, The (Pollan), 99,
    113, 227–28, 255
organic foods, 70, 157
    infection of, 139
Orwell, George, 25
osteoporosis, 147

Pachauri, R. K., 211
Pagan River spill, 178–79
pain response, 14, 37. *See also* suffering
Paradise Locker Meats, 151–56, 162,
    164, 197, 198
pathogens. *See* viruses
Perdue, Arthur, 105
PETA (People for the Ethical
    Treatment of Animals), 70–72, 95,
    97, 208, 210–11, 220, 234
pet food, 27, 28
pet-keeping, 22–24, 101, 214. *See also*
    dogs; domestication of animals
Pet Shop Boys, 71
Pew Commission, 58, 59, 87, 180, 251
pharmaceutical industry, 141
Philippines, the, 26, 28

About the Author

Jonathan Safran Foer is the author of the novels *Everything Is Illuminated* and *Extremely Loud and Incredibly Close*. His work has received numerous awards and has been translated into thirty-six languages. He lives in Brooklyn, New York.